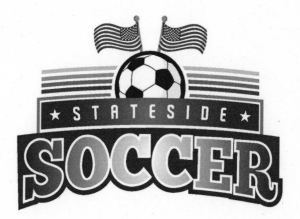

D1279741

The Definitive History of
Soccer in the
United States

TOM SCHOLES

First published by Pitch Publishing, 2019

Pitch Publishing
A2 Yeoman Gate
Yeoman Way
Worthing
Sussex
BN13 3QZ
www.pitchpublishing.co.uk
info@pitchpublishing.co.uk

ISBN 978 1 78531 521 3

Typesetting and origination by Pitch Publishing

Printed and bound in India by Replika Press Pvt. Ltd.

Contents

Dedication:

To my mum and dad, without whom this book would not have been possible to make.

Acknowledgements

THANK you to my family and my friends for their support throughout this process. Thank you to those who expressed an interest in reading this book before a word had even been written. Thank you to whoever has shown support over the past few months. Finally, thank you to the New York Knicks for providing me with some late-night company during the 2018/19 Tankathon (#TankForZion).

Introduction

FIRSTLY, I'd like to introduce this book by saying thank you to those who have purchased this particular copy. I know what you're thinking, and no I am not related to Paul Scholes, although I always tell people that just to see if I get the same *'Oh really'* reaction. I always do. But this book is not about me, and while I would love to sit down and write 130,000 words on myself (don't worry, that isn't happening any time soon), I thought it would be better if I wrote 130,000 words on something that people could find useful, and the first idea that came into my head was to write about American soccer. Not just about the NASL (North American Soccer League) or MLS (Major Soccer League) or the 1994 World Cup, but the entire history, dating from the very beginning to March 2019 when I finished this book. I realised that while there had been certain books written about certain periods in US soccer history, hardly any had been done about the entirety of it, which is the task I set myself.

I must say off the bat that some chapters will be significantly shorter than others for the simple fact that getting match reports of college games in the 1800s proved to be a lot tougher than I imagined, and other than match results, attendance figures, special signings and news about the Fall River Marksmen and Bethlehem Steel, there wasn't all that much that could've been dragged out about the American Soccer League (ASL) either. What you see in this book is the important points of those periods and none of it is my opinion. To quote Rafa Benitez, *it's all facts.* Sometimes there is a distinct lack of information that you just have to deal with, which was the case for most of the earlier years in this book, but once the NASL hits, it goes full out. There were more media outlets when the NASL dropped, meaning there were more news articles, interviews, *Sports Illustrated* columns and just a wider scope to cover the league than back in the ASL days. If they had ESPN back when Fall River had a team, I'm sure most of the early chapters would focus on that instead of mini articles in local newspapers.

When I started writing this book, I had just started *The Book of Basketball* by one of my favourite sports writers, Bill Simmons. It was unique in a way that I find it hard to put into words, but it was unlike any other sports book I had ever read and will probably ever read. Why? Because Simmons wrote about history from a different point of view to any that I've seen in all the sports book I've read, and that was as a fan. He wrote *TBOB* from a fan's point of view, but also from a member of the media's point of view and that fascinated and inspired me. Of course, I couldn't write the way he writes because he has his own unique style that can't be replicated, only copied, but I wanted to explore the idea of writing from two different perspectives. This book gave me the perfect chance to do that because I wasn't entirely sure on the whole history of US soccer – I was certainly not aware of its origins or subsequent leagues prior to the NASL, but I was confident in my knowledge of modern USMNT and of MLS. I knew a bit about the NASL era but not everything, so I got to view things from different vantage points. At one point, I found myself going down a rabbit hole that started with the American Civil War, then to the university system in the US, to looking at how the first Englishman to play in a World Cup actually played for the United States and had been signed by an American team from Tranmere Rovers. It all worked out well because there were so many interesting parts about teams, leagues, historical context, locations of certain key areas (warning: a lot of places got turned into Duane Reades). It was all fascinating and I hope you enjoy it as much as I did. It goes to show that original stereotypes of US soccer can be undone if you delve into history, but at least now you don't have to delve too much or go burrowing into any online rabbit holes because you're reading this, and you can use this as a reference point the same way that I used certain books as reference points. Soccer in the United States has a wonderfully rich history that ties in with many, many historical moments in the early years of this book, but all it takes is for one person to notice something to tell the story. Whilst I don't claim to be the only person to do this (trust me, I'm not), it's an honour to be able to tell the story of the beautiful game in the land of the free and the home of the brave because it deserves to be told. Maybe people have their mind set on *Murica* and soccer and that's fine, those people have their way of thinking and that's how they want to think, but you have to understand this: soccer in the United States didn't start with David Beckham, it didn't start with the 1994 World Cup and it didn't start with Pelé and the New York Cosmos. It started way, way before all of that happened and thankfully you can read about it here ... unless you expected a book written by a relation of Paul Scholes, in which case you're already disappointed but put that disappointment to one side and turn the page, read the story of the vast history of soccer in the United States and enjoy!

Chapter One

The Early Years – Origins

IN the US, you have your traditional sports that have a lasting legacy for many, many years. Baseball has been a staple in American society since the 19th century, going as far back as 1839, while college football emigrated from Great Britain over to the US just 30 or so years later, with the very first game taking place in 1869 when Rutgers hosted New Jersey, before the NCAA (National Collegiate Athletic Association) officially started in 1910. Sport and American culture go hand in hand, and it is still the same today, but the origins of arguably the third most popular sport for a large part of the 19th century and bordering over into the 20th century are debated regularly.

Some argue that the game of soccer was introduced to the United States via immigrants coming from Europe into Ellis Island, with thousands of immigrants coming over from countries like Italy, Greece, Austria, Hungary, the Balkan regions of Europe as well as various other parts of western and northern Europe. These were countries and areas in Europe where soccer was vibrant and the people were obsessed with it, so it makes sense that a lot of influence came via immigration, but some also suggest that in Louisiana some of the earliest games of soccer in American history were played by working-class people from the 1850s, with a lot of Scottish, French, Irish, German and Spanish families emigrating to the state and possibly influencing the history of soccer without even realising it. In Scott Crawford's Book, *A History of Soccer in Louisiana*, he suggests that the very first time modern English rules for soccer in the United States were played was in Louisiana during the 1850s, a good 20 years or so before the reported influx of immigrants at Ellis Island brought the game over, and, therefore, recognises the official birthplace of soccer in the United States as Louisiana. Others suggest that the origins lie elsewhere, in particular the eastern coast of the US and in the New England area, due to the influx of immigrants who reached the east via Europe.

Of course, as with any nation who embraced the sport, you can trace back through history and find various examples of other sports that closely represent what we now know as soccer. China and Greece had it, as mentioned before, but in America there was a game called Pasuckuakohowog, which roughly translates to they gather to play ball with the foot, but, according to the US Embassy, it was this game that was first discovered by Pilgrims that set sail into the harbours of Massachusetts in the 1620s. By all accounts, Pasuckuakohowog was an absolute mess of a game, with between 500 to 1,000 people playing at a time, multiple players wearing disguises including war paint to avoid retribution after the game had ended, with games usually lasting for hours, and in some cases even for days on end. While this is the first instance of a soccer-like game in the US, the 500 to 1,000 players, war paint and post-match feast probably isn't like anything we've ever seen in the modern world. So while it's technically the first sport like soccer that the US saw, it's only a variation and in turn was nothing like what soccer would evolve into in the 1820s. Thankfully for future generations, the numbers were whittled down dramatically and the need for masks was gone. If you two-footed someone, you had to own up to it at the post-match meal, which probably still carried on after the final whistle.

But while we take a look back at the origins of soccer, we move on in the timeline to the year 1862, in the same state as Pasuckuakohowog, but this time America got its very first organised soccer team in Boston called Oneida Football Club. Formed in 1862 by a graduate of Latin School of Epes Sargent Dixwell – a private college prep school in Boston – by the name of Gerrit Smith Miller, Oneida and Miller wanted to create an organised league in America to stop the violent and chaotic games against other schools and areas, which had their own set of rules and variations of soccer. Ironically, what Smith Miller was doing personified what was going on in the United States at the time, as the American Civil War was taking place during this period, and while the entire country was divided in two, Smith Miller wanted to split 'football' into two different sports. On one side you had what would become 'American football', a variation of rugby and a game that allowed the use of both hands and feet but prioritised the use of hands over feet. Eventually this manifested into what we now know as just plain old American football, but this is where many believe the start of that game was. On the other side, was 'soccer', a game that was mainly about footwork rather than using your hands, and again that broke off into its own game, as we are about to find out. In fact, before we get into the story of Oneida Football Club, let's take a look at the life of its founder.

Gerrit Smith Miller was born in Peterboro, New York, in 1869 and was born into quite an important family. Smith Miller graduated from Harvard University in 1894, studying botany to become a professional botanist, which he eventually did. He became assistant curator of mammals of the United States National Museum in Washington before becoming the head curator from 1909 to 1940, when he then left to work at the Smithsonian Institution. What does any of this have to do with soccer? Surprisingly, not one bit of this information has any relation to it, but Smith Miller does and his time at Harvard certainly does. To understand Smith Miller and how he got to Harvard, you have to look back at his life story, and, whilst not an awful lot is known about the early life of the future botanist and zoologist, what we do know is that he was named after his grandfather Gerrit Smith, who will go down in history as one of the leading United States abolitionists of slavery and was a candidate for the President of the United States in the years 1848, 1856 and 1860.

Just by reading about Smith, you can see that he was staunchly anti-slavery and even tried to help black slaves become self-sufficient by donating several acres of land and money to the African-American community in North Elba, New York. Whether it be financially or in land donations, Smith was a very influential figure in the anti-slave movement and was a member of the 'Secret Six', who helped fund John Brown's raid of Harper's Ferry. Brown was another abolitionist who was searching to free slaves and concocted a plan to raid Harpers Ferry, an armoury for the United States in Virginia, convinced that his plan would work and it would spark up a similar kind of uprising across the nation. He even contacted Harriet Tubman and Frederick Douglass to help him with the raid, but Tubman was suffering from an illness at the time so was unable to be of any aid, while Douglass turned down Brown's offer because he believed that the plan was going to fail. Ultimately, John Brown carried out his raid and saved a handful of slaves before being captured, charged with treason and hanged as a result of his actions. Found in his coat pocket, however, was a cheque written by Smith, which then led to the hunt for Smith. The State of Virginia were on the hunt for Gerrit Smith, and while he always denied any knowledge of the raid the State failed to fully charge Smith with any crime. However, due to the stress and mental anguish of the ordeal, Smith suffered a mental breakdown and was admitted for several weeks into the state asylum in Utica. You may realise that most of what you've just read had nothing to do with soccer, but the latter parts do (you've just got to keep with me on this one, it can get quite lengthy trying to explain everything) because during the hunt and attempt to charge and hang Smith, a young Gerrit Smith Miller was moved from their estate to Dixwell Private School in Boston to avoid getting the teenager into any trouble by association.

After making his way to Boston to avoid getting into any issues with the likeness of name to his famous grandfather, Smith Miller set about creating his organised soccer and it's at this point that we jump off the Civil War part of this story and move back on to the origins of soccer platform. It was interesting to learn about the tie between soccer and the Civil War, but now we have to leave the Civil War to one side and return to Boston, more specially Oneida. During his time at Dixwell, Smith Miller was a star of the informal style of soccer that was played in the area, bearing in mind that there weren't any formal rules for soccer at the time in any area because each area code had its own set of rules, and when you went from state to state, school to school, you could have encountered two different versions of the exact same game. At this point, despite being arguably the first 'star' of American soccer, Smith Miller grew tired of the lack of rules, the violence and the chaos and wanted to form a club made up of other prep school graduates in the Boston area, and he created what would be known as the 'Boston Game'. The Boston Game was something that acted as a precursor to other sports in America, such as, of course, soccer but also the introduction of rugby and American football, and when you read about the early history of American football in the United States and its introduction in colleges, the Boston Game is mentioned due to the fact that Harvard – the premier university team at the time – insisted on playing by these rules. While there aren't any records of other teams that Oneida played, maybe because the teams they played weren't organised sides like they were and didn't record results or find a need to record them, legend has it that Oneida never lost a game between their inception in 1862 until 1865, and never even conceded a goal. Whether this is just a rumour that got way out of hand as the years went by, we'll never truly know, but the legend and memory of Oneida remains strong in the area. Oneida – named after a lake that Smith Miller grew up near in Peterboro – played their games in Boston Common and to this day, across from Frog Pond, there is a monument dedicated to Oneida, which was erected in 1925 and an opening ceremony was held with six of the seven surviving team members attending the service. The inscription reads:

> On this field the Oneida Football Club of Boston, the first organised football club in the United States, played against all comers from 1862 to 1865. The Oneida goal was never crossed.

It's only fair that we end our little section on the very first organised football club in America by giving credit to the 16 listed members who are engraved on that monument in Boston Common:

Gerrit Smith Miller
Edward Lincoln Arnold
Robert Apthorp Boit
Edward Bowditch
Walter Denison Brooks
George Davis
John Malcolm Forbes
John Power Hall
Robert Means Lawrence
James D'Wolf Lovett
Francis Greenwood Peabody
Winthrop Saltonstall Scudder
Alanson Tucker
Louis Thies
Robert Clifford Watson
Huntingdon Frothingham Wolcott

The organisation of Oneida clearly rubbed off on the rest of the soccer teams in the surrounding areas, because soccer was initiated as an organised college sport in the US. The Civil War had ended and citizens of the United States were attempting to get back to their normal lives in whatever fashion they could, and soccer was slowly taking off in its early forms as the years went by. The first year association games held in the

United States were recorded was in 1866, and while records of this league may be sparse, there are three games involving American college sides. The first two were between Carroll College from Wisconsin going up against the Waukesha Town team, also from Wisconsin. These two sides ended their double header with a win each, while the third game was an inter-university match between two Trinity College teams, with the class of 1869 going up against the class of 1870. If you were wondering, it ended in a draw. Slowly but surely, more soccer was played in the coming years. A third match between Carroll College and Waukesha was played later on in 1866, but the score of that game is unknown to this day, so we will never know who won the final tiebreaker game in this great rivalry. In 1867 no club games were reported in the United States, but in 1868 soccer had spread out west and down south to Utah and Louisiana, mainly thanks to an influx of immigrants from Europe. Remember earlier how we mentioned immigrants had gone to Louisiana to bring soccer to the state? Well, it looks like they finally managed to organise some games with New Orleans St Joseph's Association, playing three organised club games from 12 July 1868 to 21 July 1868. Unfortunately, there aren't any recorded results for the team as their first match was registered as 'postponed', while the other two matches were unknown. A lot of these teams didn't keep records of their scores – as you're well aware by now – and a lot of their history is passed down by photographs (which can still be found online) and by word of mouth. One person said one result, who then told another person, and it took off from there. It was often difficult for teams to fully keep account of their scores, because either no one was there to note the scores down or no one was 100 per cent sure what the final scores actually were. It was a similar story in Utah, as Salt Lake City Team A played Salt Lake City Team B in February of 1868, the score was unknown, whilst in West Jordan, Utah, West Jordan Lower Branch and West Jordan Middle Branch played to another unknown scoreline. Regardless, the pattern was emerging across the country one way or another. Whether it be via immigrants from Europe, word of mouth or variations of another game a certain area played, soccer was travelling in the United States and more teams were cropping up, playing against each other in organised games. What happened next took the sport to the next level. The first ever fully recognised game of university soccer took place on 6 November 1869, as Rutgers ran out 6-4 victors over Princeton, and thus ushered in a new era.

The following year, a few more university schools joined in with the soccer fun, with seven games being played across January, October and November. Adelphi University – home to such alumni as Chris Armas, the current head coach of the New York Red Bulls, Public Enemy rappers Chuck D and Flavor Flav and Howard Stern guest Gary Dell'Abate, AKA Baba Booey – opened up the year with a fixture against a team that officially had no name, so technically isn't known by any name other than 'Unknown Team'. The first game where we can positively identify both teams, the venue and the score was between Rutgers 1874 and Rutgers 1873, with the Class of '73 running riot in a 6-1 mauling of '74. Yale, Dartmouth and Columbia would all have matches at some point during the year but, with the exception of those games, that was it for organised soccer in the 1870s. Why? Because the college/university game just collapsed. Again, it begs the question why did the game that was taking shape just collapse amongst those who organised it? Well, they adapted the Boston Game to create what we now know as American football – while a form of soccer was played and will be recognised throughout history as soccer, the universities took the next step on from what Gerrit Smith Miller and Oneida had started and took the rugby aspect of the Boston Game to form the new American football. As mentioned before, this had been growing for some time and now that it was growing on its own, separate to soccer, it split colleges and universities in two, which, in a way, was the plan all along.

It was a blow to the soccer scene in America at the time, but arguably what happened next was the second part of the new era of soccer. The universities had their time with the sport and decided to develop a new one, which was fine because college football is still alive and well now, but when working-class immigrants arrived from Europe they had not only a more refined version of soccer, but they also had little teams set up in their own communities and within their own fields of work, much like how teams across Europe and in South America were formed. The textile mills had their own team, as did the shipyards, quarries and miners, and soon enough this trend found its way across the nation. New York, New Jersey and Philadelphia were the first ones where you could see a strong development, before it spread further to the midwest, and Pacific side. The more immigrants that came to the country, the more this new culture spread, and soon enough teams were formed and started to play. But there was one problem: they had nothing to play for. The universities would play each other in a bid to show who was the stronger school, but the new community teams just wanted to have fun. These teams needed a competition and they needed a body to govern them, or to at least enforce some ground rules. In 1884 they got their wish as the American Football Association (AFA) was formed, making it the second-oldest sports league in American sports history (behind the National League in Major League Baseball (MLB), which was formed in 1876) and the oldest official American soccer league.

The same year of its formation, the AFA created the American Cup, a tournament that was the very first in the country to pit teams from different leagues against each other, and it was largely dominated by teams from New Jersey and Massachusetts in the first 12 years of the competition's existence, despite the fact that the AFA expanded itself to include teams from Pennsylvania, New York and, to a lesser extent, Texas. In the very first edition of the competition in 1885, five teams hailed from New Jersey and one from New York, with Clark O.N.T. winning the inaugural American Cup (Clarke O.N.T. stands for 'Clarke Our New Thread' which was a marketing tool for the Clarke Thread Company to promote their new product. Oh, you thought using soccer teams as a promotional tool was a recent thing?) Clark O.N.T. won the tournament in 1885, and again in 1886, and completed the three-peat in 1887 with a win over Kearny Rangers – which was a local derby – marking the first dominant team of the era, but the first victory didn't come without controversy. The very first American Cup Final in 1885 was played on Valentine's Day, with O.N.T. running out victors, but their opponents, simply known as New York, complained that they had used an illegal player(s). A replay was demanded and two months after their initial victory, O.N.T. won the cup again. No love lost there from the Valentine's Day fixture ...

The American Cup seemed to work a treat, with many sides entering, and for the first twelve years it rotated around New Jersey and Massachusetts, with Clark O.N.T. winning the first three, before Fall River domination in 1888 and 1892 as Fall River Rovers, Fall River Olympics and Fall River East Ends all took home the trophy (these were all different teams, not just one club going under three different names), which meant that two states had eight different winners across a 12-year spell, and it wasn't until 1897 that Philadelphia Manz broke up the duopoly, beating Paterson True Blues, a New Jersey team (shock) who were considered to be one of the first dynasties in American soccer, with three American Cup wins and five runner-up finishes.

Unfortunately, as the 20th century introduced itself, the American Cup was going through a turbulent time and wasn't held from the 1899 season to the 1906 campaign due to internal conflict within the AFA. On the surface, it just looks like a gap in time where an association needed to fix some issues, but in reality it proved to be a much more important moment in American soccer history as it opened up the discussion about whether it would be beneficial to have a governing body that would be able to oversee the entire United States soccer scene, as opposed to just the north-east. The opening decade or so of the 1900s would prove to be pivotal in the expansion and growth of soccer, not just in the US but worldwide, as FIFA was formed in 1904, and while the AFA was somehow gripping on to its power as the main governing body in the US, 1911 saw the introduction of the American Amateur Football Association

(AAFA) and it capitalised on what the AFA hadn't, by expanding out of the north-east, and even started its own cup to rival the American Cup called the AAFA Cup (very creative bunch).

Things in American soccer were moving at a rapid pace, a pace that was in keeping with the growth of the sport in the country. These groups didn't just form for the sake of it, there was a real demand to govern the sport across the country, and having two go head to head to essentially battle it out for the right to rule US soccer meant that the sport was on the edge of two things. It was on the edge of a golden era that would be the first 'boom period' in the country or it was on the edge of implosion. To use a somewhat modern (yet rather niche) reference, it was like WWF and WCW back in the late 90s– early 00s. Both had their core markets that they fed off, but the AAFA (the WWF in this scenario) capitalised on the mistakes that the AFA (WCW) had made, and when people started to realise that 'hey, maybe the AAFA have a better idea on how to run this joint across the country', there was only going to be one winner, and, even though both applied to be recognised by FIFA in 1912, it was in 1913 when the AAFA – which had renamed itself the United States Football Association (USFA) – was officially recognised by FIFA as the governing body and thus started to exert their influence across the United States.

Teams now had two competitions to fight for, a national team was now playing regularly after first playing against Canada in 1885 in what is widely recognised as the very first international soccer match played outside the United Kingdom, and the United States Men's National Team (USMNT, as we will refer to them from now on) toured Norway and Sweden. They weren't the only other team to tour Sweden, as Bethlehem Steel, one of the powerhouses of American soccer at the time, who managed to win the American Cup in 1914, 1916, 1917, 1918 and 1919 as well as the National Challenge Cup in 1915, 1916, 1918 and 1919, went away too, but by the time they came back to American shores what is now called the first golden age of American soccer had begun. The fact that teams were touring areas of Europe was a big enough accomplishment because not only did it show that teams felt they could go to Europe and attract big enough crowds, it also showed that these teams could go to Europe and beat the Europeans. Consider this in today's game where a semi-professional club like Hitchin Town or North Ferriby United went over to South America and took on the likes of Boca Juniors or Santos. It seems far-fetched now, but that's essentially what Bethlehem did! But if touring was the first step, the creation of the ASL in 1921 was the giant step the sport needed to take. Was the ASL the first professional soccer league in America? Some say yes, some say no, but was it the biggest and most popular? Absolutely, so popular that Scottish and English players risked FIFA sanctions for leaving their countries just to play in the ASL.

Soccer in the US during this time was huge. Maybe not as big as baseball, seeing as they were just about to enter the Lou Gehrig and Babe Ruth era, but big enough to generate attendances in the tens of thousands, attract suitable sponsors and bring in two teams who had rich backers but also rich history on the field: Bethlehem Steel and Fall River Marksmen. The two fought tooth and nail to become the era's most dominant team, but with seven ASL titles and four National Challenge Cup wins, the Marksmen were the dynasty of the 20s. The Marksmen went on tours and faced huge European names like Glasgow Rangers and Sparta Prague and managed to hold their own at times. Teams like the Marksmen and the Steel would have big effects on soccer in the coming years, both positively and negatively (which we will jump in to in the next two chapters) and during the 20s, while America was experiencing an economic boom, these two teams represented what America was about. They spent the most money on the best players to increase their chances of winning. Who did the Marksmen beat by six points to win their first ASL title? The Steel. When they retained it the following season, who was lagging three points behind? The Steel. When they completed the three-peat, who was behind them? Not the Steel, but you get the point: these two were the dominant force of American soccer in the 1920s.

While it's important to move forward with the history of soccer in the US, it's imperative to look at the ASL as a whole and how important it was to the future of the sport and the lasting effect it had on not only domestic matters for club sides, but also on an international level for the US men's national team. We've touched on Fall River Marksmen and Bethlehem Steel, but why just stop at where we did? These two teams are widely considered to be 'dynasties' in American soccer, so without further ado, it's time to get stuck into the first golden age of soccer in the United States.

Chapter Two

The American Soccer League (1921–33)

WHILE not many people remember the league or anything to do with how the league was conceived, let alone who played in it, it's important to remember that without the American Soccer League, the rest of what you're about to read may not have happened. When one looks at any historical timeline, whether that be a single country, a continent, a timeline of conflict between two nations or a sport, you find that certain incidents have a lasting effect on the rest of that timeline. Everything links together in ways that you may not have realised, and that's what makes history incredible. As for American soccer, everything you read in the previous chapter will link to whatever you read in the rest of this book, even if the link is sometimes rather blurred. One of the more important links, however, is something we touched on briefly in the last chapter, and that is, of course, the ASL. We spoke about how two teams in particular dominated the league and made themselves famous because of it, but it's a topic that needs to be discussed in more than just a handful of paragraphs because of the impact it had.

The ASL was formed in 1921 after a merger of the National Association Football League – a semi-professional league that ran between 1895 and 1898, before a second incarnation from 1906 to 1921 – and the Southern New England Soccer League – another semi-pro league that formed in 1914 and collapsed completely in 1921. While it didn't serve the entire United States, just some of the north-east, it was by far and away the most popular league because the sport was so popular in the cities where they had handpicked their teams. For contextual matters, let's take a look at the teams that started the very first ASL season:

Philadelphia Field Club
New York Field Club
Todd Shipyards FC (Brooklyn, New York)
Harrison Soccer Club (Harrison, New Jersey)
J&P Coats (Pawtucket, Rhode Island)
Fall River United (Fall River, Massachusetts)
Holyoke Falcos (Holyoke, Massachusetts)
Jersey City Celtics (Jersey City, New Jersey)

Just by looking at the teams involved, you can get an idea that in these sports-mad markets (yes, they were sports-mad back in these days, too) they would grow fond of soccer and embrace it the same way they embraced baseball, and during the ASL period the fans of these teams absolutely loved it! The league was founded in the Manhattan-based Hotel Astor, which was known for its sophistication, wealthy atmosphere, and it signified the type of owners who would be interested in such a league. (Just for the record, the Hotel Astor is no longer there; in fact, what stands in its place is One Astor Place, a high-rise complex on Times Square that includes the PlayStation Theatre, the Minskoff Theatre and the MTV Studios. If you've been to Times Square, it's the tall building next to the equally historic Paramount Building, better known as the Hard Rock Cafe building and Bubba Gump's Shrimp Company restaurant. What does this have to do with soccer? Nothing, it's just a note that if you ever walk past One Astor Plaza, you're walking past the exact spot where the first professional American soccer league was formed.) Remember, this was a time when soccer was the second-biggest sport in the entire US, behind baseball, and business in America was at an all-time high. Factories and metalwork industries were experiencing a post-First World War boom, with people inventing new ideas such as wristwatches, stainless steel and adding zippers to trousers, and citizens were spending more money than before. Because of the sheer size of the United States, it didn't need to import any materials from abroad to make anything, it was able to do it all on its own. The automobile industry, the factories and steel mills produced tons of products that could be used by seemingly everyone after the First World War, and thus the demand for more factories, more cars and more steel opened a lot of new jobs for millions of people. The stock market was booming as a result, and a lot of people were making outrageous sums of cash. One company in particular that was thriving as a result was Bethlehem Steel, who had been a major supplier of armour plating for the US Army and were profiting from that massively. One important part of the 1920s boom was the fact that, due to the amount of money companies were making, they were able to employ a large number of European workers to work in their factories. It may seem like a minor detail, but when Charles Schwab, owner of Bethlehem Steel, turned the employees team into a professional one in the mid-1910s, he went out of his way to make the newly named Bethlehem Steel Football Club.

'SCHAWB CORNERS FOOTBALL STARS', read the headline from the *New York Times*, which profiled the move from Schwab and provided a good insight into how the main information was relayed at the time.

> Charles M. Schwab, the United States Steel man has taken such an interest in soccer football that he spared no expense to get together a team which promises to surpass any soccer team in this country. The team will represent the Bethlehem Steel Works of Bethlehem, Penn. A raid has been made of all the crack soccer teams of the country and many of the stars have been signed to play under the Bethlehem colours.

> Not only does Mr. Schwab expect to have the best
> soccer team in America to represent Bethlehem, but
> he also plans to build a new athletic field for games
> at Bethlehem which will represent an outlay of more
> than $50,000. On the field will also be an up-to-date
> clubhouse for the players.

Safe to say, there was a sufficient amount of attention on
Bethlehem Steel, mainly because of their owner, their name
and the amount of money they spent on assembling their squad
(not much changes in this sport), but there was a team across
in Massachusetts who were building a superteam of their own
without the help of a steel tycoon, although little did either side
know that they were about to go head to head for the right to
call themselves the dynasty of the ASL.

Fall River has an extensive history in the early years of
American soccer, with the likes of Fall River Rovers proving
to be a successful outfit in their own right, and when local
businessman Sam Mark – who was known as a local basketball
and baseball promoter – bought out Fall River United he
renamed them the Fall River Marksmen (why were they called
the Marksmen? Was there a rich history of Civil War riflemen
in the Fall River area? Nope, Sam Mark just wanted to name the
team after himself). In true owner form, Mark was never really
a massive soccer fan, but he was attracted by the attendances
of the Fall River Rovers side who we spoke about before in the
first chapter. Mark had a plan to build a successful soccer team,
build a new stadium (just across state lines in Tiverton, RI, to
avoid Massachusetts law) and to fill that new stadium with
eager and adoring fans to rake in the cash.

Seems like a normal strategy that almost any sports team
would implement, right? Of course it is, because while Fall
River had a rich soccer history, the ASL were moving in the
direction of legitimising soccer in the US and making money
because that's what the 20s were about: making money and
being successful at the same time. Luckily for the ASL, they
had two teams who were determined to do both.

Before we dive into the Steel vs Fall River rivalry, let's take a look at the ASL as a whole to understand the context. Dissatisfaction for the way the National Association Football League was being run, plus the fact that the USFA wanted to create a unified first division was the perfect storm. The first secretary of the league was Thomas Cahill, one of the most influential figures when it comes to early US soccer history as he was the man who initially went to FIFA to get the USFA recognised as a governing body. Also, remember how the USMNT went on a tour of Scandinavia during the 1910s? Cahill was the manager of the team, guiding them to their first-ever official win under the USFA banner. Cahill did a lot for soccer in the early days, even if the peak of his influence was during the prime years of the ASL, and despite his influence waning following the ASL period. While he will be mentioned in these chapters, it's a shame that his name is often forgotten about when discussing the history of US soccer and that most people know about the 1930s USMNT at the World Cup but can't recall any players or Cahill as manager. Nevertheless, his influence was wide-ranging, and during his time at the ASL the league only grew as each year passed.

The inaugural 1921/22 season was underway, and while in the history books it'll say that Philadelphia Field Club won the very first title, it was a strange path to get to that title. Initially, the owners of Bethlehem Steel disbanded them, moving them to Philly under the name of Philadelphia Field Club. Philly FC re-signed most of the top Steel players and some top players from elsewhere, due to the wealth of Charles Schwab, and they, of course, won the ASL. But despite the success, Philly FC lacked fan support and reported financial trouble, so the owners once again moved the club back to Bethlehem under their old name, just one season after moving. So, technically, Bethlehem *did* win the very first ASL title, but under a different name and in a different city.

On the face of it, the ASL looked like it could suffer from a number of things. Sure, the winners had to relocate due to lack of fan support, the Jersey City Celtics had to fold after just five games and two more clubs withdrew from the league, but while these were major hiccups, everything else seemed to be running fairly smoothly, although only in areas where fan interest was high and owners were willing to spend that little bit extra to push their team over the finish line. But the 1922/23 season promised to be of a better standard and more competitive. A new Philadelphia team was added to the league under the same Field Club name, while Paterson and Brooklyn introduced new teams, with Sam Mark making his impact after taking over the newly renamed Fall River Marksmen – who finished third from bottom in 1921/22. For the first time in ASL history, we had the Marksmen and the Steel going head to head in what would be the beginning of the first major rivalry in US soccer, and perhaps the first time two potential dynasties had come up against one another at this point in time in US sports in general. The Red Sox and New York Yankees weren't completely contending due to the fact the Yankees took Babe Ruth off the Sox, while the Yankees didn't have any serious long-term competition for quite some time. Fall River and Bethlehem Steel, you could argue, was the first time the US had seen anything like this.

So, who would come out on top of the Marksmen and the Steel rivalry in its infancy? Well, neither one of them. J&P Coats of Pawtucket won the league by just two points, ahead of the Steel, winning 21 of their 28 games in this season and scoring 68 goals in the process. The Steel, as mentioned, were just two points behind and seven points ahead of the Marksmen, who improved considerably from the previous year, making 25 points up to finish third in the league. Of course, with Sam Mark wanting to make his team a powerhouse as quickly as possible, he made three key signings that changed their history quite considerably.

Harold Brittain, Alex Kemp and Billy Orr were brought in for the 1922/23 season, with Brittain coming from the Steel/ Philly FC (after they had lured him over from Chelsea, London, a few years before), while Kemp was a Scottish-born defender who had come over from Canadian sides Grand Trunk Railway (fun fact, the Grand Trunk Railway inspired the name of the 1970s American rock band Grand Funk Railroad as the line ran through Flint, Michigan, where the band was from. This is the kind of cutting-edge insight and historical accuracy you should expect from this book) and Boleil. These three signings, especially Brittain as he finished top scorer in the first season with a mightily impressive 24 goals in 17 games, would prove to be vital in the building of the Marksmen dynasty, but also they would prove vital to how other teams would try to build their own teams. All three signings weren't American, or at least they weren't American born, and they brought with them the experience of growing up in England and Scotland. Other clubs, mainly those who were tied in with owners who made their money through industry, started to look overseas for help in their factories and for those with experience in the textile industry, mainly in the English county of Lancashire and Scottish valley of Clyde. Thus, there shouldn't be a surprise that teams like the Marksmen, the Steel and the Boston Wood Workers – named after their owner G.A.G. Wood – decided to spend a lot of money to make their teams better, because why wouldn't you? You have the ability to fund a superteam of sorts, with the ability to lure better players from areas such as Lancashire and Clyde to work in their factories and provide a good level of talent in their own teams. In the book *Boston Ballparks and Arenas* by Alan E. Foulds, he talks about the introduction of the Boston Soccer Club, formed by Wood in the 1920s.

> In 1924, G.A.G. Wood formed the Boston Soccer Club. The new entrant stirred things up. Gate receipts for the entire league that year doubled from the year before. The team's president, Wood, said, 'We spent a lot of money because we realised that nothing was too good for the Hub.' Wherever the team travelled, fans came out to see the Wonder Workers – the name was unofficial but, according to contemporary reports, well deserved. Most players were either born in Scotland or had Scottish ancestry.

The introduction of the Wonder Workers in 1924 signified the growth of the ASL. Owners like Wood, Mark and Schwab decided that, to grow the league, you needed to spend money on new playing fields and increasingly better playing talent than what was already in the league at the time, and now with the new stadia and better players, the fans started to come in droves. This kind of thinking was implemented initially during the 1923/24 season when the Marksmen lifted their first ASL title, beating Bethlehem Steel to the top spot by six points, with the Steel on 38 and the Marksmen on 44. When people write extensively about dynasties they often use the line 'little did this time know what they were about to achieve', but the fact of the matter is Fall River Marksmen knew exactly what they were about to achieve. How did they know this? Because success is exactly what they set up for by bringing in the foreign imports and building a new stadium for more fans. It sounds simple, but Sam Mark bought Fall River to win and to make money. To win, you have to spend money, which is exactly what they did.

Their 1923/24 success in the ASL was just the first half of their triumphant double, as they defeated Vesper Buick (yes, another sponsored team. As the famous quote goes, 'they'll be going wild in the streets of Vesper Buick tonight') in the final 2-4, with all four goals coming from three scorers born in England and Scotland. Brittain scored for Fall River, as well as Glasgow-born Johnny Reid and a double from Fred Morley, who was a prolific forward for the likes of Reading, Blackpool and Brentford and was born in the town of Burslem, England (home of former Motorhead bassist and vocalist Ian 'Lemmy' Kilmister). Oh, before we move on ... who did Fall River beat in the semi-final? Bethlehem Steel. They just can't stay away from each other.

As attendances grew larger and the demand for more ASL soccer grew along with it, the regular season games were extended from 28 games to 44, meaning we got a lot more soccer, a lot more goals and a lot more money from the fans. Three more teams were added from the Massachusetts area resulting in more local derbies – if people weren't hooked on it already.

New Bedford Whalers (two-time champions of the old Southern New England Soccer League), G.A.G. Wood's Boston Wonder Workers and the Providence Clamdiggers arrived in the league, along with two other teams from New York and Philly – Fleisher Yarn, former winners of the American Cup in 1923 and the first National Amateurs Cup in 1924 – meaning the league extended from just eight teams to 12, and this could arguably be called the start of the peak years for the ASL, with very good reason as well. The increase in goals helped massively, with 906 being scored across the 12 teams, and attendances ranged between 8,000 and 10,000 on a regular basis. The ASL was outdrawing the fledging National Football League (NFL) at the time, and teams like Fall River would often outdraw the Boston Red Sox at a time when baseball ruled America.

Thomas Cahill went on record to say that 'soccer is making great progress and in the not too distant future will be second only to baseball as the leading pro game', which may sound like a bold statement now, but consider this: the NFL was barely even a flicker of what it is now, the National Basketball Association (NBA) was a good 20 years away from forming and basketball wasn't as popular as soccer was, so only baseball rivalled soccer in the sporting hierarchy. So while it may seem outlandish to suggest this now, back in the 1920s and the heyday of the ASL, Cahill probably wasn't far off in his prediction. He was suggesting that soccer was growing and based on evidence from the 1924/25 season, he was going in the right direction – as was the sport as a whole. We already know that the recent additions to the league weren't afraid to spend the money needed to be competitive, in particular in Boston where we know that Fall River and the Wonder Workers were ready to spend, but perhaps not many anticipated quite how much they would spend. Teams weren't afraid to spend big and sign players from clubs like Glasgow Rangers (which the Wonder Workers did when they signed Scottish international Tommy Muirhead as their player-manager), but one loophole that caused a lot of upset was that these clubs would sign players to play for their teams, all while working at the factory of their owner. For example, the Boston Wonder Workers managed to sign another Scottish international in the form of Alex McNab from Greenock Morton, paying him $25 a week (just under $1,500 in today's money) to play and work in Wood's factory. McNab spoke about his move to the United States to a newspaper reporter at the time:

> I was offered only four pounds a week (by Greenock Morton for the 1924/25 season). I don't think that is anything like a decent wage. And when I asked to be put on the transfer list I was told a sum that nearly took my breath away. It was more than 1,500 pounds. Fifteen hundred pounds, who's going to pay that for me? It was obvious that the sum was prohibitive and that I was being so tied down that I could not do anything other than sign for Morton. Well, I was determined not to do that. I went to work in my engineering yard and one day a cable from the other side (America) arrived. It was an offer of around 12 pounds a week to work and play football. I jumped at it.

Employing people to work in your factory was fine. Signing players to play for your club was also fine. Employing people to work in your factory AND play for your club, not so fine, so the clubs got into serious trouble. Multiple meetings were held between the USFA and FIFA to order these teams, who had become known as 'American Menaces' in Scotland, to stop signing players in this manner. It's easy to blame one or two clubs for doing this, but the reality is that most clubs, or at least most that won or challenged for honours, were doing the same thing. Was it ethically right? No, but no one seemed to care. The players didn't care because they were getting paid absurd amounts compared to what they got back home, the fans didn't care because their team had outstanding players and were playing very good soccer and the owners didn't care because the players were happy – their teams were playing entertaining football and the fans were arriving in their droves to watch. It was a perfect storm that would only hurt the league a few years later, but until that time arrived the ASL and its participants wanted to reap the benefits.

Bear in mind that in the off-season of the 1924/25 season a lot changed, and this season was meant to be the pinnacle of the ASL, or the start of the prime years. The Wonder Workers had signed new players to challenge for the title in their first season, including the likes of the aforementioned McNab and Muirhead, alongside Johnny Ballantyne from Partick Thistle, even though the Scot was already under contract with Partick. Ballantyne knew he would be criticised for the move when he said to the *Sunday Star*:

> Oh, I got this offer only the other day and it was at the last moment that I was determined to go. I have written to manager Easton about it and I hope that he will receive my letter sympathetically. I have no doubt that I will be criticised for having departed so suddenly but then the offer came suddenly and I had to make up my mind quickly. I hope to make 12 pounds a week here in America. What chance have I got of doing that here?

Former Manchester City and Fall River man Mickey Hamill joined up as well to create a line-up that threatened to go head to head with the likes of Fall River and Bethlehem Steel. Speaking of which, those two clubs were aiming to set the standard in the ASL, and while Fall River largely kept the same team that won the title in 1923/24, the Steel made a few acquisitions that meant they had as good a chance as any to walk away as the champions. Whitey McDonald, Bill Carnihan and Bob McGregor formed a midfield that would become synonymous with outstanding creativity, with all three having tons of ability in their locker, but arguably their most valuable signing came from New York City when they picked up the top scorer from the previous season, Archie Stark. Without giving away too much of what happened during the course of the season, Stark proved to be an incredible signing as he set record after record in US soccer. With the creativity of McDonald, Carnihan and McGregor behind him to give him chances galore, Stark set the record for most goals in a single US soccer campaign with 67 in 44 games (a ratio of 1.5 goals per game) and bagging eight hat-tricks along the way, including four goals on the opening day against Philadelphia. This free-flowing, attacking style of play meant that while Fall River had the team chemistry and title-winning experience to go back-to-back, the Steel had the firepower to out-score any team and could be unplayable on any given matchday. So, with teams spending a lot of money to build teams that could catch up with the one team who didn't spend all that much, where would the title end up?

For the second time in a row, Fall River captured the ASL title, but only by three points, and amazingly they did it despite having two fewer wins than second-placed Steel. The Steel scored 14 more goals but conceded 15 more than Fall River, whilst losing five more games, which is where the title swung in the Marksmen's favour. Title experience had won over lavish signings, but it wasn't all about the Steel and Marksmen. The Brooklyn Wanderers managed to finish in third place, one point ahead of the Wonder Workers, despite all the money that was spent by Boston. That being said, it wasn't all bad for Boston as they managed to win the Lewis Cup, beating Fall River 2-1 in the final.

Wait, wait, wait, the Lewis Cup? Yes, a new competition designed by the ASL clubs to go up against the Open Cup – the more traditional cup competition in the US – in a way to make their own schedule a bit easier to handle, seeing as they were required to participate in the Open Cup despite the fact the games were right in the middle of their ASL schedule. Named after one of the league's co-founders, Edgar Lewis, the cup never really managed to rival the history and legacy of the US Open Cup, but it proved to be a huge factor in why soccer would change at the turn of the decade, and while ASL boycotted the 1925 Open Cup to stage their own Lewis Cup, it was the start of something that would be brewing up inside US soccer for the next few years, but that's something we will get into later ...

After scoring 113 during the season, with Harold Brittain, Tommy Croft, Harry McGowan, Bill McPherson and Dougie Campbell all scoring double figures for them, the Fall River Marksmen managed to make it three ASL title wins in three consecutive years, setting a new record for total points in a 44-game season with 72, winning 30 games, drawing 11 and losing only twice. Even more incredibly, they broke the record for most goals in a single season by bagging 143, but only had two players in the top-scorers list. Tec White finished fourth in the charts with 33 goals in 39 games, while the only other player in the top ten from the Marksmen was the ever-consistent Harold Brittain, scoring 21 in 35. But if anything it goes to show how the quality of the league improved over time and how the influx of foreign imports raised the standard so much that teams were scoring well over 100 goals per season and players were getting goal figures into the 30s and above (to put that into context, only two players have ever scored more than 34 goals in a Premier League season – Andy Cole and Alan Shearer – and even they only beat Tec White's record by one goal. That's impressive enough, but when you consider that only Dixie Dean in 1927/28 has come close to breaking Archie Stark's record of 67 goals in a single season – Dean got 60 – it makes it all the more incredible).

By this time, the ASL had established itself as the premier soccer league in the United States. You can tell just by the amount of money spent, number of fans through the gate and the types of players scoring outrageous amounts of goals that the soccer was of high quality, or at the very, very least it was entertaining to watch. It was around this time that famous teams from Europe started to sail over to challenge the best of the ASL. The first to travel over was the well-known Czech side Sparta Prague, who had formed a new look side post-First World War, nicknamed 'Iron Sparta' due to the strength of the club during the 1920s and 1930s when they dominated their domestic league, winning six titles across the two decades including a back-to-back triumph in the 1925/26 and 1926/27 seasons. While they may not have been a club side like Real

Madrid, Manchester United or Inter Milan, they certainly proved a strong test for the ASL sides, who were considered to be good teams but never ones to trouble the mighty Europeans. The other team to come over from Europe that summer was a team by the name of Hakoah Wien, an all-Jewish side who went on a ten-game tour of the US, with the peak of this tour coming at the Polo Grounds in Manhattan against an ASL New York All Star Team, which drew some outrageous crowds for the time. The three games that Hakoah played in New York generated crowds of 25,000, 30,000 and 36,000, but the All Star match brought in 46,000 paying customers, a record for spectators at a soccer match in the US at the time.

It was vitally important for Hakoah to tour the United States, primarily the Jewish population in the north-east. Hakoah means 'strength' in Hebrew, and many teams went on to adopt the name. The players were pleasantly surprised by the lack of anti-semitism they faced on the tour, and some even stayed in the United States and signed on with some of the teams because they enjoyed it so much! Some of the players that stayed Stateside eventually created a new team in 1928 called New York Hakoah and won the US National Challenge Cup the following year. The tour unfortunately lost Hakoah Wien a substantial amount of money (it was rumoured that the club lost around $30,000, leading their president to resign once he got back to Vienna), but despite this, and losing a few games, the style that both Hakoah and Prague played left an imprint on the game in the US. Pete Renzulli, the goalkeeper for the ASL New York All Star Team, was quoted as saying, 'Hakoah had the ball for around 87 minutes of the game', yet the ASL NY All Stars hit them on the counter three times to win 3-0. It was a productive tour and it was definitive proof that the teams and players in the league were improving, and that the ASL was at the peak of its powers, being able to take on European teams who had experienced success on the continent and convincingly beating them.

But the change experienced during these tours wasn't just a fad, it spread throughout the league and it didn't just affect the style of play or the players that stayed in the United

States from Hakoah, the ASL even experimented with the rules afterwards. For example, they introduced the idea of having in-game substitutions, which was way ahead of its time, especially when you consider that in the English Football League subs weren't fully introduced until the 1965/66 season (just in case anyone was wondering, the first sub in the Football League was a gentleman by the name of Keith Peacock, who came on for Charlton Athletic to replace the goalkeeper on the day, Mike Rose, against Bolton Wanderers. Peacock would eventually leave south-west London to join the Columbus Magic in the second incarnation of the ASL and the Tampa Bay Rowdies indoor side. See, this stuff all links together one way or another!). Another new rule that was introduced was the goal judge to decide whether the ball had crossed the goal line or not, similar to what they have in the National Hockey League (NHL) these days and almost like what you see on the touchline during Champions League games, except the ASL officials actually did something. Curiously, something that is often called for in modern-day soccer in England was implemented during this season of the ASL – they added a 'penalty box' or, as it's more commonly known, a sin bin. It must be noted as well that these changes didn't stick around for very long, and were ultimately scrapped at the end of the 1926/27 season, but we will get on to what happened after this current season later on ...

For the first time under their Bethlehem Steel name in the ASL era, they won the league by a resounding nine points over the Wonder Workers, scoring 114 goals in the process (one fewer than the previous season, but the scoring figures this season were very odd – hang on with me before I get to the scoring charts) and conceding a league low of 52. Whilst the Steel were reclaiming what they felt was rightly theirs, the Marksmen were doing what the Steel had done the season before and finished third in the league table but won the US Open Cup, thumping the Detroit-based Holley Carburetor 7-0 in front of 10,000 spectators.

The Steel's league victory was in large part down to their prolific duo up front, Archie Stark and Tom Gillespie

– who was brought in from English club Preston North End after spells up in Scotland (surprise, surprise) – with the two scoring 56 goals between them during the season, and Johnny Japp, George Forrest and Malcolm Goldie amassing 36, meaning that 92 of the 114 goals were shared amongst just five players.

Now, if you heard that stat about a team like Pep Guardiola's Barcelona from the late 2000–early 2010s you'd be in awe of what they'd managed to do (the treble-winning Barcelona side of 2009 had Lionel Messi, Thierry Henry and Samuel Eto'o all reach double figures in La Liga as they scored 72 of the 105 goals in the league that season, meaning just 33 goals were scored by players other than those three), but for the Steel it had almost become an expectation because of the players they had at their disposal (some extremely talented foreign imports) and the money they threw at winning this title and the cups during the era.

So while it had taken them a few years to knock the Marksmen off their perch, and even though they had won five US Open Cups during their existence, you could argue that it was this league title that secured their status as one of two main dynasties of the early 20th century in US soccer. And the fact that the two were going head to head with each other at the time was very good for the ASL and soccer as a whole, but even though in public the soccer was great and the fans were in love with their teams' star players, it was after the 1926/27 season that things started to change drastically.

During 1927, the ASL was at the apex of its popularity and, by the looks of it, the league could only go in one direction – forward. It was by now the second-biggest sport in the United States behind baseball, with history suggesting that the ASL was as close as any league could get in any sport to MLB, considering the popularity of soccer and the crowds they getting. There aren't too many links between MLB and the ASL during this time period, but there is one connection that would prove to be a fatal one, even if at the time it looked like it could have been revolutionary.

Charles Stoneham, a native of New Jersey, was known for being the owner of the New York Giants baseball team (now known as the San Francisco Giants in MLB) and eventually became the owner of another New York sports team, the New York Nationals (formerly known as Indiana Flooring, who finished fifth in the 1926/27 season). During his time as owner of the Giants, he oversaw three World Series titles in 1921, 1922 and 1933 before his death in 1936, but it isn't his time with the Giants we are focusing on, it's what he did during his tenure as Nationals owner that eventually started what would be called the Soccer Wars (there's a whole chapter on that coming up), and the changes he tried to introduce into the league despite the controversy it was always going to cause. Stoneham had the idea to essentially let ASL teams boycott the US Open Cup in order to focus on the ASL season, like if the owner of a Premier League team wanted everyone to boycott the FA Cup and League Cup in order to concentrate their energy solely on what made the most money for everyone, the Premier League itself. This wasn't new territory for the ASL, who had previously withdrawn from the competition during the 1924/25 season. It caused a bit of tension – and not for the first time – between the USFA and the ASL, but the ASL clubs quickly returned to the competition despite the introduction of the Lewis Cup.

As Colin Jose says in his book, *The American Soccer League: The Golden Years of American Soccer 1921–1931,* when talking about the prime years of the ASL:

> The halcyon days of the ASL, when soccer's popularity was growing by leaps and bounds, lasted from the summer of 1924 until fall 1928. At the time it must have seemed that the game had finally arrived and had a bright future in the United States. But unbeknown to all, in 1928 and 1929 there were some very dark clouds on the horizon. The beginning of the end of the American Soccer League began in the summer of 1928 when Charles A. Stoneham, the owner of the New York Giants baseball club (now the San Francisco Giants),

who also owned the New York Nations (formerly Indiana
Flooring) of the American Soccer League, made a series
of proposals. Among these proposals was one suggesting
that the league withdrew its teams from the United States
Open Cup, unless the national governing body agreed
to play the competition in the spring, following the ASL
season. The USFA refused. Ironically, the Nationals were
the holders of the Open Cup at the time, having won this
competition, regarded as the national championship, the
previous spring.

Mr. Stoneham's proposal was adopted by the
ASL and all the clubs were ordered to withdraw from
the Open Cup, much to the displeasure of the USFA.
However, three ASL Clubs – Bethlehem Steel, New York
Giants and Newark Skeeters – defied the league ruling
and were subsequently suspended by the league. The
USFA ordered them reinstated and the ASL refused. The
ASL was then suspended by the USFA but continued to
operate as an outlaw league.

And just like that, the Soccer Wars began, but while all the off-
field problems were occurring between the two federations, it
was easy to forget that the ASL was still in operation during
the 1927/28 season and had their new changes in order. A big
change that was introduced was splitting the league into two
halves and, no, not like a Western Conference and an Eastern
Conference, but two separate leagues of the same teams,
before going into a play-off system based around the best six
performing teams over the course of the entire season, both the
first and second halves. In the sole wildcard tie Bethlehem Steel
defeated Stoneham's New York Nationals 6-1 on aggregate to set
up a meeting between the Steel and the Wonder Workers, while
the New Bedford Whalers went up against the Marksmen to see
if Fall River could regain their crown from the Steel's clutches.
In somewhat of a shock, both the Marksmen and Steel went out
at the hands of New Bedford and Boston and the two dynasties
were out. Was it a shock based on the entire season? No, because

the winners of the ASL in the first half of the season were the Wonder Workers, while the Whalers beat the Marksmen to top spot in the second half, despite having one less point (one less point? Well, the Marksmen had played one more game than the Whalers in the second half due to the fact that Philadelphia were suspended after 10 games and the league asked Hartford to resign to balance up the league, but the Whalers finished top on account of having a better win percentage of .680 to the Marksmen's .673. A fine margin, but a very confusing one too). Despite the confusing way that the league was decided, the play-off final was a very exciting game, as Boston faced off against New Bedford. Boston upset the Whalers with a hat-trick from Scottish striker Barney Battles Jr (a player who would go on to score 41 goals in 116 games for Boston, 133 for Hearts in 148 games while also representing both the United States and Scotland in his career) to give them the win on the day and their first ASL title. Some 987 goals were scored across both the first and second halves of the season, and it was one of the New Bedford strikers who won the scoring title as Andy Stevens, who already had a scoring title under his belt, finished one goal ahead of Max Gruenwald of the Giants, with Stevens hitting 30 goals in 46 games. Again proving the quality of the league and the quality of the goalscorers, Stevens finished top with 30 goals but only five goals separated Stevens and the rest of the top seven, with 12 players in total hitting 20 or more in this campaign.

The Giants won the National Cup that year, while the Steel claimed the Lewis Cup for the very first time (spoiler: it would be the only time they'd ever reach the final of the Lewis Cup) as they defeated Boston in the final. But as the Soccer Wars escalated, the league suffered as a result. Three teams would leave the league prior to the 1928/29 season and, in one particular case, would hurt the league in a big way – a way that perhaps they didn't anticipate, but when Newark Skeeters, the New York Giants and the Bethlehem Steel all departed the ASL, there was a gap that needed filling. These three teams eventually joined up with teams from the Southern New York

State Soccer Association to form the Eastern Professional Soccer League (EPSL), a league that only lasted until 1929. But while the Steel weren't officially part of the ASL at this point in the timeline, it's important to remember the impact they had on the league and soccer in the United States.

Nine league titles, five National Challenge Cups, six American Cups, one Lewis Cup and one Allied Amateur Cup. In all 22 trophies from 1914 to 1929 – including five runner-up places in the league in 1916, 1918, 1923, 1924 and 1925, along with a runner-up spot in 1917 in the National Challenge Cup and another runner-up spot in the American Cup in 1920. In such a long period of time, to be so successful was extraordinary. They had the backing of Charles Schwab, but they still managed to use the money wisely to bring in the right kind of players. Archie Stark and Tom Gillespie formed a brilliant partnership towards the latter stages of the ASL years, and they had innovators of soccer in the early years of the 20th century like Harold Brittain, who, while he was more well-known during the ASL days as a Marksmen, started his career in the United States with the Steel during the 1920/21 season. He may have only been with the club for a solitary season, but that year practically set the foundations for what was to come during the 1920s for the Steel, even if it meant that they had to compete against Brittain and the Marksmen to claim the ASL crown. To end the spell of a great ASL side like the Bethlehem Steel in the way that they did was not only untimely, but it didn't suit the way the club held itself during the successful years. If they had walked away before the Great Depression, that could be understood due to the financial constraints during the time, or whether they won the league title and decided to walk away, as odd as it would have been, it could have made sense that they'd walked away on top. But to be expelled? It's a shame they had to be expelled to end a great and successful era of a famous team of trailblazers, but that was the state that US soccer was in at the time. Whilst there still was an ASL season to be played, it wouldn't be the same without the Steel. In fact, without the challenge of the Steel, the Fall River Marksmen claimed yet another title, this time winning both the first half of the season and the second half, thus rendering a championship play-off irrelevant. Reigning champions New Bedford left the league in mid-March – 14 games into the second half of the season – to join the Steel in EPSL II, and while the official record books show that the New York Giants, Bethlehem Steel and Newark Skeeters finished bottom, second bottom and third bottom respectively, it wouldn't be a full season. Some big names were departing over what was essentially a power struggle started by the New York Nationals owner Charles Stoneham, who saw his side beat New Bedford in the Lewis Cup.

That being said, the goalscorers still managed to find the back of the net, with five players hitting 30 or more goals and Werner Nilsen of Boston and János Nehadoma of Brooklyn tied at the top with 43 goals apiece. It wasn't a bad time for goal scorers, but in terms of the way the league was heading and what was going on around the league, it meant the beginning of the end for the ASL. It was a crazy time around America, not only in sports but in day-to-day living for ordinary citizens. A final ASL season happened in fall of 1929, whilst the Soccer Wars were ongoing, with the Marksmen once again winning by three points over Providence (who were now calling themselves the Gold Bugs). The Fall River Marksmen would prove to be the final winners of the ASL before the end of the Soccer Wars, which concluded in October 1929 (but there is more too discuss on that, which you'll see in the not-too-distant future), and, ultimately, this was it the for the very first incarnation of the ASL.

The ASL gave the United States two of its first 'superclubs', so to speak. When you think of a dynasty or a superclub, your mind goes to Sir Alex Ferguson's Manchester United, Gregg Popovich and the San Antonio Spurs, Magic's Lakers, Kobe and Shaq's Lakers, Bird's Celtics, Tom Brady and the New England Patriots, Lionel Messi and the Barcelona teams of the late 2000s and early 2010s, these are eras not only associated with stars but with success. Bethlehem and Fall River had both. Their success and star names got overshadowed by Lou Gehrig,

Babe Ruth and the New York Yankees because baseball was the dominant sport, so it made sense, but history seems to have lost how important these names were to soccer in the United States. Trailblazers is a term that shouldn't be used all the time, but in this case that's definitely the right phrase to use. Fall River and Bethlehem set a standard so high, not only on the pitch, or with their state-of-the-art playing fields, or even how they recruited players from overseas, but they tried, so much, to make soccer a success during the 1920s.

This was during a time when, in sporting terms, popularity was up in the air. Babe Ruth was tearing it up for the Yankees but soccer in the north-east area was thriving. The NFL wasn't in a position to fully take over or challenge MLB and the NBA didn't even exist yet (let alone the ABA (American Basketball Association)), so it begs the question what could have been if the ASL hadn't folded in on itself. If they had just waited to iron out a few issues and capitalised on the 1930 World Cup, would NASL have needed to start up in the glitzy, expensive and attention-grabbing way that it did? Unfortunately, as we all know, it didn't quite pan out this way. In time, we will look deeper at how the ASL folded and what happened to American soccer after the Soccer Wars, but firstly we have to focus on the positives. Cast your mind back to 1930. The ASL would go on to have a huge impact on the very first FIFA World Cup, but would the United States of America make any kind of impact on the competition? This was a nation dominated by pitchers, shortstops and home-run hitters, not midfielders and goalscorers. It was a shock to almost everyone, but it's an incredible story of how an amalgamation of stars came together to create the most successful USMNT performance in a World Cup to date.

Chapter Three

The First World Cup (1930)

IF there was ever a time or tournament to showcase how influential the ASL was to United States soccer, the World Cup in 1930 was the ideal opportunity. The league was booming domestically – or at the very least was on the comedown from its boom period – soccer was making a claim to be the second most popular professional sport in the country and the United States loves the opportunity to be the best in the world at whatever they do. The World Cup offered the United States the chance to proclaim themselves to be the best in the world at soccer (unlike England, who decided that they were the best in the world at the sport but didn't *actually* need to prove it) and they had the chance to show, albeit to a rather small audience, that the ASL and the United States took the sport very seriously. But the World Cup was completely different back in 1930; in fact, it wasn't just FIFA that hosted the tournament back then (it was originally an Olympic event that was brought together with the help of FIFA and its members, but technically the first two incarnations of the World Cup weren't solely run by FIFA). To understand the scale of achievement that the US national team had during this World Cup, you have to understand the context of the soccer world at the time and why it took the USMNT so long to even be on a par with their result and finish from 1930 (spoiler alert: they haven't even matched their finish from 1930, making 1930 an even greater achievement in some aspects). And not only do you have to understand the soccer world at the time, but you have to understand just how the World Cup – and the Olympic event that was run in its place from 1920 – was formed. In fact, there is a strong case that if it wasn't for the city of Los Angeles, we may not have had a World Cup in 1930, and we may not have had the World Cup as we know it today.

History records that from 1900 to 1920, the Olympics held soccer tournaments in their games due to the popularity of the sport at the time, with Great Britain winning three gold medals, Canada, Denmark and Belgium all winning one and Uruguay winning the final two gold medals in 1924 and 1928. As we all know, FIFA was formed in 1904, and FIFA had tried to organise a tournament in Switzerland for nations who weren't part of the Olympics, but despite their best efforts the tournament was considered a failure because – to be quite frank – they didn't really know how to organise a tournament at this point as they were only in their second year of existence. The Olympics was still the pinnacle of all sports including amateur soccer. FIFA knew they had the right to host their own tournament, but it wasn't the right time, and it wouldn't be the right time for another 24 years; however, that didn't stop them from getting their feet wet a bit with the help of the Olympics and the IOC. It was like sitting at the side of a pool and dipping your toes in. You do it to get acclimatised to the temperature and when you're ready you jump in. That is essentially what FIFA did with the help of the IOC. FIFA used the 1920, 1924 and 1928 Olympic Games to acclimatise themselves with regards to how to run an international soccer tournament, and then when they felt ready they jumped into their own pool with the World Cup. FIFA had the three previous Olympics under their belt, but it wouldn't be until the days of two Frenchmen when FIFA would take the next big step. Jules Rimet, who was FIFA president from 1921 to 1954 (the longest stint to date by any FIFA president) and his good friend Henri Delaunay, who was the secretary of the FFF (French Football Federation) and was officially the secretary from 1919 until his death in 1956, serving alongside Rimet who was the FFF president at the same time as running FIFA from 1919 to 1942, would begin discussions about staging their very own tournament in Antwerp in 1920, the same time as the Olympic Games, and this extract from the great Brian Glanville's book *The Story of the World Cup* explains the process of what Rimet and Delaunay wanted to discuss:

> In 1920, at FIFA's Antwerp congress, concurrent with the Olympic Games, the idea of a World Cup, previously much debated, was accepted in principle. In 1924, at the Paris Olympics, the FIFA meeting discussed it in more serious detail, while a dazzling and hitherto obscure Uruguay side walked off with the soccer tournament. Two years later, at FIFA's congress, Delaunay proclaimed: 'Today international football can no longer be held within the confines of the Olympics; and many countries where professionalism is now recognised and organised cannot any longer be represented there by their best players.'

It was around this time when FIFA started to make changes, and it was around this time when Los Angeles helped push along the invention of the World Cup. At their own congress in 1928, FIFA decided to host their own tournament and needed to pick a host nation, with the Netherlands, Italy, Spain, Sweden and current two-time Olympic champions Uruguay keen on hosting. What also helped FIFA in this case was the Olympic Games of 1932 being awarded to Los Angeles in 1927. As soccer was not as popular across the whole of the United States (the ASL was huge, but you can't hold an Olympic Games only in the north-east in a country that is 3.8 million square miles, even if that part of the country is soccer mad), the Los Angeles Olympic Committee decided to not include soccer in their 1932 games, with some saying it was an attempt to try to boost the popularity of American football instead. This was the straw that broke the camel's back and it gave FIFA the impetus to push on with their World Cup idea because they wanted to prove that, despite what the Los Angeles Olympic Committee thought, soccer was the world's game. FIFA took matters into their own hands and it changed world sport forever. Without this rejection the world may never have been given the gift of the World Cup, yet this rejection brought further thought to a FIFA World Cup and the congress started delegating who would host the 1930 edition, and it also started the discussion of which nations would take part in the tournament.

It wasn't so remarkable that the holders of the Olympic crown, Uruguay, would be hosting the tournament, but what was remarkable was the promises that the country made in order to do it. Bearing in mind that at the time of the first World Cup the country only had a population of barely 2 million people, Uruguay offered to pay all travelling expenses for the nations who competed and their hotel expenses too. Not only that, but they promised to build their new Centenary Stadium in the middle of Montevideo to celebrate their 100 years of independence in 1930. In modern times, building a new stadium is standard practice for hosting a World Cup, but Uruguay promised to have it built within eight months of the project starting, including three months of torrential downpours. No other European nation could match the enthusiasm and promises made by the Uruguayans, so the Dutch, Swedes, Italians and Spanish all pulled out of the running and also pulled out of even competing in the competition, which posed yet another threat to the first World Cup. Two months before the start, FIFA was without a single European nation, with the aforementioned potential hosts pulling out, as well as Austria, Hungary, Germany, Switzerland and Czechoslovakia all refusing to travel. The British nations were not even in FIFA at this point (the nations had differing views about what defined an amateur player and a pro, so they missed the first three World Cups and didn't become a member until after the Second World War), Belgium, Romania and Yugoslavia weren't entirely sold on the idea of travelling halfway across the world just yet, as were France but they essentially had their arms twisted by Rimet. Ultimately, both Belgium and Romania adhered to pressure from higher powers – Belgium from FIFA vice president Rodolphe William Seeldrayers and Romania from their own king, King Carol, who was very involved in the sporting culture. Although he wasn't hugely popular in Romania, the king granted amnesty for all Romania footballers, and he even picked the Romania team himself and pressured the employers of the players to give them time off to go to the World Cup. Yugoslavia also eventually accepted the invitation to play. So, why were so few Europeans at the first World Cup? Was it a protest about one of the Euro nations not being awarded the tournament? Was it too expensive? Well, no. It was neither (remember, Uruguay offered to pay for travel and hotel). It was simply because it was too far. The reason why so few European countries were staying at home was because to get to the World Cup in Uruguay they had to take a boat. The journey lasted just over two weeks. The major problem that these nations (and players) had was getting time off from their main job, and two weeks' leave was hard enough, let alone getting another two weeks just to travel to Uruguay as well, then two weeks to travel back home. It was a headache that certain countries didn't want to have or couldn't afford to have, at least from the players' point of view.

This played into the hands of the United States and is how they managed to get invited to the inaugural competition. There were numerous open spots allocated to nations like Mexico and the US, who both took the same boat journey to Uruguay (by the way, their journey took 18 days) and were kept apart in the seedings, mainly because it took FIFA longer than it should have to realise that there needed to be a grouping system in order to actually make it a knockout competition. Uruguay, Argentina, Brazil and the United States were seeded, and there were four groups – group 1 contained four teams, and the other three contained three teams. The four group winners progressed to the first knock-out round or, as it was known in this very small World Cup, the semi-finals. With the groups drawn and travelling arrangements made, all that was left was the selection of the United States squad, which was concocted from all over the country and some different backgrounds, birthplaces and heritages. To simply say that the ASL had an effect on this USMNT squad would be an understatement, with the 15-man squad being made up almost entirely of players in the ASL. Of the 15 players going to Uruguay, 14 were plying their trade in the ASL, with the solitary non-ASL player playing in the St Louis League. Of course, when you have one major league dominating the majority of soccer in one country, that league will almost certainly provide the overwhelming number of players in that country's national team, but it was still a positive note in the ASL's history books. The competitive nature of the league, coupled with the talent that was already in the league and perhaps going to the World Cup together as a team, helped the internationals brace themselves for the challenge of going up against South American nations. But as well as their talent, there was also something that made some of the players stand out even more. Some players weren't born in the United States, nor did they have American parents, but they qualified for the national team due to being in the country long enough to officially be classified as a US citizen or, to give it its official term, they were 'naturalised'. For example, George Moorhouse was born in Liverpool, England, and had played two professional games for Merseyside club Tranmere Rovers between the years 1921 to 1923, then he briefly emigrated to Canada before moving south of the border to join the Brooklyn Wanderers of the ASL at the age of just 22. Ironically, his first cap for the US came against Canada in 1926, and by the time the World Cup came around Moorhouse was 29 years old and had lived in the US long enough to qualify for the national team. This wasn't a rare case for most players in the squad either, with six English- and Scottish-born players being involved. It wasn't a case of 'these guys are good, let's pick them because no one will put two and two together', they were genuinely allowed to play for the US.

The stories of some of these players are fascinating and it speaks volumes about how US soccer was at the time, as English- and Scottish-born players were accepted into the squad without any issues or problems, because they had been recognised as Americans for long enough. If anything, it tells the story of how America can be when it mixes those of different birthplaces under one banner. The majority of these men weren't what could be described as 'full-blooded Americans' but that probably makes this team more 'American' than anyone realises. A bunch of people from various nations working together to reach a goal that previously some would have considered unreachable? That sounds like what America should be, which this 1930 side perfectly encapsulated. There is more information on some players, simply due to their status after this World Cup, while information on others is sparse, but here are short profiles of every member of the 1930 USMNT World Cup squad.

Goalkeeper: James 'Jimmy' Edward Douglas

Standing at six feet, two inches and born in 1898, Douglas was the imperious and experienced goalkeeper selected to marshal the US backline in the World Cup. Born on the banks of the Passaic River in East Newark, New Jersey, and a 30-minute walk from where the New York Red Bulls now reside in Harrison, Douglas was born and bred in the Garden State and started his career with the Central Juniors Youth Club in Jersey when he was just nine years old, before spending the next 14 years or so moving around various youth teams across the state, including Ryerson, Antlers, Erie and Swanson. But at the age of 24, Harrison took a chance on Douglas and made him their goalkeeper in the ASL. However, despite being signed by a club that openly paid players, Douglas wanted to remain an amateur and refused to accept any payment for his time at the club. In his debut season for Harrison, Douglas made 14 appearances before being signed by Newark Skeeters (at the time they were simply known as Newark FC), playing with them for two years and making 43 appearances. Douglas's stock was rising every season and eventually he earned a move to the New York Giants.

After spending two years with the Giants, Douglas made the big jump to the Fall River Marksmen and became the first player in this US squad to represent the Marksmen at the World Cup. In fact, Douglas had two spells with the Marksmen, first in 1927, ending his first spell just a year later, and then a second time in 1929, making a total of 39 appearances. Maybe not a lot, but enough to make an impact for them, and, despite moving around various clubs in just eight years, Douglas was always a reliable goalkeeper for his clubs and for his country too. Ending his career in 1931, Douglas eventually made nine appearances for the United States, including the 1930 World Cup, actually being the most capped player in the US squad at that particular World Cup (he only had five caps, but international games were played rarely at this point in time) and was inducted into the National Soccer Hall of Fame in 1954, capping off a solid career with many top teams in the ASL, as well as being a trailblazer when it came to the USMNT.

Defender: George Moorhouse

Moorhouse was the first member of the squad not to be born in the United States, despite spending the majority of his life in the States. Starting his career with Tranmere Rovers in the Third Division of the English Football League, making two appearances in two years for Rovers and not being too far from his hometown of Liverpool (Tranmere is near Birkenhead, and technically is in the Wirral not Merseyside, despite only being separated by the River Mersey). Moorhouse originally emigrated from England to Canada in the early 1920s, but he eventually made his name with the Brooklyn Wanderers, making three appearances in 1923, before going on to make a stunning 203 appearances for the New York Giants from 1923 to 1930, scoring 32 times from left-back. His 203 games for the Giants predominantly came in the ASL, but when the Giants were expelled from the ASL in 1928, Moorhouse stayed with the club in their season and half in the EPSL before returning to the ASL when the Giants were reinstated. In terms of the USMNT, Moorhouse made his full debut in the 6-1 demolition of, ironically, Canada in November 1926. He didn't play in the next two US games in 1928, but he was called up into the squad and made history as the very first English-born player ever to play in the World Cup. The English-born full-back carried on playing for the USMNT until 1934 when he finally decided to concentrate on his time with the New York Americans – a team that played in the second, and least successful, incarnation of the ASL. Unfortunately, and tragically, Moorhouse never got to see himself inducted into the Hall of Fame as he passed away in Long Beach, New York, in 1943 at the age of 42 (conflicting reports suggest that Moorhouse either passed away in 1982, claimed by the Hall of Fame, or in 1943, claimed by some historians, including Colin Jose in his History of the ASL). He was officially named a member of the Hall of Fame in 1986.

Defender: Frank 'Frankie' Vaughn

Known as a one-club man for his entire playing career, Vaughn spent his playing days with Ben Millers of the St Louis Soccer League, but there is very little information on him. He was described as a successful player by the US Soccer organisation. Born in 1902 in St Louis, Missouri, Vaughn was a full-back who was inducted into the Hall of Fame in 1986. The Ben Millers were the powerhouse of St Louis soccer throughout the 1910s and 1920s, before breaking up in the 1930s, winning multiple league titles along the way, so while we can assume that because of his involvement in the 1930 World Cup squad, plus his age (he would have been 28 during the World Cup so would have been in his prime years during the 1920s success of the Ben Millers), Vaughn has four league titles to his name and potentially a National Cup, his name was not registered as a member of the Ben Millers roster for the 1920 National Challenge Cup win, nor was he registered for their runner-up spot in the same competition in 1926. That being said, he was listed as a member of the St Louis All Star Team that went on tour in Scandinavia in 1920. So, using the information we have we can assume one of two things:

Vaughn was a member of the Ben Millers side who won the double in 1920 and was left out of the National Cup squad due to a misprint, or he was a very reliable role player who was picked for the All Star Team to make up the numbers, but given his longevity at the Ben Millers it's more likely that he was an integral part of the team and was left out of the squad either by a misprint or was rested/injured. Ultimately, Vaughn never actually made an officially recognised appearance for the USMNT, playing only in friendlies that weren't official games, but he was inducted into the St Louis Hall of Fame in 1972, 14 years before the National Soccer Hall of Fame recognised him.

Defender: Alex Wood

Alex Wood was born in Lochgelly, Scotland, in 1907 before moving to the United States when he was 14 years old with his parents. The Wood family moved to Gary, Indiana, and he joined Emerson High School before gaining his US citizenship just a year later. Wood's first club was known as the Bricklayers and Masons, who he helped reach the final of the 1928 National Challenge Cup before losing to the New York Nationals. It wasn't until 1930 that Wood turned into a fully fledged professional player, when he joined the Brooklyn Wanderers, playing 31 games in one season, but scoring just twice. This was the last club that Wood played for in American, as unforeseen circumstances forced his move back to the United Kingdom. The Wanderers folded in 1931 and with most teams in the ASL II at the time either folding like the Wanderers or merging with other teams, Wood took a gap year in his career to pretty much figure out what he wanted to do. With a World Cup appearance under his belt and recognition for being a professional, Leicester City brought him to Filbert Street in 1933, where he played 52 times before making the move across the Midlands to join Nottingham Forest in 1936. Wood played a solitary season for the Nottingham club before moving to Colchester and winning the only trophy of his entire career: the 1938/39 Southern Football League title. He ended his playing career in the south of England, but Wood soon moved back to Gary, Indiana, to work for US Steel Corp, where he retired from work altogether in 1970, before joining the Hall of Fame in 1986. Thankfully, Wood got to see his induction in 1986 as he sadly passed away at the age of 70 just one year later.

Midfielder: Andy Auld

Auld was another Scotsman who emigrated to the United States, but perhaps few stories in this World Cup squad are as amazing as his when it comes to what they experienced and how they managed to live their life. Hailing from Stevenston, Scotland, Auld began his career with Stevenston FC at the age of 11 in 1911, before leaving the set-up just two years later. It was six years before Auld started playing for his next club. Why? Because he was drafted into the military and served during the First World War whilst still in his teens! The reason he left Stevenston FC in the first place was because he needed to complete his national service, and he wouldn't be let out of the military until a year after the war had ended. After that he joined Ardeer Thistle (who are still going, playing in the Scottish Junior Football Association West Region League Two). He remained with Thistle for three years before moving to Glasgow club Parkhead, where he spent two seasons before crossing the Atlantic to try his hand in America. However, unlike many of his peers in Scotland, Auld didn't move for the soccer. He moved to Gillespie, Illinois, in a bid to start a new life in the States, but the lifestyle didn't suit Auld, who quickly packed his things and planned a move back home to Scotland. However, what happened next was a complete accident and it ended up changing Auld's life for good. Auld made a stop in Niagara Falls to visit his sister, who lived there at the time and eventually got around to playing a pick-up match in the area. There just happened to be a scout for the ASL club Providence Clamdiggers, and that scout managed to convince Auld to abandon his trip back to Scotland and sign for the Diggers, which he did. Six seasons and 277 games later, it proved to be a good move from Auld, who became a legend in Providence soccer history due to his commitment to the clubs he played for and his longevity, playing for the Diggers and then sticking around when they renamed themselves as the Gold Bugs. Auld was also a legend for the USMNT, mainly for his performances in the 1930 World Cup, but while he retired in 1935 to make money in the sheet metal business, Auld was finally inducted into the Hall of Fame in 1986, putting the cherry on top of what was an outstanding career and an even more incredible life.

Midfielder: Jimmy Gallagher

Another player born in Scotland and another one who made his way to the United States at a young age, Gallagher emigrated to New York with his mother at the age of 12 in 1913. He joined his first club in 1919 – Tebo Yacht Basin of the New York State League – and would eventually go on to win the 1921 league title with the club. Of course, bigger things were on the horizon for Gallagher and he earned a move to J&P Coats of the newly formed ASL, spending two seasons with the club and winning the title in his final year. The next few years meant a fair amount of chopping and changing for Gallagher, who would initially join the Fall River Marksmen in 1923, before leaving them after just two games to join the New York Giants. He didn't last long with the Giants either, as he then left them in the summer of 1924 to join Fleisher Yarn, and even then he only stayed for a season as he then joined Indiana Flooring (if you're keeping track, that's five ASL teams in two years). But it was around this time that Gallagher cemented his legacy as one of the greats of American soccer, as he went on to make 75 appearances for the club before they changed to the New York Nationals, where he is recorded as having made 144 appearances between 1927 and 1930, before yet another name change saw Gallagher make 68 appearances in two years for the now New York Giants. This meant that in his 11-year ASL career, Gallagher made a staggering 346 regular and post-season appearances, listing him third on the list of all-time American soccer appearances before Chris Henderson knocked him down a place in 2006.

Five caps and one goal for the USMNT saw Gallagher entered in to the Hall of Fame in 1986, but his consistency, longevity and professionalism in such an early period in the sport's history in the United States makes him a legend in any era.

Midfielder: Philip Sloane

Born in New York City in 1907, Philip Sloane was the joint-fourth youngest player in the 1930 squad, but while he made the squad his career was a short-lived one, not because of any tragedy or anything along those lines, it was just a case of bad timing. Sloane was a multi-talented athlete and, whilst studying at Manhattan's High School of Commerce, he earned varsity letters in the disciplines of baseball, soccer and basketball and eventually graduated St John's University in 1929 with a degree in law. This is obviously a fantastic achievement, but even Sloane admits that the degree made it tough to have a proper crack at a soccer career, once saying:

> Life was hectic then. I played professional soccer on the weekends, worked during the week and went to evening classes at St John's University Law School.

Sloane was playing for New York Hakoah at the time and was inadvertently a victim of the Soccer Wars as the owner of the Hakoah, Maurice Vandeweghe, also owned another team in the ASL and had to sell one or the other. He sold Hakoah, meaning Sloane had to jump ship and join the Giants. When Sloane returned home from the 1930 World Cup he found that the ASL had changed and he joined the Hakoah All Stars for a season before playing the last seven years of his career with New York Brookhattan. But if there was one story that summed up Sloane's career – the bad timing, and the misfortune of being in the wrong club at the wrong time – it was how he was inducted into the Hall of Fame. Sloane was the last surviving member of the 1930 World Cup squad, but an article by FIFA. com suggested that he didn't appear in the Hall of Fame until 1996 because no one knew where he was! Most had assumed that Sloane had passed away and the ceremony went on without him, but when Jim Brown died in 1994, news broke that Brown wasn't the last surviving member, Sloane was, and while it may have taken a decade to officially see him into the Hall of Fame, Sloane enjoyed his moment as being the 'Last Survivor', as FIFA called him in the article.

Forward: Mike Bookie

Much like Sloane, Mike Bookie was a multi-talented athlete in his home of Pittsburgh, Pennsylvania, beginning his career as a baseball player in his home town, where he was listed as a shortstop. Not long after that, Bookie took up soccer and joined his first cub Jeannette in the early 1920s, before making the jump to the ASL and joining the Boston Wonder Workers. In the record books, it shows that Bookie only played five times for Boston, scoring just one goal, before moving to join Vestaburg. Little is actually known about Vesteburg other than in the solitary year that Bookie was with the club, they won the 1925 West Penn Challenge Cup and reached the quarter-finals of the National Challenge Cup. He returned to the ASL with the New Bedford Whalers at the end of 1925, but only played four games for the club before once again deciding to leave and play for three more clubs – American Hungarian, Cleveland Slavia and Pittsburgh Curry Silver Tops. He was playing with Slavia when he got the call-up to join the World Cup squad, but Bookie's career was unfortunately cut short due to the Second World War, when he enlisted to join the US Army in 1944. He was tragically, and accidentally, killed when he was shot by a machine gun in a training simulation. Of course, Bookie will always be remembered as a member of the 1930 World Cup squad and was inducted into the Hall of Fame in 1986.

Forward: Jim Brown

Jim Brown was a wonderful player who was born in Scotland but found his way to the United States for reasons other than soccer. He managed to make himself a legend almost by sheer accident and luck. Born in Kilmarnock but brought up in Troon (a small town in South Ayrshire that was the home of golfer Colin Montgomerie and future NASL man Stevie Nichol), Brown was the oldest of four boys, two of whom went on to play professionally as goalkeepers. When Brown was just 12 years old, his father left the family to start a new life in the United States, and it wasn't until 1927, when Brown was 19, that he went to America to try to find his father. While he never played organised soccer at home in Scotland, Brown found that he had quite a talent for the sport when he played for Plainfield Soccer Club and Bayonne Rovers. During this time, Brown was working on the production floor of a steel factory, but that would soon be put on hold when Newark Skeeters acquired the services of the Scot, where he scored 12 goals in 42 games. Brown then went on to feature for the New York Giants, New York Soccer Club and Brooklyn Wanderers before the ASL collapsed. While it may seem like we've rushed through his career in America, there is much more to come in the second half.

Brown was called up to the US World Cup squad, not based upon where he was born, nor his citizenship, but due to his father's citizenship (rules were a lot more relaxed back in those days when it came to representing nations, although Brown was awarded his citizenship in June of 1930, just before the World Cup started). The Scot played in every game during that tournament and his performances for the United States earned him a move back to the United Kingdom, but this time to Manchester United. When the ship bringing the US team back from Uruguay neared the dock, multiple representatives from English and Scottish clubs awaited Brown in a bid to try to sign him for their team, but Manchester United manager Scott Duncan had other ideas, taking a tugboat out to sea and signing Brown on the ship before the liner had even managed to dock! Brown made an impact in the north-west of England, scoring directly from a corner on his debut for United after just 90 seconds, and he finished with a solid record of 17 goals in 40 games before the club sold him to Brentford due to Brown's outspoken wish for a players' union. A £300 fee was paid by Brentford for Brown, but the board at the West London club fell out with him due to his union demands and sold him to Tottenham Hotspur not long afterwards. Brown only played four games for the first team in his one season with Spurs, leaving the club to go semi-pro with Guildford City of the Southern Football League, where he scored an incredible 148 goals in 150 games. Injuries forced him to retire after 1941, and Brown was inducted into the Hall of Fame in 1986 before he died in 1994 at the age of 85 back in New Jersey.

Forward: Tom Florie (Captain)

The captain of the side, Florie was born in Harrison, New Jersey, to Italian parents, and had a youth career in soccer. He could have had a more impressive start to his professional career, but Florie was drafted into the Navy during the First World War, delaying his soccer career for a few years. Florie didn't join a team until 1922 when he signed up with his local side Harrison, playing three games in what was a short season for the forward, before joining American AA in the West Hudson Amateur League (WHAL) for two years. His stock rose in the WHAL and his performances obviously impressed Providence FC as they picked him up for the 1924 season, where he stayed for the next four and put in a litany of top performances, establishing himself as one of the top forwards in the latter years of the ASL. After 166 games for Providence, Florie joined New Bedford Whalers II in 1928, making 121 appearances for them, scoring 47 times, before a brief stint in the spring of 1931 with Fall River FC, before Fall River and the New York Yankees merged to become the New Bedford Whalers III. Florie stuck around the ASL until almost the very end, before going to the Pawtucket Rangers in the second ASL, and he ended his career in 1934 after his second World Cup. Picked for his experience and his leadership qualities, Florie was an integral part of the squad and, of course, he was inducted into the Hall of Fame in 1986 as well.

Forward: James Gentle

Gentle's career in soccer was short, with very few appearances recorded during his time in the game, but that didn't stop him from picking up the bronze in the 1930 World Cup and also making an appearance in the 1932 Los Angeles Olympic Games, picking up another bronze medal, but this time as part of the US men's field hockey team. Gentle grew up in Massachusetts and went to the University of Pennsylvania, where he would go on to play American football as a freshman at the school, but he quickly changed over to soccer and track & field for the next three years at Penn University, making first-team All-American honours for soccer in both 1924 and 1925. Gentle graduated in 1926 with a degree in economics, and also had a fondness for acting as he was the class president for the Mask and Wig Varsity Club.

One thing that makes Gentle such an intriguing case was that he only ever played one game of soccer for an organised team back in 1925 for the Boston Wonder Workers and wouldn't play for another team until after his graduation, joining the Philly Field Club in 1926. So, if he hardly played at all and spent most of his time in university studying economics instead of playing, how did Gentle get his spot in the squad? Well, he just so happened to be the only member of the team – playing staff or management – who was fluent in Spanish, which was key considering they were going to a Spanish speaking country for about a month or so. Gentle's soccer career faded after the World Cup and he joined the Army Reserve in 1931, making time for his field hockey exploits and working at Mutual Life Insurance Company, before being called into action during the Second World War in the 36th Infantry Regiment. After multiple battles across Europe, mainly Italy, Gentle and his regiment joined General Patton's forces to move across Europe and into the Rhineland. Gentle survived the war and was named US trade and industry officer for the American occupied zone of Germany, before retiring from the army in 1956 with the rank of colonel.

Forward: Billy Gonsalves

When you're described as the 'Babe Ruth' of any sport, you must be a superstar, right? In the case of Billy Gonsalves, this seemed to be true as he made a huge impact from the late 1920s until his retirement with Newark FC in 1952. There was a reason Gonsalves was left out of the last chapter, and that's because it was only fair to give him a profile like this instead of just highlighting one or two moments of his career, especially when you consider that his stand-out and prime years came at the same time as the Soccer Wars, which overshadowed his performances.

Gonsalves was the seventh of nine children in his family, with his parents emigrating to the United States two years before he was born, and, despite being born in Rhode Island, Gonsalves grew up in Fall River, Massachusetts, and was a considerably strong athlete, excelling in boxing, baseball and soccer before embarking on a career in soccer that took him from various youth clubs in his area to Boston Soccer Club in 1927. In his first season with the Boston club, they won the ASL title after the 19-year-old Gonsalves contributed six goals in his 20 appearances, with his debut coming on Christmas Eve when he managed to find the back of the net. Gonsalves spent one more year with Boston before moving home to join the Fall River Marksmen, where he became the star man in a team that had traditionally been one of the biggest and most successful in America. Across his three-year stay with the Marksmen, Gonsalves scored 69 times in 116 games and led the team in assists, forming a deadly partnership with fellow 1930 World Cup squad member Bert Patenaude (we'll get to him in a minute), and he managed to deliver two National Challenge Cups in his time with the Marksmen. It wouldn't be long until the ASL started to collapse and Gonsalves started looking around for new clubs to join in more stable conditions. He carried on playing in the St Louis leagues, but he never rediscovered the form he had towards the latter days of the ASL with the Marksmen. He retired from soccer in 1952, two years after being part of the inaugural class for the Hall of Fame, and his personality and career was summed up by Steve Holyrod, who said:

> Gonsalves was the consummate gentleman on the pitch: legend has it he was never cautioned or ejected from any match for rough play or ungentlemanly conduct.

A legend, a gentleman and an icon of early US soccer history.

Forward: Bart McGhee

A history maker born in Edinburgh, Scotland, and raised in a soccer family, Bart McGhee was essentially born with a ball at his feet. His father, James McGhee, had played for both Hibernian and Glasgow Celtic before taking the manager's role at Hibs's arch rivals Heart of Midlothian. His brother Jimmy was a forward for the Philly Football Club. In fact, the reason Bart had managed to come to America was because of his father's resignation at Hearts, with his dad leaving Scotland to find a new life in America, and it was two years before Bart and his family joined James in the US in 1912. For the majority of his youth, Bart played for various youth clubs including New York Shipbuilding, Wolfended Shore and Philadelphia Hibernian (wonder if the name helped him get a spot on this team?) before finally going pro with New York Field Club in 1922, ten years after his arrival. For the next few years, McGhee jumped from team to team in order to find the best fit for himself. He had a stint with New York Field Club for two seasons and a solitary year with Fleisher Yarn, which meant that Bart was looking for his third team in as many years, but the next stop on his journey would prove to be the most important in his club career. After Fleisher folded, Bart spent two years with Indiana Flooring, then the infamous Charles Stoneham bought Indiana and renamed them the New York Nationals, with whom Bart made 253 appearances, scoring 97 times. He had the 1928 National Challenge Cup in his trophy cabinet as well as the 1929 Lewis Cup, before retiring from soccer after the 1930 World Cup. The World Cup would be his crowning moment, scoring the first US goal in the tournament and only the second goal ever in World Cup history, and he finished his club career with 127 goals in 350 ASL appearances. When you grow up in a family full of people involved with soccer, scoring in the World Cup, winning the domestic cup and playing 350 games is an amazing career to look back on.

Forward: Arnie Oliver

Possibly the best nickname out of anyone in the squad, 'Lucky Arnie' had a 13-year soccer career and was about as reliable a player as you could hope for in a squad, even if he never made the most appearances. Oliver was born in New Bedford to British immigrants and began his soccer career at the age of 14 with Quisset Mill in the New Bedford area before joining amateur club Shawsheen Indians in 1925, playing five times in one season. In 1926 Oliver turned pro with the New Bedford Whalers, but he failed to keep his place in either the Whalers team or the Hartford Americans, finding his home with J&P Coats. Arnie scored 38 times in 58 games for J&P across two seasons, but he finished the 1929 season back at the Whalers, where he failed to score in his five appearances. Two spells with the Pawtucket Rangers and one season runs with the Marksmen, Gold Bugs and Santo Christo saw an end to Oliver's short and sweet career, but his impact as a reliable squad option both at club level and for the national team won't be forgotten any time soon.

Forward: Bert Patenaude

With some players there are only a few words that can describe the type of player they were and the kind of career they had. In the case of Bert Patenaude, he was an absolute stud who could sniff out a goal even if he had a blocked nose, no matter the team or occasion. Born in Fall River in 1909 (making him the youngest member of the World Cup squad at the age of 20), Patenaude signed his first-ever professional contract in 1928 at the age of 18 with Philly Field Club, and he made an immediate impact. He only played eight times but scored six goals before being sent out to J&P Coats for a one-game loan. For whatever reason, Philly didn't keep Patenaude, despite his sensational start, and in 1928 he returned home to join the Marksmen. In just three years he became perhaps the deadliest goalscorer in the ASL at the time, alongside his partner in crime at both club and international level, Billy Gonsalves. At the end of his three-year stay with the Marksmen, Patenaude finished with a stunning record of 114 games played, 112 goals scored, two ASL league titles and two National Challenge Cup wins. If you were looking for a legend of early soccer in the US, chances are you wouldn't find anyone with a more apt CV than Patenaude. As the ASL collapsed, he bounced from team to team, still scoring plenty of goals as he passed through the Newark Americans, St Louis Central Breweries and Philadelphia Passion, before ending his club career in 1936. But while his club career was incredible, it would be at the 1930 World Cup where he cemented his legacy as a true legend. The first ever hat-trick to be scored at a FIFA World Cup? That was by a certain Bert Patenaude, scoring a treble against Belgium following his goal against Paraguay, meaning his four goals in the 1930 World Cup is still the best total by an American player at any World Cup. Patenaude stayed in Fall River until his passing in 1974, but he will always be remembered as a history maker and a true legend of US soccer.

Forward: Raphael Tracey

Very little is known about Tracey in terms of his overall appearance numbers and goal stats, but what we do know is that after being born in 1904, Tracey grew up in St Louis, Missouri, and made his start in soccer with the St Louis Vesper Buicks, where he would last just one season with the club but still made a huge impact. While the official total of goals is unknown, reports suggest that Tracey was the second-highest scorer on the team that season, but that didn't stop the Vesper Buick's from releasing him at the end of the campaign. There doesn't seem to be any reason why they did, but that allowed Tracey to sign for the Ben Millers and see out the rest of his career with the club. Joining in 1926, Tracey stayed with the club until his last officially recorded season of 1932. He failed to win any silverware, but made a big enough impact to play in all three of the US games in the World Cup. Most famously, Tracey will be remembered for breaking his leg during the semi-final against Argentina and playing on until half-time. Bearing in mind he broke his leg just ten minutes into the game, it's unclear whether this was an act of immense bravery or an act of intense stupidity. Either way, it added to the legacy of Tracey, who was inducted into the St Louis Hall of Fame in 1973 and the National Hall of Fame in 1986.

Manager/Head Coach: Robert Millar

You can't have a team without a coach, and what better coach to have than someone who hails from what seems to be a hotbed of soccer talent, both on and off the field. Millar was born in Paisley, Scotland, which is the home of former Burnley boss Owen Coyle, Aberdeen manager Derek McInnes, former Spurs and Chelsea player Gordon Durie, Tranmere Rovers boss Micky Mellon, Champions League winner Paul Lambert, Scottish World Cup hero Archie Gemmill and former Hearts manager Robbie Neilson, but perhaps Millar should be recognised a bit more than he is because, when you look at his career, you can't help but be somewhat amazed by what he managed to achieve. Starting his professional career with St Mirren in Scotland, Millar soon made the trip to the United States in 1911, joining Disston AA. For whatever reason, Millar never liked to stay with one team for very long, playing for 10 clubs in eight years, with the records of his five appearances and one goal for the Bethlehem Steel in 1918/19 still intact. It wasn't until the first season of the ASL that Millar's statistics became available, when he scored 10 times in 21 games for J&P Coats, before jumping to Fall River, New York Field Club and New York Giants in a short space of time. His next move to Indiana Flooring, however, would prove to be a big one for Millar as he didn't join as just a player, he became player/manager of the club. His scoring record at the time was exemplary (29 goals in 57 games across two seasons) but the Soccer Wars in 1928 saw Millar depart his post as he wrote to team management saying:

> I hereby advise you that I must refuse to continue as playing manager of the New York Nationals Football Club. I hereby tender my resignation, because to engage further in unsanctioned soccer football will materially endanger my status in organised soccer and will thereby affect my future livelihood as a professional soccer player. You have not lived up to the terms of my contract, which call for me to play and manage under the rules and regulations of the USFA, and by forcing me to engage in outlaw soccer, you are endangering my means of gaining a living.

This allowed Millar to take up the role of US national manager from 1928 to 1930, guiding his team to an historic semi-final following a career that saw him play with 16+ teams in, at the very least, five US leagues, and he had two seasons at the start of his career at home in Scotland. People find it hard to have a lengthy career as a player and then as a coach, but Millar did both and occasionally did both at the same time ...

Now that you've been introduced to every single member of the 1930 United States World Cup squad and their manager, it's time to dive right into the World Cup itself and see quite how extraordinary it was that the United States managed to make history in more than one way. It would be the first time the World Cup banner would be raised and it certainly wouldn't be the last, but without a qualification stage to get to the finals as we know it now, who were the other nations who were at this tournament and how did the groups line up?

Group 1:
Argentina
France
Chile
Mexico

Group 2:
Brazil
Yugoslavia
Bolivia

Group 3:
Uruguay
Romania
Peru

Group 4:
Belgium
United States
Paraguay

As mentioned before, there was one group of four teams and the rest had just three teams, with the winners of each group heading into the semi-finals. This meant all you really had to do was win your two group games and one knockout round to be in the final, which may change how people view the whole 'they got into the semi-finals' if they only had to play two games to get there. But even if they only had to play two games in the group stage, you look at how the United States played, who they played and the performances they put in during those wins and you can see why they were ranked third in the competition as the best semi-finalists. The first opponents on their list were Belgium and it proved to be a historic day for the Americans, and one that shouldn't be forgotten in an historical sense, but also in a sense of how they outperformed a top-class side. The United States were a strong, imposing and powerful team, nicknamed by the French as 'the shot-putters'. Made up almost exclusively of ASL players who came up against tough opponents seemingly every week, it should be of no surprise that physically the US had an advantage over other nations. Other nations may have had the silk and flair that they would eventually build around in the future, but the US laid down a marker for being tough, courageous and having a never-say-die attitude, but they also had players who could flick their own switch and go from a battler to a match winner almost in an instant. Of course, being tough only gets half the job done, and in the opening game against Belgium on 13 July the United States showed that they weren't just at the World Cup to make up the numbers. They were there to compete.

Some 18,346 spectators crammed themselves into the Estadio Parque Central in Montevideo to watch the United States face off against a Belgian team that had had to be convinced to even travel to the World Cup. Led by their team manager Millar (sources have rarely agreed on who the official manager of the US national side was at this World Cup. Some sources have it as Jack Coll – who was the team physio – and Wilfried Cummings – who was the team's general manager as opposed to the on-field manager. FIFA have Millar down as the head coach, so we will stick with that) and accompanied by their famous fight song, 'Stein Song', the US were ready to battle the Belgians on what was a damp and soggy pitch. There had been a mixture of both rain and snow fall during the match itself, and the conditions didn't exactly suit what the Americans were used to, so they had to take about half an hour to acclimatise to the conditions, rethink whatever strategy they may have had at the time and push through. Thanks, in large part, to their defensive backline and goalkeeper, the US kept the Belgians out, and on the half-hour mark, the Americans got their goal through Bart McGhee. It couldn't have been an easier goal for Bart, as he was in the right place at the right time to tap in the ball after it had rebounded down off the crossbar following a thunderous shot from Billy Gonsalves. This is the first part of any historic meaning to this World Cup, because for the longest time it was claimed that McGhee's goal was the very first in World Cup history. It would be fitting for this chapter if that was the case, but unfortunately for America the honour of first-ever goal goes to Laucien Laurent of France, who scored after 19 minutes in the French win over Mexico on the same day as the US vs Belgium match. Now, one record the US can have is the first goal scored by a nation outside Europe in a

World Cup. Is it a record for the sake of having a record? Most likely, but when you say it out loud it sounds very impressive (at least to some it will).

The American onslaught continued when, on the stroke of half-time, Belgium made a massive mistake. It's a mistake that often happens during a game and it's reprehensible when it happens, but when Belgium tried to play a high offside trap against US captain Tom Florie, the ref didn't whistle. The Belgians stood there, arms raised and looking expectantly at the referee to give offside, but the call never came, and while the Belgians were stood there looking like a bunch of workers waiting by the side of the street to hail a cab, Florie kept rushing towards goal and finished well to double the US's lead. This World Cup business seemed to be an easy ride, or at least the Americans were making it look that way. After the half-time interval, it all went smoothly for the US and they even added a third when a great piece of wing play from the soon-to-be-in-demand Jim Brown gave Bert Patenaude the easiest of headers to seal the win. The wing play and subsequent lob from Brown was described by GM Cummings as 'one of the most brilliant plays of the tournament' and it helped cap off what was not only an important win but also a stylish win. They may have been known as the shot-putters for their strength and physique, but the Americans showed that even the brutes of soccer can play beautifully.

The first-ever recorded clean sheet in a World Cup game went to the Americans, and in the second group game against Paraguay another record was set by the US. The very first hat-trick was scored in a World Cup by Bert Patenaude on 17 July 1930 in Montevideo, and it was indicative of how the US played on the day. Fast, strong and free-flowing soccer blew Paraguay away, but goals from Patenaude would be the centre of controversy for the next 76 years. We know now that Patenaude was the hat-trick scorer, but there was some confusion over who scored the second US goal in the 15th minute. In 2006 the award of the first hat-trick was taken from Argentinian Guillermo Stábile and given to Patenaude. The goals were not too dissimilar to what was scored against Belgium, but the confidence was oozing out of the United States, promoting the *New York Times* to run this headline:

US FAVORITE TO WIN WORLD SOCCER'S TITLE

Was it optimistic? In retrospect, any nation that has its own media proclaiming they are the favourite for an international title pretty much always ends badly, but at the time you can see the reasoning for the optimism.

> The United States team, because of its splendid showing in the tournament, is favoured to carry off the world's championship.

So said a different *New York Times* article, and considering that they had just posted up two convincing 3-0 wins and that little, if anything at all, was known about their semi-final opponents Argentina a fair amount of reasonable optimism seemed justified. It's not like these days when anyone can know everything about every team; the fact that Argentina were a threat was unknown, they were in blissful ignorance if you will. Did the 6-3 win against Mexico not give the US warning that Argentina might be a good side going forward? The chances of them scouting the Argentinians was very slim, but given what happened in the semi-final it made the *New York Times* look somewhat foolish in their claim that the US were the favourites. In front of an estimated crowd of around 80,000 people, in rainy conditions following torrential downpours the night before (this isn't an excuse, both teams had to play in the conditions), the game turned violent very, very quickly. The US were on the back foot pretty much from the 10th minute onwards because Raphael Tracey had his leg broken, and not long after that Andy Auld had to deal with a terrible mouth injury after being kicked square in the face. Jimmy Douglas, the US goalkeeper, went down with an injury as well, and by the end of the game the US had just eight players on the field, but they had a fighting chance at the half-time break as they were only one goal down, scored by Monti in the 20th minute. But after half-time, whatever resistance was left in the battered United States team soon evaporated when the fast attacks of the Argentinians was too much for them to handle, and ultimately the South Americans won 6-1. Not impressed by the vicious nature of the Argentinian players and the standard of refereeing from Belgian Jean Langenus, US team physio Jack Coll ran on to the pitch and threw his medical equipment at the referee. Coll had used the equipment enough during the 90 minutes so decided to give it one last throw on the pitch for good luck. Unfortunately, while many across Europe and South America were impressed by what they saw from the United States, the same cannot be said for the media back home, with one *New York Times* columnist suggesting:

> The Americans should take up Field Hockey instead of Soccer, because it's more natural for an American to use a stick or implement in his hands than it is to depend on his feet or his head.

This was a chance for the United States to fall in love with soccer. But it was just the wrong time and the wrong generation. Even though they fell at the semi-final hurdle and were largely battered and embarrassed by a far superior Argentina side, it was still a great tournament for them. If this had been in the 20th century where the attention is always on soccer, it would have been so much different. But it wasn't the case, and the US soccer team would have to wait until 2002 to even come close to matching the third-place finish from 1930 (they reached the quarter-finals against Germany in Japan/South Korea, and to date that's the second-best finish by any American team in a World Cup). The US would have been heroes in the eyes of fans if they had reached the semi-finals in 1994. In 2002 they were agonisingly close to beating eventual finalists Germany in the quarter-finals, and if they had won that game, they'd have been much fancied against Turkey in that final four. But that should not affect the importance of the 1930 World Cup.

Babe Ruth and Lou Gehrig were coming to the end of their careers and America needed new sporting heroes. If more attention had been paid to the World Cup, those new heroes could have been Billy Gonsalves, Jim Brown, Bert Patenaude. The team was full of players who were extremely talented and at the top of their game (remember, the Manchester United manager hired a tugboat just to speak to Brown first), but instead of flourishing following a successful World Cup campaign in which Europe and South America were impressed by how they played, the soccer world in the United States decided to, essentially, go to war with itself. Federations weren't happy, team owners weren't happy, clubs were merging together, clubs from other nations didn't approve of how they signed players and FIFA had to be called in to resolve the many issues that were brewing. It got so bad that some of the US players returned home without a club or played for new clubs that had merged while they were away. What exactly happened to ruin what could have been the golden era of soccer in the United States? Welcome to the Soccer Wars, and the fall of America's soccer leagues.

Chapter Four

The Soccer Wars and the Fall of the Amateur Leagues

THE US had shown that, despite only playing a handful of games, they could perform at a high level against very good opposition. Soccer, in theory, should have grown exponentially after this tournament. Instead what happened affected the sport (and general sporting landscape) for years and years. It changed how we see the sport now, it changed how the sport is run and governed immediately after, and it changed how it's run now. The Soccer Wars changed everything.

In almost every sport, there comes a time period where the 'real world', so to speak, has an impact on the sporting world and, on the odd occasion, vice versa. For example, the athletes in America at the time of writing who are kneeling during the US national anthem in protest of police brutality amongst other issues has changed how many people watch and react to the NFL, the 1968 Black Power salute from Tommie Smith and John Carlos, or from a wider point of view the various wars that affected sport such as the two World Wars, the Falklands (Tottenham Hotspur duo Ossie Ardiles and Ricky

Villa were booed due to the English conflict in their home country of Argentina) and we are still yet to understand the full ramifications of Brexit on the United Kingdom and Europe in terms of how the sport will operate and what changes will be made. When reality comes into contact with sport, more specifically soccer, history suggests that it never really ends well (or at least it changes the course of that sport's history, even if it is just briefly) and that's certainly the case here. As we touched upon in the American Soccer League chapter, the Soccer Wars changed soccer in the US, forcing the game to take multiple steps back in its development, taking it from being the second most popular sport in the entire country behind only baseball (and it had the legs to take on baseball too after the 1930 World Cup) to being rock bottom. However, the impact of the Soccer Wars wasn't solely down to soccer itself. The real world had its say, and the Great Depression had an effect on not only citizens who lost jobs, but also the owners of companies, who lost money. Those people may have been persuaded to invest in a growing sport like soccer but were now either not willing to spend any money on a sport that was surrounded by infighting amongst those who governed the leagues or they didn't actually have any money to spend on sports anymore. How big an effect did the Great Depression have on soccer in the US? Would the ASL still be going strong in this day and age if there wasn't in-fighting amongst governing bodies and club owners? These are all questions we intend to get to the bottom of by the end of this chapter by looking at how the leagues were affected and looking in more detail at the Soccer Wars. Who were the key figures? What were the main motivations for the infighting? And what happened after the Soccer Wars concluded?

To understand the full story of the Soccer Wars, one has to trace back all the way to the mid-1920s. You could go back to the start of the 1920s and look at Charles Schwab, the steel magnate who made millions upon millions of dollars making and selling steel. He formed the Bethlehem Steel company and poured a lot of money into making them the force they went on to become.

Schwab helped to build the skyscrapers and bridges we know today, such as the Chrysler Building, the Empire State Building, Madison Square Garden, the Waldorf Astoria, the Rockefeller Centre, the George Washington Bridge, the Golden Gate Bridge, the San Francisco Municipal Railway and the Hoover Dam. While Bethlehem Steel didn't build these on their own, they provided important steelwork to the construction. It wasn't just a run-of-the-mill company that made a few dollars here and there putting up office blocks, they were recognised as the premiere steelwork company in the entire United States. So, why does any of this matter with regards to soccer? Does the construction of the Empire State Building really matter? Well, yes and no. It gives us an idea of the type of companies and owners who were investing in soccer at the time and shows that important, influential and rich people were interested in investing because it was a growing sport and, in some regards, it was a way to flex their financial muscles, much like we see owners do in the modern game.

Owners like Schwab were interested in the sport because it was growing at a rapid rate and soon, because of their influence, the fans were rushing in to see the star players that were signed with the new money that was injected into the league. The owner of the Marksmen, Sam Mark, had the same idea. You spend money to make money, and by spending the money on new players, the club made money by winning trophies and with the fans paying whatever it took to see the club. It was a sound business strategy that was working, and other rich people around the country wanted a piece of the action. They wanted the chance to show how rich they were, even if they didn't really have that big an interest in soccer. In sports, yes. In soccer? Maybe not. One owner who comes to mind fairly quickly when thinking of jumping on the ASL bandwagon is one Charles Abraham Stoneham, owner of the baseball team the New York Giants. We already know what Mr Stoneham was like but this section from an article from the *Society for American Baseball Research* describes Stoneham as:

Short, stout and jowly, Good Time Charlie Stoneham embodied a Jazz Age stereotype – cutthroat businessman by day, boozy bon vivant by night. Even before he took over the Giants in January 1919, Stoneham was a familiar name to the readers of New York City tabloids. Beginning with the well-publicised suicide of a mistress in 1905, Stoneham's messy personal and business life was periodically in the news. Thereafter, the Giants principal owner had to contend with federal indictments, civil lawsuits, hostile fellow magnates, and troubles with booze, gambling, and yet more women. But during his 16-year tenure as club president, the Giants achieved more success than the club had had under any prior regime.

For a compulsive gambler like Charlie Stoneham – he was a regular at racetracks, casinos and other gaming haunts – stock speculation/bucketeering converted his pleasure in endeavours of chance into a livelihood, and he prospered spectacularly. In time, Charles A. Stoneham & Company would expand operations to Boston, Providence, Chicago, Detroit and elsewhere, in addition to maintaining the home office in New York City's financial district. By the advent of World War 1, Stoneham was rich, so well off that he could reportedly afford to lose $70,000 to Arnold Rothstein's Partridge Club playing roulette one evening – over the telephone! But gambling was hardly Stoneham's only vice. He was also a heavy drinker and fond of the opposite sex. With second wife Hannah safely stashed in their Jersey City home, Stoneham nightly prowled the Manhattan demimonde, usually with drink in hand and often with a chorus-girl mistress on his arm.

By all accounts, not the kind of guy you would expect to be investing tons of money into soccer. When your nickname is 'Good Time', chances are you're not going to live a life without a few secrets hidden away. Nevertheless, the character of

'Good Time' Charlie Stoneham would continuously creep up around the ASL throughout his time in soccer and, depending on your point of view, it was hardly ever positive. Stoneham was influential in the origins of the Soccer Wars, and the back end of the golden age of soccer was due, in part, to his influence. Was his finger in every pie at the time? No, but his fingerprints were all over the Soccer Wars crime scene. So it begs the question how exactly did the soccer wars come about? Because it wasn't just something that happened overnight, it had been brewing for some time and it's always intriguing to go right back to the very beginning and dissect what went wrong. You have to go back to before the ASL was in its prime, to 1924. It all started with the National Challenge Cup. It was a beloved domestic cup tournament in which clubs from across the nation competed for a trophy to proudly display in their cabinet for the next 12 months, although it wasn't loved by everyone. The 1924 edition of the tournament saw the ASL clubs boycott the National Challenge Cup because of a conflict of scheduling, complaining that it was too close to the schedule of the ASL games, meaning clubs had to spend more on travel and the players were more likely to get injured. We've covered this back in the American Soccer League chapter, but in the context of the Soccer Wars story it was important to mention it as it pretty much planted the seeds for what would happen in the future. In the 1925/26 season, the ASL clubs came back to the competition and the USFA promised that they would cut down their own take on matchday revenue and tournament winnings from 33 per cent to 15 per cent, but meetings were still planned to sort out any potential worries the ASL and the USFA had between each other. These meetings prompted a headline in the *Bethlehem Globe* newspaper on Thursday, 14 May 1925, which read:

> EXPECT A HOT SOCCER MEETING
> USFA Will Hold Annual Conference In New York Next
> Week.

The soccer world knew what was going to be discussed and they knew it would probably get quite tempestuous. The rest of the article read like this:

> Several important issues promising heated debates are on tap in soccerdom, when the moguls gather for their annual meetings. Next week the U. S. F. A. will have their annual confab at New York and early in June the American Soccer League will have their annual session in the metropolis. Both these meetings indirectly have much to do with the Bethlehem Steel team.
>
> Among the problems that the National Commission will battle are several that have to do with the American Soccer League and the most important probably will be in making concessions demanded by this professional loop. Disagreement on certain matters resulted in the American Soccer League withdrawing all of its clubs from the national cup competition and unless the concessions are adhered to, it is quite certain that the league will again decide to paddle its own canoe and again conduct a cup competition limited exclusively to the American Soccer League clubs.
>
> The American Soccer League will ask representation on the national council and equally as important will be a revision of the usual split of the gate receipts for the semi-final and final in the cup tie play. Heretofore the division of the gate receipts gave the association 33 1/3 percent. That is what the league objected to and has admitted a proposition whereby if the commission percentage is cut to 15 percent, assurances of these strong professional clubs in the cup competition will be given.
>
> Since from a financial standpoint as well as otherwise the national cup tie play fell flat during the last season, it is expected that the National Association concede to the demands of the league. The election of officers is another important issue.

When the National Association is done, the American Soccer League executives will warm up for their annual debate, including the election of officers, and some spirited doings are also hinted for this meeting. Doings, it is whispered, that might result in a drastic change in the executive board. Also with the division of receipts of the home games.

It is understood that there is a movement on foot and stimulated by Mr. Bagnall, of Fall River, to cut the division of the receipts to the visiting club from 20 percent to 10 percent. In the New England district, where the attendance numbers in the thousands, this issue will, no doubt, receive support. However, the clubs of the Metropolitan districts, including Philadelphia and Bethlehem, are expected to strenuously oppose such a change. The present basis of 20 percent to the visiting clubs has been proven highly satisfactory, and if continued, the revenue derived by the clubs that do not draw the biggest gates is certain to inspire an effort in securing players to strengthen their teams. At least, that seems to be the sentiment in Bethlehem. The Steel Workers have always been a big attraction in the New England cities, and as such, should be considered accordingly. In fact, it is believed that the attendance records for league games have been established with Bethlehem the opposing team.

At the very least, the issues that the ASL and USFA had with each other were out in the open. A dialogue had been opened and everything seemed to be going back to the way that everyone was used to. The ASL teams were back in the Challenge Cup, and the USFA were glad to have them back. But during this very same time period, there was another issue involving the USFA and the ASL, but this time FIFA were involved, and it looked very, very serious. Remember how the ASL clubs used their riches to sign players from Europe into their league? Remember how Scottish and English clubs nicknamed some of the ASL clubs 'American Menaces'? Well, some clubs in Europe *really* didn't like how the ASL clubs operated and called FIFA in to try to sanction the American clubs and to order the clubs to adhere to international contract rules. Surely it would just be a slap on the wrists for the ASL/USFA or a hefty fine, but FIFA had other ideas. FIFA instructed that the clubs stop signing players in the way that they had been doing or risk USFA expulsion from FIFA, thus meaning the ASL would not be officially recognised as a professional soccer league. The ASL and USFA would pretty much fail to exist if FIFA banned the USFA, and US soccer would have zero power or influence in world soccer, which obviously meant that the ASL and USFA had to work something out in order to protect the league and the governing body. The league and governing body did manage to keep on the good side of FIFA and survived any major sanctions, but the infighting between the ASL and USFA had just begun. They could only delay their internal issues for so long and just one year after FIFA tried to step in to balance out the financial might of these US clubs (which most European clubs couldn't compete with when it came to keeping players or signing them), the metaphorical waste hit the fan that was US soccer. But, no one really knew it at the time. It just sort of ... happened. The league was at its all-time high, business was booming, both in the real world and in soccer, yet it was all on the verge of crashing down. Why? Because the infighting between the ASL and USFA – spurred on by the owners of the clubs who wanted the maximum they could get in terms of financial gain – heated up, and in 1928 it boiled over.

In 1928 'Good Time' Charlie Stoneham got his messy and controversial hands involved in issues and in places one would suggest they didn't necessarily need to be. Stoneham set about with his plan of persuading the ASL clubs to boycott the National Challenge Cup, just like they had done before in 1925, but this time Stoneham wanted the ASL clubs to leave the competition permanently. Why did Stoneham want to remove the ASL clubs from the most prestigious competition in North American soccer? Was it purely out of spite because of how the USFA behaved towards the ASL, or was it purely down to money and the scheduling, like it had been in 1925? It all harks back to when FIFA got involved with the transfer dealings of the ASL. The ASL club owners felt that the USFA's reaction and subsequent 'bowing to foreign authority' was weak so they were inspired to seek a solution or alternative that freed them from the limitations and restrictions from both FIFA and the USFA, inspired in part by how MLB pretty much ruled themselves. Stoneham, who obviously owned a fairly successful baseball team, wanted his soccer team and league to be run in a similar fashion. To put it bluntly, some ASL owners wanted to run their team in a league that had zero influence from anyone outside of the United States of America. In modern times, it sounds ridiculous to say that soccer can't be influenced by anyone outside of the US – in particular Europe – but when those in charge of the clubs aren't used to anything different, it's the least that you can expect.

But what Stoneham wanted to do with the breakaway clubs was actually quite interesting and could have made the sport a more national sport, rather than just regional, and while he went about it the completely wrong way, it could have been a huge success. What Stoneham suggested was that the ASL branch off from just the north east of the US and move more towards introducing a midwestern league, with a grand final being played between the winners of the north-eastern ASL and the midwestern ASL, which could replace the National Challenge Cup and prove who was the *best* soccer team in the United States. It sounds interesting, and if you consider that Stoneham and the rest of the ASL owners wouldn't be content with just two leagues, they would more than likely branch off into other regions such as a west coast league, a southern league, a north-western league, all with the winners of those leagues going into one competition to prove who was the top dog. If this plan was to work, it would take a heck of a lot of time to implement it, and it would have huge ramifications for US soccer. On the face of it, it is similar to what actually happened in the English Premier League, where club owners got together and formed a breakaway league from the English Football League in 1992, taking their new television deal with Sky TV with them, but while they moved away from the Football League and the Football League governing body, they still remained a part of the FA, because if they removed themselves from both the Football League and the FA, they wouldn't be officially recognised as a professional league by FIFA. Now, that plan ended up working, but with the ASL they just wanted to leave the USFA completely and form their own governing body. To do this and still be recognised as a professional league was more or less impossible, unless FIFA themselves ratified you as a governing body, as they did with the USFA. The ASL felt like the USFA had stabbed them in the back by siding with FIFA, while the USFA felt that, for the long-term benefits of the game in the United States, they had no other choice than to side with FIFA or risk being expelled from the organisation. It made sense for the USFA to side with FIFA, but the ASL didn't see it that way.

Stoneham managed to persuade most of the ASL clubs to boycott the National Challenge Cup, claiming that if the USFA didn't reschedule the competition to the end of the ASL season they would leave the competition completely. There were just three exceptions – Newark Skeeters, New York Giants and, most notably, Bethlehem Steel. The ASL responded to this by expelling the three clubs from the league and once again brought on the wrath of both FIFA and the USFA who sided with the three 'outlaw' clubs, claiming that the league's actions were out of bounds and essentially excluding it from world soccer. To put it simply, because of their actions, FIFA and the USFA acted as if the ASL did not exist. It *had* existed at one point in time, but as of 1928 the league was no more (at least in their eyes). The Soccer Wars were well and truly in full effect, and both sides were feeling it. For some, the reaction from the ASL was a shock and seen as extremely harsh, especially from the *Bethlehem Globe* who spoke of their surprise at the treatment of their local club:

Local Management Amazed at Drastic Punishment of League President

'We are amazed at the action and regret very much the steps taken,' was a statement from the Bethlehem soccer team in commenting on the action of William Cunningham, president of the American Soccer League, suspending Bethlehem, the New York Giants and Newark FC, and fining each $1,000 for refusing to withdraw their entry in the National Challenge Cup competition.

'We took such steps as we believed our interests warranted when we entered the cup tie and the sentence of the league may mean a legal entanglement in the interest of the respective clubs,' the statement continued.

Just why the local management plans have not been divulged and probably will not be until official notification of the punishment meted out is received from league headquarters. Up to noon such notification has not been received. Before the Bethlehem team left for the New Bedford invasion over the weekend an effort was made to confer with the league president and a telegram was wired inviting such a conference. However, there was no reply to the telegram but when the club returned home yesterday noon a letter was awaiting.

There is considerable speculation on what action will follow. There is talk of a new league and this is most likely. It is understood that quite a little missionary work has already been done in this respect and if a new circuit is organised it will be a more compact loop with all of the New England clubs eliminated.

For some time the contention has been that invasions of the New England states are far too expensive and at the same time consume entirely too much time. This opinion is not alone entertained locally but practically by every other club in this district.

When Bethlehem played New Bedford and Providence over the weekend the team sounded sentiment in that territory, which strange as it may appear, seemed to be heartily in accord with the action taken by Bethlehem.

There is a feeling throughout the circuit that several clubs have entirely too much influence in directing the operation of the league and one of these alleged clubs is Fall River.

Several instances are advanced in which the Marksmen seem to have a controlling power and one of these, in which the league has taken no action, involves Bethlehem. It is learned that Fall River agreed to a transfer price for the services of Malcolm Goldie, former Bethlehem outside left, but yet the Marksmen have made no remittance and at the same time are playing Goldie regularly.

Advices received from Philadelphia indicate that a new league would be favoured and if one does materialise application for a franchise will be immediately made. In fact it is understood that enough clubs are already available for a new circuit.

A new league was on the verge of being started up by the USFA called the Eastern Professional Soccer League, which in the end would only exist for a season and a half from 1928 to 1929 with the sole purpose of going head to head with the ASL. The EPSL was formed on 8 October 1928 in the Cornish Arms Hotel in New York City (just in case you're wondering, the hotel's address was 322 West 23rd Street. The 13-storey building is no longer used as a hotel, and instead it is a Duane Reades at the bottom and the other 12 floors are very expensive apartments) with a league comprised of eight teams: the three expelled ASL teams, four from the Southern New York Football Association (New York Hispano, New York Celtics, Philadelphia Centrals and IRT Rangers) and one newly created team, the New York Hakoah. Meanwhile, the ASL were submitting their request to join FIFA, and, predictably, FIFA rejected their request. It was all a bit childish and no one really benefitted from any of the moves that were made, except for maybe the three teams the ASL banned. Even though they eventually ran riot over the EPSL because they were light years ahead of their competition with much better players, they never actually took a side in any of this. They could have stayed with the ASL and made more money, but no one was sure about the future of the league given the USFA and FIFA had basically abandoned them, and they wanted to play in a league that was professionally recognised. Soccer in the United States should have been thriving, but all the hard work done by the likes of Thomas Cahill was unravelling. Another article written by the *Bethlehem Globe* on 29 December 1928 spoke about the support the USFA was receiving from FIFA and how the ASL didn't have the backing of anyone, which in turn led to the next step in the Soccer Wars.

Pledge Support to National Body

All bodies affiliated with the United States Football Association will shortly receive a communication from headquarters presenting the attitude of foreign soccer bodies in regard to the controversy in this country. Rumour that the American Soccer League and its promoters in its plan to organize a national association to conflict with the U.S.F.A. would be welcomed into the good graces of the Federation Internationale de Football Association are refuted in letters received by Sec. Thomas W. Cahill, of the national body, copies of which he is sending to all organizations associated with the U.S.F.A. In regard to the recognition of the suspension of players engaging in American Soccer League soccer Mr. Cahill is in receipt of the following letter from F. J. Wall, secretary of the English Football League: 'I have received letters of 10th of November which shall have consideration. In the meantime I confirm the principal of reciprocity as between your association and ourselves on these matters.' A communication from the Federation Internationale de Football Association refutes the statements being made that the F.I.F.A. intends to appoint a commission to investigate the affairs of the United States Football Association. This letter reads: 'With regard to the troubles in your country you need have no doubt that the F.I.F.A. stands behind you and will support you.'

Licked at Every Turn

Thus far it would seem that the national body and the newly formed Eastern Soccer League have emerged on top in all arguments. Legal action taken in filing injunctions to restrain players from participating with Eastern Soccer League clubs have been dismissed, which in reality is a moral victory for the new soccer organization and the U.S.F.A. Two of these injunctions were brought in New York, one by representatives of the Brooklyn Wanderers and the other by the New York Nationals. The players involved played and will continue playing in the new circuit. Now with sentiment from foreign associations pledging support to the U.S.F.A., the rival faction has been beaten at every turn in waging warfare.

While the USFA had the support of FIFA, both their EPSL and the ASL were suffering financially, with both the USFA and ASL losing respect from their peers across the world and doing immense damage to their image. If anything is ever dubbed a 'war' of any kind, it always means that both sides lost in one sense or another. In this particular case, both sides knew that they were struggling, and, whilst they didn't always see eye to eye, they needed each other to maximise what they had. The ASL needed the USFA in order to regain its status as a professional league and the USFA needed the ASL to add another string to its bow on a worldwide stage, allowing it to boast one of the strongest leagues outside of Europe at the time. Both sides knew they needed each other, but little did they know what was just around the corner in soccer and in the real world.

When the New Bedford Whalers left the ASL to join up with the USFA in 1929 with no announcement whatsoever (they just upped and left, no warning given to the ASL), it sent shockwaves throughout the soccer world. The USFA had a huge scalp from the ASL, who in turn had to call a meeting to essentially reassure themselves that no other club would leave them and join the USFA. Fans at Fall River Marksmen matches were clamouring for a reconciliation between the ASL and USFA, but rumours at the time suggested that unless the two joined up again the ASL was as good as dead. On 9 October 1929 the ASL signed an agreement to return to the USFA soccer fold, and just a couple of days after the EPSL season had come to a climax the three teams that the ASL had expelled were back, but in the newly formed league called the Atlantic Coast League. Peace had been found between the two after four to five years of animosity, albeit more out of necessity than want. The USFA had 'won' the Soccer Wars, but what had they actually won? The ASL was down on its knees when it came to finances, with multiple teams also having trouble paying the bills, and some were even forced to expel themselves from the league and fold their clubs completely. They were back together, but at what cost? Neither side knew what was about to hit them. What happened next? The Great Depression came and took every last penny that anyone had, starting with the owners of large businesses including those like Bethlehem Steel.

When the Great Depression hit, it hit the whole of the United States like a rock hitting a glass house. Its effect was felt in every walk of life in America, but at first people didn't really know what to expect. In fact, no one had any idea what was going on, let alone what it would lead to. In retrospect we can look back at this decade-long period and accurately depict what caused the Depression and the after-effects, but no one can accurately depict what it was like to live through that time period. We can analyse the effect it had on human beings, companies and the stock market, but we can't weigh up quite how significant it was for people in terms of living day to day not knowing if they would have any food or drink, or whether they would ever get a job. In the 21st century we know the Depression ended, but in 1929 no one knew anything. They didn't know when it would end, if it would end at all, and it was symptomatic of what the American way of life had become. The amount of money in the country that was the cause of such great hope and optimism inadvertently caused the polar opposite and sparked arguably the most significant stretch in time for the United States in its history. It was a time known as the roaring 20s, when people were seemingly ecstatic every minute of every day, with businesses booming like never before after the First World War. Between the years 1920 and 1929, the total wealth of the United States more than doubled due to industries such as the steel and iron works, and automobiles were coming into the mainstream with the big three companies of General Motors, Chrysler and Ford dominating the financial world. Beautiful art deco-style skyscrapers were built in cities like New York City to emphasise the wealth that was available, and due to the increase in steel production from companies like Bethlehem Steel, it seemed that every man and his dog could own a skyscraper if they planned it out correctly.

But what made the 1920s so extraordinary is that every man and his dog *could* invest in whatever they wanted, with the general population able to buy stocks in whatever company they wanted to on the stock market, which was centralised in New York City's New York Stock Exchange (NYSE) on Wall Street. The NYSE had experienced a major change within a few years in the 1920s because everyone had jumped on the stock market bandwagon and there were peaks and troughs of extremely good trading days where a lot of money was made and extremely bad trading days where a lot of money was lost. The stock market wasn't a new invention, it had been integrated in some fashion across the world, but never in the United States had it experienced growth like this before. The post-world war recession (a natural occurrence whenever a war is fought) was forgotten about and the public seemed to think that the only way to forget about the tragedies was to spend. And spend they did! It all worked in a cycle. For example, let's take the three car companies we mentioned earlier, Ford, Chrysler and General Motors. They were starting to move with the times and create more automobiles for the public, who bought these cars as the need for one increased over time. Due to the consumers buying more cars to suit their needs, the car companies were making more money, making them more valuable on the stock market. People would buy the stocks of Ford, Chrysler and General Motors because these companies were pumping out more cars for people to buy, even if they were creating more cars than there were people! Then you take Chrysler and General Motors (more specifically Chrysler), who made so much money that they started construction on what would become the tallest building on earth (for 11 months), the Chrysler Building in New York City. Aided by the steel works of Bethlehem Steel, they managed to start construction in 1928 and finished the building in 1930. That's four major companies who benefitted hugely from the upturn in spending: Ford, Chrysler, General Motors and Bethlehem Steel. There were many more things that made tons of cash, but you get the point.

There was an economic recession in 1921 after the conclusion of the First World War that was allowed to run its course without any interference from political parties or anyone like that, the country just let it go and within 18 months it was all over. From that moment on, the wealth in the United States grew larger and larger every year, with the tax reports from the Treasury Department claiming that in 1921 there were 21 millionaires in the US, 75 in 1924 and 207 in 1926. This was at the exact same time the ASL was experiencing its influx of wealth from their respective club owners.

In 1927, the Treasury reported that there were an estimated 15,000 millionaires across the United States, and one billionaire. There was money everywhere, and as a result the prices of everything went up. Cars, houses, food, clothes, shares, stocks, land, it was all rising. Would it come to an abrupt end soon? No one at the time thought so, because the last time there was a recession it was over in 18 months.

Those involved didn't feel like they had anything to worry about, which explains why everyone was spending a lot of money, including the ASL clubs, who were outspending their European rivals – who were far bigger in terms of historical value and standing in the soccer world – because of the market boom. Owners had more money to spend on improving their team, and as a result of their teams' success their companies became more profitable. But because of the expansion of the stock market and rumours floating around about share prices, stock started to tumble down in relation to its real value. A lot of profit made by these companies was going towards bonuses for executives and their salaries skyrocketed as a result of good business. All of this led to a stock market crash. While the majority of the 1920s was filled with mass production and positivity, 1929 changed all of that. Production was down, wages were down and the number of people in jobs was down as well. The market started to experience changes that no one knew how to deal with, and on a day now known as 'Black Thursday', 12,894,650 shares were traded on the stock market. 'Black Thursday' was followed by 'Black Monday', then came the fatal and now infamous 'Black Tuesday', where 16,410,030 shares were traded, meaning billions of dollars were lost and everything was financially obliterated. Everything that people didn't think could possibly happen, happened, and it happened in the worst way imaginable, with millions of people across the US out of jobs. Those people who lost their jobs had invested in the booming stock market amidst the rise of Wall Street, but they had lost everything. Every penny they had, gone. Why? Because *too much* money was being made.

The rise of the stock market correlated with the rise in financial power, interest and standard in the ASL. But then companies lost money, meaning they had to rely heavily on fans to pay any price to come and watch them play in order to pay the players, but the fans weren't able to buy tickets. They were only just about able to survive, let alone watch a soccer match. Coupled with the pettiness and infighting that the Soccer Wars brought, and interest in the sport was dwindling. There isn't actually an official record of how much owners of ASL clubs lost during this time period, but it was enough to cause some teams to fold. It wasn't just the ASL and soccer that was affected in sport either, baseball had just as hard a time with regards to their attendances. The summer before the stock market crash there were five MLB teams that averaged over 10,000 spectators every single game, but within three years of it only two teams averaged 10,000, the Chicago Cubs and New York Yankees. Just one year after that the Yankees led the league in highest average attendance with 9,707, meaning they were down 50 per cent from the summer just before the crash.

It didn't help that the league had gone through hell (that they put themselves through) and were trying to re-establish interest in a league that was fading anyway, but the Depression made a difficult task ten times harder. Baseball managed to survive the Depression harmed but not on its last legs. Soccer wasn't so lucky.

The league tried to regain some form of popularity and excitement, but the name changes between the Atlantic Coast League and the American Soccer League didn't help, and when your league is comprised of only eight teams and a handful capable of putting together a squad strong enough to warrant a title charge, it makes the competition a little boring. All this happened after the success of the 1930 World Cup, which was the peak of soccer during this era. The ASL flourished, but the World Cup should have been what lit a fuse underneath the sport in the United States. Instead, the domestic league was a shambles and the attention of the public was elsewhere, and understandably so. As a result of both the Depression and the lack of fans, the legendary teams such as Fall River Marksmen and Bethlehem Steel started to disappear. The Steel had worries about the construction side of the company so disbanded the soccer team, while the Marksmen renamed and reformed as the New York Yankees (possibly in a bid to fool fans who wanted to see the Yankees baseball team and not soccer – it didn't work), and, just like that, the two biggest names in American soccer history at this point in time were gone. If they had been around

40-odd years later when the NASL kicked off, who knows what may have happened because what the Steel and Marksmen did was no different to teams in the 60s, 70s and 80s, they were just ahead of their time and became victims of that. On 4 January 1932, only 3,000 fans attended the last-ever ASL championship match in New York City between the New York Giants and New Bedford Whalers, the Giants winning 9-8 on aggregate. It was almost too fitting a tribute that the ASL would close its doors on the golden age of soccer with a high-scoring game, and while soccer didn't die after this game, it had been put on life support. Soccer wasn't completely gone, though, it just marked the end of the golden age of US soccer of the 1920s and early 1930s. However, the semi-professional leagues that were formed in the years following the Depression failed to even come close to what the ASL had promised and delivered less than a decade before. It wasn't nearly as exciting, talented or rich as the first ASL, but at a time when America needed any form of league, it provided a source for soccer. World Cup legends Billy Gonsalves and Bert Patenaude played in the ASL II, but even they couldn't garner a similar kind of interest as the ASL. However, the large number of semi-pro players in the league actually meant that other amateur leagues across the US were able to compete with the ASL II in the National Challenge Cup. There was a distinct lack of imports and no superteams like the Steel or Marksmen, which allowed for a much larger and equal playing field. This would have been amazing to see, with upsets happening in the cup every year, and the National Challenge Cup was creating its own history. But if an upset happens in the National Challenge Cup and there are no fans to see it, does it even happen? There may be records of it, but there is no 'I was there when so and so beat this team' moments because no one was going. And that is the sad part of it all. There is nothing wrong with playing as an amateur or at a semi-professional level, but if there are no fans to cheer you on and witness historical moments, that's when you know the sport is in a bad place.

Big teams from Europe would occasionally travel over to the United States for tours like they had done in the past, and the crowds flocked to see the likes of Liverpool and Manchester United because they thought it would be the only time that they would see actual top-level talent. The games were usually exciting and well attended, even if the European sides wiped the floor with the American teams, but what else was to be expected? It's sad that in modern America, the American Soccer League has been forgotten.

In many ways, it was ahead of its time, but as Gregory Reck and Bruce Allen Dick say in their book *American Soccer: History, Culture, Class*, it's more down to cultural amnesia than anything else:

> The history of the American Soccer League and the 1930 US National Team is part of this country's sports amnesia. When one of the foremost historians of US Soccer, Colin Jose, was conducting research on the ASL in 1969, he received a list from the league at that time detailing the winners of the ASL championship. The list started in 1933. Imagine his surprise many years later when he came across articles in the New York Times chronicling the ASL of the 1920s. 'How could this be?' he asked, when according to the ASL's own records the league began in 1933. Intentionally or not, the ASL had erased its official memory of the best years of its existence.
>
> Whether cause or effect, this institutional amnesia is linked to the space occupied by soccer in the popular consciousness of the US sports fans. In the minds of most Americans, soccer is a recent foreign import into a sports landscape long occupied by baseball, basketball and American football. Both contemporary advocates and critics of soccer argue that the sport's marginal space results from its 'recent' appearance in the United States, since there is little room for a 'new' sport given that the Big Three have always dominated that landscape. The history of US soccer through the 1920s paints a very different picture, however.

Because the past is always reconstructed through the lens of the present, this amnesia – or, to some, dementia – may be related to the current cultural space occupied by US soccer. The criticism identifying US soccer in these early days as a foreign sport peopled with foreign players is patently false. By the close of the 1920s there were as many, if not more, native-born players in the ASL and on the US national team than players born abroad. Recognising the success of this era might require rethinking the case-based formula for success that typically dominates the soccer landscape today, which is reason enough for those who have an investment in the contemporary structure of US soccer to conveniently forget the past.

The golden age of US soccer has almost been forgotten about, either by choice or for other reasons, but if anything it should be the best example possible of how to run the sport, even with its major flaws, because those flaws would eradicate the errors that are being made in today's game.

US soccer kept trying with its various amateur leagues, but the sport was hit heavily by the Second World War and, of course, was delayed by a number of years. Could it have learned lessons from the NFL, bided its time over the Depression years and build up from the colleges, building new players and fans? It might have worked, but it's impossible to say definitively if it would have because the two leagues were structured differently. Ice hockey and basketball either had no following or were in their infancy around the time of the Depression, so soccer had a head start on all sports other than baseball, but they couldn't quite get to grips with a new wave of soccer.

Soccer kept fading away into the background as more leagues were created to try to drive interest, before collapsing due to financial difficulties, and all the while the NFL, MLB and soon to be NHL and NBA were creating their leagues and building the fanbases where soccer had done in the past. Soccer and baseball set the standards for American sports at the turn of the 20th century, but just 30 years into the timeline, only baseball was professional out of the two. Thomas Cahill never saw his dreams fulfilled and when he passed away in 1951, he had seen a lot but sadly missed out on so much. The question isn't 'what happened to soccer in the United States', it should be 'what could have happened in soccer in the United States if it had stayed professional and survived the Depression?' That's a question that we will never know the answer to.

But its popularity did start to increase again, with success at college level as soccer was introduced as an official sport of the NCAA and the famous win at the 1950 World Cup over England which shocked the entire tournament after the US had been reduced to total underdogs. Soccer in America really could have been massive. So surely you'd think that after what had happened in the 1920s the soccer world in the United States wouldn't make the same mistake again, would it? Surely not. There was no way they could spend, spend, spend on players after what had happened before ...

Chapter Five

The Rise and Fall of the NASL (1968–84)

THERE was a chasm between the culmination of the Second World War and the 1960s in US soccer. Amateur leagues were still playing and trying their hardest to garner as much attention as they possibly could, all while trying their best to stay afloat financially and not fall into the perils that faced previous clubs in the American Soccer League. The Great Depression had seen interest in soccer dwindle and, despite various amateur leagues still being active and certain members of the famous 1930 World Cup squad still being active and playing in those amateur leagues, no one could really recreate the same sort of ambition, buzz and excitement. The ASL II didn't have the same pull for star players as the original ASL, nor did it have the financial power to allow clubs to create the same kind of 'super teams' we saw at the time as well. Post-Second World War, soccer was relatively quiet in the US, and other sports were making their mark on the culture in a post-war environment that was up for grabs. Baseball was still top of the tree with the integration of ethnic minorities (the 'Negro League' ended in 1951 and players like Jackie Robinson, Hank Aaron, Willie Mays and Earnie Banks all joined Major League Baseball and had Hall-of-Fame careers) at the forefront of their move into a post-war world, while expansion out west meant that it was now being played countrywide and available to a wider audience. The NFL had ridden the harsh waves caused by the Depression and was slowly building on the foundations they had set, with the sport being televised regionally and, most importantly, nationally to a much wider audience, which took the NFL to the next level, and their merger with the AFL (American Football League another football league led by Lemar Hunt, someone you'll hear from later on) meant that the NFL was the only rodeo in town, and the invention of the Super Bowl meant football had gone from being a sport primarily played by college students and amateurs to being legitimately the second biggest sport in America, if not the biggest and most popular at the time. The NBA was formed in 1946 and grew to be the most significant basketball association in the world, with players like Bill Russell, Bob Cousey, Bob Pettit, Elgin Baylor, Wilt Chamberlain, Oscar Robertson and Jerry West transforming the sport, inspiring many young children, no matter what race, to pick it up. It only got more popular as time went on and had usurped soccer as the game that anyone could play in the street, with basketball courts being erected in playgrounds and everyone trying to copy the moves of their favourite player. Post-war America had three legitimate powerhouse sports with the NFL and NBA only growing larger and larger as they expanded into new markets, created new stars and created new ideas like the All Star Game/ Pro Bowl and Slam Dunk contests (the ABA had created that first, but thanks to the popularity of 'Doctor J' Julius Erving, the NBA 'borrowed' the concept once the two leagues merged) giving people something to be wowed by.

While this was happening and baseball was still known as 'America's Pastime', soccer was nowhere to be seen. These other leagues had taken the leap of faith, going from primarily college-based and NCAA sports to being professional, with superstar players and television spots to advertise everything they had on offer, whereas soccer went the opposite direction. It already had a professional league that wowed paying fans, who flocked to their local stadium to see high-scoring games, but the sport eventually had to go amateur to stay alive and it was a bonus when it was accepted as an NCAA sport. The NFL, MLB and NBA used the NCAA to draft in the young prospects and create the next generations of stars, whereas soccer used it as an avenue to just play, which was just one of the issues the sport faced. If the golden age of soccer had come after the war, things would have been different. Maybe soccer would have had its very own Wilt Chamberlain or Bill Russell, Jim Brown or Johnny Unitas, Yogi Berra or Mickey Mantle or Jackie Robinson or someone who could inspire an entire generation to go outside and pick up a ball. In the years that these sports were creating generational superstars, soccer was still trying to find its feet and trying to figure out what step to take next. Would they pour all their money into one big league and hope people liked it, similar to the ASL, or would they adopt a four-tier league system like, for example, in England where you have four tiers of the Football League and each year teams are promoted and relegated depending on their results. Would promotion and relegation even work in a nation where bad teams are usually rewarded with the best young talent instead of going down a league? These were all questions that soccer faced in a time where they were not only catching up with the rest of the soccer world, but they were catching up with their own country. But while they may have looked at the English Football League for inspiration, it was England that had inadvertently inspired the powers that be to take another dive into soccer in 1966. The World Cup had a deep history in the United States and the 1966 edition proved to be the catalyst for a new generation of soccer in America.

FIFA make a sanctioned documentary on a World Cup in every year that the competition is played. The tradition started back in 1954, when Switzerland hosted the finals and West Germany won their first World Cup, with a film called *German Giants*. Fast forward 12 years to when England hosted and won the competition in 1966 and the film *Goal* was produced and shown around the world. Predictably, it was popular in England, but it was in the United States where eyebrows were raised. One million people tuned in to watch the film highlighting the 1966 World Cup (maybe one million isn't massive compared to the shows at the time, but it was still a large audience for a sport that, at the time, wasn't considered major in the US), which led many American sports investors to believe that the soccer market was there to be taken over. It was untapped, and had been for a very long time, but the viewing figures of the World Cup film showed otherwise, at least in the eyes of the investors. Was it an upturn in popularity that could immediately skyrocket the sport to the heights of baseball, football and basketball? No, but it was a start. And for those investors who wanted to make as much money as possible, a start was all that was needed. It took less than a year for two leagues to form in the US, one named the United Soccer Association (USA) and the other called the National Professional Soccer League (NPSL). The former was recognised as an official league by FIFA and consisted of teams that were brought over from Europe and South America and rebranded as a local American team, with players from the original clubs. The league was created by a consortium named the North American Soccer League – a group of sports entrepreneurs led by Jack Kent Cooke, who owned the Los Angeles Lakers and NHL side Los Angeles Kings, with the help of Lamar Hunt and Steve Stavro – and was sanctioned almost immediately by both FIFA and the USSFA (United States Soccer Football Association renamed from the previous USFA). They were forced to speed up the process of forming their league due to the swift formation of a rival league, the NPSL. The NPSL was different to the USA because it wasn't officially sanctioned by FIFA or the USSFA, meaning they were dubbed the 'outlaw' league, much like the ASL was during the Soccer Wars. But if the NPSL was an 'outlaw' league, why did the USA feel pressured by them to speed up the formation of their own league? Well, it's plain and simple – television. Despite not being recognised by FIFA or the USSFA, the NPSL's broadcasting rights were bought by CBS. This is why there were only imported teams in the USA instead of new, local clubs being formed – the league was worried that if they didn't keep up with the NPSL and the television coverage they were receiving, they would fall into irrelevancy. The imported teams were hastily readied for the season, with teams from around the world agreeing to take part. Here are the teams that lined up in the inaugural USA season and their respective partnered teams:

Boston Rovers – Shamrock Rovers (Ireland)
Chicago Mustangs – Cagliari (Italy)
Cleveland Stokers – Stoke City (England)
Dallas Tornado – Dundee United (Scotland)
Detroit Cougars – Glentoran (Northern Ireland)
Houston Stars – Bangu AC (Brazil)
Los Angeles Wolves – Wolverhampton Wanderers
    (England)
New York Skyliners – C.A. Cerro (Uruguay)
San Francisco Golden Gate Gales – ADO Den Haag
    (Netherlands)
Toronto City – Hibernian (Scotland)
Vancouver Royal Canadians – Sunderland (England)
Washington Whips – Aberdeen (Scotland)

The idea of having these teams come to America and play what would essentially be exhibition games was to get the fans accustomed to the teams and the sport while also giving the franchises adequate time to sort rosters, sign coaches and players and build an actual team instead of rushing one together to start the 1968 season. The league started playing on 28 May 1967 with the Houston Stars bringing in a crowd of just under 35,000, but while the Houston franchise was able to bring in a big crowd, the rest of the league failed to match their figures and the first USA league season ended up with an average attendance of around 8,000. There was some serious talent on show as well, with the Cleveland Stokers having World Cup winner Gordon Banks between the sticks, and the legendary Inter Milan and Juventus striker Roberto Boninsegna finished as the league's top scorer with 10 goals playing up front for the Chicago Mustangs. Did every team put out their strongest possible 11 in every game? Some would say no, because to those teams coming from Europe it was their off-season, they wanted to rest their stars. It was natural for these teams to rest players, and it probably did affect the attendances once the novelty of the sport wore off, along with the insecurity of not knowing who would be on the team next year, so fans almost certainly must have wondered what was the point of cheering for these guys if they'll just leave at the end of the season.

The NPSL, on the other hand, got off to their start on Sunday, 16 April 1967 with a total of 46,547 fans flocking to various grounds across the country to see the 'new' sport of soccer. Unlike the USA, who brought in imported players to fill their league, the NPSL gave new franchises the chance to build their teams from the get-go, and, while the NPSL may not have had the immediate star power that the USA had, they still had very talented and accomplished players to build a steady league around, such as Aston Villa legend Peter McParland, former West Ham and Villa man Phil Woosnam, who was player-manager of the Atlanta Chiefs (remember that name, he will come up again in a big way very soon) as well as two former Real Madrid players in Juan Santisteban and Yanko Daucik. Were they the same star names as Gordon Banks and Roberto Boninsegna? No, but they didn't need to be. The NPSL planned on having these players build a base for their franchises instead of playing a season, packing up their things and going back home, never to be seen again. It also helped that the NPSL had the CBS contract for two years, as it helped them win a new audience. However, it actually did more harm than good, because CBS just did not know how to run a soccer broadcast.

With Jack Whitaker and former Tottenham Hotspur captain Danny Blanchflower leading the broadcasts, CBS were quite picky about how they wanted to show the NPSL games. Firstly, something that is known in infamy and still thrown at the US game as a negative was how CBS instructed referees to slow play down and stop play as a whole to allow commercials to be shown on air. Not during the half-time break, not at full time or pre-game, but during the match itself. It was nothing short of a stupid idea (there's a good story that we will get on to later about commercials in soccer during this time period that showcased how stupid and brainless the idea was). Referee Peter Rhodes once spoke about how he was instructed to force players to fake injuries and stay down longer in order to allow CBS the time to play a commercial, then let them get back up once it was over. One game that stands out in particular for this featured Rhodes in a match in May 1967 between the Pittsburgh Phantoms and the Toronto Falcons where 21 fouls were called. That doesn't seem like anything other than a hard, dirty game, but 11 of those fouls were called to allow CBS to show a commercial. It led some people to question whether CBS had *too much* of an influence on the matches themselves, and while this technique of filling time with commercials may work in leagues where timeouts are prevalent, like the NFL and NBA, or where there are a lot of breaks in play, like in MLB, it just didn't work in soccer. It wasn't the only mistake that CBS made, but it was the one that stuck in the mind forever and had a lasting impact in the wrong way. The first game shown on CBS was the match between the Baltimore Bays and Atlanta Chiefs, where Blanchflower and Whitaker ran the broadcast as the usual tandem of Whitaker being the play-by-play man and Blanchflower analysing the game and picking out the positives and negatives of what he saw. No different to how any other sport works now and even how they worked back then, but Blanchflower's style didn't suit CBS. In an article in *Sports Illustrated* from 10 June 1968, Blanchflower talks about how the network tried to get him to change his tone and thoughts on where the sport was heading in America at the time.

JUST ONE TRUTH FOR ME

It never really worked. I probably should have known that from the beginning, had I given it more thought, but I doubt if that would have changed my feelings. I'm not the sort to go into anything with a pessimistic attitude. Even now I want to believe that enough people in America want an honest outlook in their sporting affairs, enough, that is, to get it. At least I hope they will give my opinions fair consideration.

Maybe I should have been more concerned that night in February 1967 when I met Jack Dolph, the director of sports for CBS TV, in the foyer of London's Savoy Hotel. His words do seem more significant now. I remember his brief apology for having little time to spare before he rushed me through a mixed bag of questions concerning American soccer and my possible role as a television commentator, and how something in my answers perturbed him. 'You're a spellbinder with words, I'll admit,' he finally said. 'But, to be honest, you frighten me.'

His fears were spellbound, apparently, because a month later a press conference was held by CBS in New York to announce my appointment as 'colour' man for the network's latest venture in sport, the televising of NPSL games. None of the press corps seemed upset by my answers on that occasion, but they did have some doubt about my fate with CBS. 'You'll ruin him,' one lady reporter said to Bill MacPhail, the CBS Vice-President for sports, over a drink at Toots Shor's after the conference. 'Look,' MacPhail said to me across the table, 'if we say a word to you, you have my permission to phone her.'

I wondered if he had forgotten that when I was summoned to his corner office on the 26th floor of the CBS Building just a few weeks later. A couple of his aides were sitting around, and there was a slight air of embarrassment.

'We didn't like part of your commentary on Sunday,' one of them said.

'What was that?' I asked.

'You criticised the St Louis goalkeeper. Couldn't you have been more positive?'

'No,' I replied. 'He made a mistake.'

'That's not what we mean ... you could have said it was a good shot.'

> Someone told me later that the team owners did not
> like my comments and that CBS thought I was knocking
> the product.

Blanchflower's commentary was popular amongst fans and viewers because it was somewhat controversial and offered an insight into the game and what was actually going on. Remember, this was the captain of the Tottenham Hotspur side in the early 1960s, who won the first league and cup double in English soccer in the 20th century, so he probably knows a fair amount about the game. Clearly he wasn't what CBS wanted and they replaced him with Mario Machado, a commentator who would go on to commentate at four FIFA World Cups and had a love for soccer, so at least CBS got that one right!

Despite the broadcasting controversies and everything off the field, the NPSL kicked off with 10 teams split into an Eastern Conference and a Western Conference, with the winners of each respective conference facing off at the end of the season to see who the superior team was (exactly like the USA league would do it, although neither side stole the idea from the other, it was just the logical final to have). With six points for a win, three for a draw and none for a loss, the end of season table threw up some incredible stat lines, but before we go deep into the league season of both the USA and the NPSL, let's see who the ten NPSL sides were heading into 1967:

Atlanta Chiefs
Baltimore Bays
Chicago Spurs
Los Angeles Toros
New York Generals
Oakland Clippers
Philadelphia Spartans
Pittsburgh Phantoms
St Louis Stars
Toronto Falcons

The final table saw the Baltimore Bays finish top of the East with a staggering 162 points and the Oakland Clippers finished top of the West with an even better 185 points from just 32 games (putting the ridiculousness of the points system into perspective, the Phantoms finished bottom of the East with 132 points, while the Toros finished bottom of the West with 114). The Clippers went on to beat the Bays to win the one and only NPSL title, while over in the USA it was a Californian double in soccer as the Los Angeles Wolves defeated Washington Whips 6-5 after extra time at the LA Memorial Coliseum in what could perhaps be the wildest final ever played, with two players scoring hat-tricks, three penalties given (two were scored), four goals scored in four minutes during the second half and both teams scoring in extra time, with an own goal being the decisive winner. Just like their rivals the NPSL, the USA also had its one-and-only season in 1967, but why? Why did both of these leagues, who fought to be the main soccer league in America, just stop after one season? Because instead of butting heads against one another, they joined forces to create what they both wanted in the first place – one major US soccer league called the North American Soccer League, or NASL for short. In 1967 the second soccer boom erupted, but no one knew at this point. To them, they were still building, but this merger would go on to bring so much attention and fame to America, and it all kicked off in 1968 when the very first NASL season was sanctioned and ready to bring soccer back to the American masses.

In 1968 the NASL started with 17 teams split into two conferences of nine in the East and eight in the West, merging eight NPSL teams along with nine teams from the USA league. Pittsburgh and Philadelphia folded following the culmination of the NPSL, with three USA teams folding too (New York, San Francisco and Toronto). With some teams reportedly in $500,000 worth of debt, it came as no surprise that the two merged together to 1) create a bigger, more profitable league and 2) cut back on costs drastically. Club owners didn't really know the market they were trying to create cash from and almost went into this venture blind, and when they realised how much money they'd lost they set about trying to figure out what had gone wrong. Had they overestimated the market following the 1966 World Cup? Perhaps. Did they try to cash in on the excitement and enthusiasm caused by that World Cup? Absolutely, but rather than taking the logical step and informing fans about the sport itself, and accept that, while some may be more informed than others, the large majority of fans needed to be eased into soccer, the owners assumed that, like in baseball or basketball, fans would rush and buy season tickets. They pinned a lot of hope on the season ticket sales, but people didn't really know what they were buying season tickets for yet, which meant that even more money was lost. Another move that the NPSL and USA made was to tap into the 'ethnic' market, because they felt that the immigrants who had come to America loved soccer back home, so they'll definitely love it now, but people from Britain, Serbia, Italy, Germany etc. could tell the difference between good soccer and just putting one or two foreign players into a mediocre team in an attempt to boost attendance figures. With the lifeline of merging together to create the NASL, it provided a second opportunity for these owners to learn from their mistakes and create a bigger and better league that could fulfil the soccer needs of people from overseas who live in America and educate those who are curious as to what soccer is. A bunch of home-grown players mixed in with top overseas talent would have been a good way to integrate new fans, but nevertheless the league didn't heed that advice. Instead, they formed the NASL and a new era had begun.

Backed once again by the CBS television deal, the NASL was screened with all 17 teams in action, with the league keeping the same points format from the NPSL days. In a bid to keep markets fresh and to avoid two teams playing in the same city, a lot of shuffling was needed to get the league to where the owners and commissioners wanted it to be. The Chicago Spurs moved to Kansas City and joined the Western Conference to allow a new Chicago team, the Mustangs from the USA, to join the East. The Los Angeles Toros departed the City of Angels to move to San Diego, allowing the Los Angeles Wolves to take over. The New York Generals were allowed into the league once the New York Skyliners had folded, and the San Francisco Golden Gate Gales moved to Oakland, which then allowed the owners of San Francisco to purchase the controlling interest in a Vancouver franchise. With all the franchises in place, CBS ready to broadcast and the teams ready to play, the first season of the NASL was up and running, and it was a class above anything either the NPSL or USA leagues had produced.

The NASL had an influx of foreign imports that helped the quality drastically, similar to the ASL. Whilst one of the criticisms of the original NPSL and USA was the foreign players taking over from home-grown talents, it's perhaps ironic that the foreign imports were one of the reasons the league had some interest. Maybe it wasn't the fact the players in the NPSL and USA were foreign, perhaps it was because the imports in the NASL were just ... better? Was that the case? The NASL had their first-team All Stars and second-team All Stars, none of which were American. For instance, Janusz Kowalik, a Polish striker who finished top scorer in 1968 with 30 goals for the Chicago Mustangs, was named in the first team All Stars, while Vava, who had won the World Cup with Brazil in 1958 and 1962 and was the first player ever to score in two separate World Cup Finals, was a second-team All Star. Europeans such as Tony Knapp who played in England for the likes of Leicester City and Tranmere Rovers and former Chelsea and Brentford defender Mel Scott got picked for the All Star teams, proving that fans were interested in the talent from overseas and that it worked having them there. Even in the dugouts, foreign talent was brought in. The Vancouver Royals had appointed the legendary Hungarian striker Ferenc Puskás to be their new manager in 1968, but with some level of controversy. Puskás had originally been the manager of the San Francisco Golden Gate Gales, but when the merger took Puskás to Canada, he had to be joint head coach with future England, Ipswich and Newcastle manager Bobby Robson. Obviously, having two head coaches wasn't allowed at the time, so one had to make room for the other, and when Robson was offered the assistant role he resigned and moved back to England to manage his first club, Fulham.

This really was a league built – at least on the playing side of things – on imports. Sure, there was some home-grown talent thrown in, and players who could qualify to play for the US national team, but the fans came for the play makers, the entertainers, they wanted exotic names who had the flair to match. The owners thought the foreign imports with their flicks and tricks would be enough, but they were wrong. The Atlanta Chiefs, coached by Phil Woosnam, who had become the NASL commissioner by the end of the season, won the league after defeating the San Diego Toros 3-0 in the two-leg affair, and a crowd of 14,994 fans witnessed the triumph. It was the highest gate for the entire play-off rounds, despite the imports, despite the CBS contract and despite the owners thinking they knew what the fans wanted, and clubs were in trouble. Big trouble. A total of 1.19 million people went to at least one of the 254 NASL games played during the 1968 season, which on the face of it seems quite a good number. But that number looks less impressive when you see that the average gate was 4,699, down 17.5 per cent from the last NPSL season. It was also reported that the average attendance clubs needed to break even was 20,000, so they were 15,301 off. Every club had lost at least $200,000 during that season, and Woosnam had the seemingly impossible task of convincing club owners to stick with the NASL and the soccer 'experiment'. Five owners were convinced to stay, but ten clubs folded. The first season of the NASL had been a total disaster. While on paper the idea of having top imports play in your league could have worked, when you have to establish the sport to a whole new fanbase it takes more than that. The owners set their sights too high and paid the price (literally) for it. This is where Phil Woosnam comes in and has to effectively change the entire NASL or risk the league being kicked out of the house before it's even had time to take off its shoes. It was an unenviable task, but if anyone could do it, it was Woosnam.

Welshman Phil Woosnam made his career as a striker with Leyton Orient, West Ham United and Aston Villa, whilst also completing a degree in physics, captaining his university team and completing his military service at a young age alongside Manchester United legend Duncan Edwards. In 1966 he emigrated to America to join the Atlanta Chiefs soccer club despite interest from Chelsea. Woosnam decided that, even though he hadn't actually signed any form of contract with the Chiefs, he couldn't back out of his verbal agreement with the franchise and started a new life in America. Whilst he was officially hired as the head coach, he still played as a striker for the team and scored the first goal in their first home match and won NASL Coach of the Year after guiding the Chiefs to the inaugural NASL Championship. Woosnam, who had been considered underrated in the United Kingdom, forged a reputation as a mastermind almost immediately after winning the title, and he also managed to beat Manchester City – his first-ever professional club – in front of a packed stadium, with Manchester City manager Malcom Allison claiming that the Chiefs 'couldn't even play in the England Fourth Division'. Manchester City had just had a tough season, and they eventually claimed the First Division title, but they failed to beat Woosnam's Chiefs. Fatigue and competitiveness may have been a factor in the result, but to the eyes of many Woosnam was *the guy* to bring US soccer back from the dead. As the 1969 season started with just five teams, Woosnam could have jumped ship. His exploits as Chiefs' head coach had given him the chance to contend for the job as manager of two English First Division clubs, but he turned them both down. He stayed because he wanted to change the perception of soccer in the United States and grow the game exponentially, just like Thomas Cahill with the ASL. He said:

> We hadn't failed because of the sport, we failed because the wrong circumstances prevailed. We had to work to change the circumstances. In my heart, I knew the sport was good enough.

Woosnam enlisted the help of former chief soccer writer of the English newspaper the *Daily Express* and general manager of the Baltimore Bays Clive Toye to assist him in running the league, ensuring that the Bays would remain part of the NASL, and with Toye by his side Woosnam set about trying to convince other clubs not to abandon ship. He demanded that clubs reduce their player salaries and cut down on costs across the board in order to keep their operations well under the allotted $200,000.

In order to build up their squads, and in order for Woosnam to get more teams into the league, he adopted the USA's strategy from 1967 and split the league into two halves. In the first half of the season the league would be represented by imported clubs from Europe and South America, while in the second half games would be played by the 'real' teams instead of imported players. This gave the league and Woosnam enough time to bring in new franchises and allow those franchises to sign players to their rosters. Woosnam hoped that the imported players would create a buzz around the NASL and bring fans back in for the second half of the season, when they would have an actual team to root for.

The International Cup, as it was named, didn't quite work out the way Woosnam wanted it to. West Ham, under the guise of Toye's Baltimore Bays, faced off against Wolves, who reprised their team from the USA league, but instead of Los Angeles it was Kansas City, and it only drew just over 5,000 fans. In England, such a match – which featured World Cup winners Geoff Hurst, Martin Peters and Bobby Moore – would have drawn at least 50,000. However, it bought the league and Woosnam some time to balance to books, establish a starting point for the league to build upon and helped it escape death. Kansas City won the International Cup with little to no fanfare because, to be quite frank, nobody cared. CBS had pulled out of their television contract and showed no interest in soccer at that time, so while Woosnam and the NASL lived to fight another day, it only took a year for it all to look like they were on the verge of going back to square one in 1970.

The Baltimore Bays told the NASL halfway through the 1969 season that they had no plans to return in 1970, which put a massive dent in Woosnam's plan. You can't run a league on just four teams. So, Woosnam decided to hatch a plan in order for the NASL to escape the clutches of death for a second straight year. He hid the Baltimore news, not telling anyone that they were leaving, and managed to bring in the Rochester Lancers and Washington Darts from the ASL II, meaning that once Baltimore left, the NASL would have six teams. Woosnam convinced the two new franchises to pay a $10,000-dollar franchise fee for their 'promotion' to the NASL, and the league was extended to 24 games. The schedule included play-offs and a second International Cup, but this edition had a twist to it. The six regular NASL clubs would face-off against touring teams from abroad, with the games counting towards the final NASL standings. Coventry City, Hertha Berlin, Varzim of Portugal and Israeli club Hapoel Petah Tikva would play against the six NASL clubs, with the exception of Hapoel vs the Dallas Tornado because the Dallas owner Lamar Hunt felt that a match against a team from Israel would not be the wisest move for him considering the ties he had with an Arab oil business. Perhaps not the most morally correct policy, but at least any potential catastrophes were avoided as a result. The Washington Darts took home the International Cup with a 2-2-0 record and went on to finish top of the three-team Eastern Conference, so they would play fellow newcomers Rochester in the championship match. The Darts had the best points tally in the league with 137 (still six points for a win at this point in the timeline) yet managed to lose the first leg 3-0 and the second leg 3-1. Washington had the most points, scored the most goals, conceded the fewest goals, had the second-highest goalscorer in the entire league (Leroy DeLeon with 15), had statistically the best goalkeeper in the league (Lincoln Phillips) and kept a record 12 clean sheets in the process, yet lost in the final against a team that barely scraped a 0.5 per cent win rate.

The league was hanging on for dear life as Woosnam and Toye kept thinking of ways to reinvent the wheel and bring stability to the NASL. The 1970 season was a good starting point. They may have only had a few teams in the league and attendances during the season had grown by eight per cent in comparison to the 1969 season (in fairness, the 1970 season had 61 more games than the 1969 season so it wouldn't be entirely fair to judge the two, but the 1970 season didn't have the World Cup winners that played in the shortened 1969 season, but either way an eight per cent boost is a good thing). Brazilian-born American international player Carlos Metidieri finished joint top of the goals and assists charts, the very first native-born Rookie of the Year was crowned with Jim Leeker of the St Louis Stars picking up the award, and Pat McBride, another American, was featured in the NASL All Stars second team. (Instead of just having a top scorers list and assist leaders list, the NASL combined the two; for example, Leroy DeLeon of the Darts was the second-highest scorer in the league but finished fourth in the goals and assist charts because he only made one assist. Each goal counted as double, which is why he finished fourth, and Metidieri, who scored one fewer but had six more assists, finished joint top with 35 points.) Speaking of which, the NASL All Star side ended the semi-successful season for the league when they squared off against Pelé and Santos at Chicago's Soldier Field in front of 13,222 fans, losing to the Brazilians 4-3.

Regardless of the increase in attendance and a rise in home-grown players getting game time (although the St Louis Stars had 19 Americans in their squad, and there were only two others outside of this team), the biggest moment of the season didn't even happen on the pitch. It didn't even happen between any of the players. In fact, one of the people involved was jazz producer Nesuhi Ertegun, who made albums with Ray Charles, Bobby Darin, Louis Armstrong and John Coltrane, and he was incredibly influential in taking the NASL to the next level. He was a music producer and executive vice president of Atlantic Records – a subsidiary of Warner Communications – and he was a massive soccer fan. Ertegun had met Woosnam at a cocktail party hosted by the Ertegun family for the 1970 World

Cup. Toye had contacted the legendary British broadcaster David Frost about owning a soccer team in the New York area, as both he and Woosnam felt the league needed to expand here in order to grow. Even though Frost loved the sport, he declined the offer, but instead directed Toye and Woosnam to Ertegun. Woosnam went down to Mexico to watch the semi-finals and World Cup Final between Brazil and Italy, and after watching the final he heard that his former boss at West Ham United Ron Greenwood was in the area, so decided to try to find him. Once he had located Greenwood's hotel in Mexico, Woosnam was pointed in the direction of the Ertegun cocktail party, only he didn't know it was Ertegun who was hosting. Woosnam knocked on the door and politely said, 'Hello. I'm looking for Ron Greenwood, my name is Phil Woosnam.' A fairly short man opened the door. It was Ertegun. The pair got chatting and Woosnam soon realised that Ertegun was somewhat interested in running a soccer club in New York. It was a chance meeting that seemed destined to happen. The stars aligned at the perfect moment to change American soccer history. God bless David Frost and Ron Greenwood.

The world probably didn't realise how important this meeting would be in changing soccer both on and off the pitch. Ertegun spoke with the powers that be at Warner and convinced them that because soccer was the biggest sport in the world it had potential to be the biggest sport in America (and very lucrative financially). Woosnam expected Warner to be sceptical of soccer, but the company was fully on board with the idea of having a New York soccer team. It was imperative to have a franchise in New York considering the melting pot of cultures that reside in the five boroughs alone, let alone the entire state. At the time, three million children across the United States were playing soccer, and the number would only grow if the NASL started to introduce new teams in larger markets such as Los Angeles, New York, Dallas – areas where the sport could really take off and become ingrained in a community. The players of some franchises already spent time in communities trying to spread the word, now imagine that in a market like LA or New York? This is the thinking that the league and Ertegun had about a New York franchise, which is what sold the rest of Warner on the idea. Steve Ross, CEO of Warner, was convinced that soccer was destined to grow and brought together a bunch of other like-minded and wealthy individuals to pledge $35,000 each in order to meet the NASL asking price of $350,000 (paying $25,000 for the annual fee), including the Ertegun brothers, the chairman of Warner Jay Emmett and chairman of Warner Brothers Studios Ted Ashley, who had just made a killing from of a documentary called *Woodstock*. The trouble was, the men realised that it may not have been the smartest thing to invest in, perhaps due to the intense finances involved. So, instead, they transferred the ownership of Gotham Sports Club (the name used for the ten-man buy-out) to Warner Communications, meaning Warner Communications owned the rights to the new franchise. Then another issue dawned on the owners. They didn't have a name for this franchise. They knew it would be called the New York *somethings* but they didn't know what the *somethings* was going to be. The Giants, the Knicks and the Yankees had already been taken, as had the Rangers. What about the New York Metropolitans? That was a good choice, but it was such a good choice that back in the early 60s the New York Mets baseball team took that one too, so that was off the table. By this time, Ertegun and Woosnam had agreed that bringing Clive Toye on board as the first general manager was a smart move, and Toye started to think of names for the team. What suited a New York sports team without being too corny and still being original? Ertegun tried to help with suggestions such as the New York Lovers and the New York Blues, but it didn't fit (thankfully); then Toye had a lightning-bolt moment:

> So I thought, what's bigger than 'Metropolitan' and came up with Cosmopolitan ... that fits New York. But we can't call them the Cosmopolitans or the Cosmopolites. Suddenly, it clicked. The Cosmos.

And just like that, the New York Cosmos were born. On 10 December 1970 the NASL officially welcomed the latest franchise into the league. But the team needed players. Woosnam couldn't do it because it wasn't his job, that responsibility laid on the shoulders of Toye, who employed a fellow Englishman by the name of Gordon Bradley to do it, who'd moved to the United States to play as a defender for the Toronto Stars alongside greats of the game such as Stanley Matthews, Johnny Hayes and a certain Danny Blanchflower. Bradley earned himself a move to the New York Generals as a defender after a knee injury prevented him from continuing as a striker, and during his time with the Generals he had the pleasure of man-marking Pelé during his time at Santos. Bradley stuck to Pelé like a stamp to an envelope, prompting Pelé to ask Bradley at half time, 'If I go to the bathroom, will you come to?' After being appointed player-manager of the Cosmos following the Generals folding in 1968, Bradley began to assemble his squad, including fellow Englishman Barry Mahy and Jan Steadman from Trinidad, both of whom had been his team-mates at the Generals. Without the prospect of huge wages and based solely on the enthusiasm of the franchise, Bradley was able to form his squad in time for the start of the 1971 NASL season, even if it was filled with castaways from other teams.

The 1971 season started with much enthusiasm, despite Kansas City folding prior to the opening game. Woosnam brought in two more franchises on top of the Cosmos from north of the border, with the Toronto Metros and Les Olympique de Montreal – or Montreal Olympic, as they would be called – both joining to really make it a 'North America' league. The league once again kept with the 24-game structure, and added four touring sides to make up the International Cup, with Hearts from Scotland making an appearance along with Lanerossi from Italy, Apollon from Greece and Bangu from Brazil. Dallas and Rochester put in good showings against the tourists, both going 2-0-2 with them, but Atlanta were crowned International Cup champions with their 2-1-1 record. Atlanta went on to win the Southern Division of the NASL, with the

Dallas Tornado finishing second, while Rochester Lancers and the Cosmos would finish first and second in the Northern Division. This set up a rather exciting-looking post-season, with a best-of-three series being implemented in every tie, as well as sudden death (golden goal, basically). Dallas defeated Rochester in the first semi-final, despite losing the first game 2-1 after 176 brutal minutes, topped off when league MVP and top scorer Carlos Metidieri scored the winner. Dallas would take the next game 3-1, while the all-important winner-takes-all game in Rochester was another brutal marathon, going 148 minutes. Dallas sneaked through with a 2-1 win (148 minutes isn't that bad, it's 28 minutes less than the first game – bunch of amateurs). Atlanta swept away the Cosmos in their best-of-three, but, while Atlanta were the superior side and deserved to go through (without conceding a goal too), the fact that the Cosmos got to the play-offs in their inaugural season was a cause for celebration. They also had the Rookie of the Year in Randy Horton – who also came second in the scoring charts – and managed to draw nearly 20,000 for their clash against the Rochester Lancers. It was impressive and certainly something to build upon, even if they didn't win the series in the end.

Dallas faced-off against Atlanta in the final, with the Chiefs taking the first game 2-1 after a goal in the 123rd minute from supersub Nick Ash, but if anything had been learnt from this post-season, it was that Dallas loved the long games. Their two-hour game with the Chiefs spurred them on even more, and they took the next two games 4-1 and 2-0, meaning the team that had finished ahead of Dallas by one point missed out on championship glory. The 1971 season had been successful for the NASL, with an exciting post-season the pinnacle of it all. Attendances had risen by 31 per cent from the previous year and the average gate jumped from 3,163 to 4,154. With the help of the Cosmos, who were widely thought to be building something big at the time, the league started to spread its wings a little bit more. And the new post-season changes of the best-of-three and sudden death must have worked to make things a bit more exciting for casual fans, judging by the attendance figures. But there was still work to be done and Woosnam knew it. He wasn't the type of person who could sit back and enjoy past success because he had a vision for the future. This was step one on the road to recovery, and he knew that in order for the league to grow he needed to keep taking it step by step. Into the 1972 season, things continued to change in a positive way. For the first time in the league's history, no franchise folded prior to the opening game. The league was still only made up of eight clubs (Washington did move to Miami, but the team remained the same) and the season was cut down to just 14 games, but that was to stabilise potential issues with travel costs. The NASL was looking upward and the 1971 season was the starting point. They just had to hope that the buzz carried over into the following season.

There weren't that many new additions in terms of playing staff into the league for the 1972 season, with teams opting to build on the previous campaign instead of massive overhauls. The Cosmos added a couple of new players into their line-up, including Washington midfielder John Kerr, who was described as being dominant at the time, as well as Josef Jelinek of Czechoslovakia, who actually played in the 1962 World Cup Final, and one more player by the name of Werner Roth (fun fact about Roth, in 1981 he would go on to play Baumann, the German captain, in the film *Escape to Victory*). The Cosmos were strong, Atlanta had kept most of their core from the season before and wanted to build through consistency, while St Louis were making a great impact with Pat McBride, Willy Roy, two British players called Wilf Tranter and John Sewell, and rookie goalkeeper Mike Winter creating a superb line-up that had a blend of youthful exuberance and experienced knowledge of how to get over the line and get the job done. In fact, the Stars would go unbeaten in their first five matches, losing just four of their 14 games in the league that season. Before moving on to the play-offs and analysing everything else from the 1972 season, there is one piece of innovation that the league tried to implement – an offside line 35 yards from goal. Across the world, the offside rule applies to the entire half, but the NASL thought it might be interesting to see the attacking possibilities if you place a line 35 yards from goal, meaning no player can be offside until they have crossed that line. So, if you're 40 yards out and the defence tries to play the offside trap and catches you, you're safe, but if they tried that same move five yards further back, it's offside. It had the blessing from FIFA, who probably saw it as a testing ground for new rules, like we would see in modern times with a sin bin, or VAR (Video Assistant Referees) being used to see how it works and iron out the kinks before unleashing it on to a wider audience. It was openly ridiculed by the world because it seemed so outlandish – not many realised that back in 1923, the English FA proposed the same sort of idea but with a 40-yard line instead, requesting that the new rule be implemented to 'reduce the number of stoppages and permit of the game being carried on more consecutively and with more satisfaction to the spectators'. Not so innovative from the NASL, but also not so stupid to suggest such an idea. But the question at this point remains, did the offside line improve goalscoring games? Initially, no. Due to the fact that it took a while for players to grasp the idea having played with the regular offside law their entire lives, the first couple of games were low scoring affairs, but once players got the hang of it play improved. Defenders learnt to drop deeper to avoid the risk of being caught with a high line, which meant that creative attacking midfielders and strikers had so much more room to operate. Goals were scored, players expressed themselves and it made the 1972 season a bit more enjoyable, even if others across the world didn't take to the idea.

The New York Cosmos, in only their second season in the league, would finish top of the Northern Division with 77 points. (Remember, six points for a win, three for a draw and up to three bonus points for the first three goals. Extra bonus points for more goals added a bit more substance for the whole offside line business.) They scored 28 goals in 14 games, and the league's top scorer and assist creator Randy Horton, who finished top of the charts with nine goals and four assists, was in the team. As for the Southern Division, that would fall the way of the St Louis Stars, who built on their core of McBride, Roy and Winter and beat the Dallas Tornado by nine points, scoring just 20 goals but having the tightest defence in the league, letting in just 14. Attendances were up with the Toronto Metros, who finished bottom of the Northern Division, averaging 7,173, and the Stars averaged slightly more at 7,773. The shortage of games in comparison to 1971 meant that the overall record was down, but the percentages were up by 15.1 per cent in terms of league average, which was another step in the right direction. Ever so slightly, the league was creeping up there with fans, and the more traction and attention the league got, the more people wanted to watch. If they had a television contract, would they have drawn more fans? Would fans go to games or watch them from home? Maybe not having the deal was a blessing in disguise at this moment in time with regards to bringing in hardcore fans who wanted to come out of interest, but having a New York team and Dallas team in the play-offs going up against each other was always going to bring fans in regardless.

A crowd of around 5,000 saw the Cosmos despatch of the Tornado 1-0, thanks to a strike from Kerr, who proved to be a valuable signing, but the fun didn't stop there for the Cosmos, as they awaited the winner of St Louis vs Rochester, which promised to be a great game. Despite scoring the same number of goals as the Stars during the course of the season, the Lancers of Rochester were no match for St Louis, who beat them 2-0, setting up the tie that the fans wanted. The best of the north vs the best of the south – New York Cosmos vs St Louis Stars, when 6,102 fans packed into the Hofstra Stadium on Long Island, New York, to see the Cosmos win in the dying minutes courtesy of a penalty from Jelinek to bring the championship to New York in just their second year of existence. The league will never admit that they wanted New York to win, but deep down one would imagine that they wouldn't have been displeased if their biggest market happened to win it. New York loves winners, and now the Cosmos were one of the winners to add to the city's distinguished list. The league was full of All Stars, with their teams being announced at the end of the season. Headlining the All Stars that season was a young Scot playing for Montreal named Graeme Souness, who went on to have a great career at a club wearing red on Merseyside. The team also included another player later associated with Merseyside, John Best, who started his career with Liverpool but made seven appearances with Wirral-based club Tranmere Rovers (the same club as George Moorhouse from the 1930 World Cup squad – someone should honour Tranmere for that), as well as the usual suspects like Sewell, Kerr, McBride and Cosmos star Horton. The only thing that the league would perhaps be criticised for at this point in time was the lack of Americans coming through. They tried to introduce a college draft system but it didn't stick to soccer the way it does with basketball, baseball and American football, because the talent is worldwide so there really isn't a need for a draft to fill out your first team, you can just sign the youngsters to youth contracts instead. The league did need more home-grown talent, not in the 'let's get rid of foreigners' kind of way, more of a 'let's give our kids something to aim towards and something to work for instead of losing them to another sport.'

1973 was set to be the year that Americans finally made an impact on the NASL, it's just that not many people had realised this yet. There was a lot of young American talent around, someone just had to 1) find it, 2) find the diamonds in the rough, 3) sign the diamonds, 4) play them and 5) win. In fact, the following season, with more Americans on the field, more fans sat in the stands to watch. Thankfully, for those young college kids who played soccer, they had a league that now believed in them. No one would have believed it years before, but the NASL was about to have its very first American top goalscorer, three Americans in the top 10 of the scoring charts, an American as the best goalkeeper, an American Coach of the Year, an American Rookie of the Year, four Americans on an All Star team and six Americans playing for the winning championship team. Safe to say, 1973 in the NASL was the year of the Americans, and it all started in Philadelphia.

Philadelphia proved to be a safe haven for young, up-and-coming Americans looking to get a head start in soccer and the NASL, but ironically enough the city may not have even had a team if it wasn't for the Super Bowl. A man by the name of Tom McCloskey was looking for tickets for the Super Bowl, and when Lemar Hunt heard of his dilemma he devised a plan and made an agreement with McCloskey. Hunt offered McCloskey the nine tickets he was after under one condition, he would buy an NASL team for Philly. McCloskey needed the tickets and had money to burn following his stellar business with his construction company. If it wasn't for those tickets to the Super Bowl, Philadelphia wouldn't have had the Atoms in their sporting city, and the NASL wouldn't have been able to bring in a franchise that not only added to a big, traditional soccer market, but it added another franchise to use as a prototype for the future. The Atoms had to form a full squad by 1 May and McCloskey appointed the vice president of his firm as the general manager of the franchise. Bob Ehlinger had zero soccer experience and was only familiar with college football, but he decided that it was probably a good idea to hire a manager. Surprisingly, it was. In fact, they not only hired a manager who was sceptical of the NASL and was unsure about the longevity of the league itself, but they hired an American, but to many fans this actually outweighed any doubts or negatives. Al Miller was brought in from Hartwick College in New York and was immediately sent out to sign English players from the English leagues, while also being under instruction to acquire as many talented Americans as he could. The Atoms went to England to train with Southport of the English Third Division, taking a few players back with them to bolster their numbers. Mixed with a great balance of English and American players, the Atoms brought an excitement to Philly that hadn't been seen in soccer for years, and that's not hyperbole either, the attendance figures back this up as well. Some 21,700 fans flooded in to see them during the home opener, and they went on to average 11,501, a fantastic number for a debut season, but while they were making waves both on and off the field, the Atoms weren't the only ones to feel a buzz and excitement around soccer. Miami, now owned by Joe Robbie, who also owned the NFL's Miami Dolphins, drew 12,766 for their opener and averaged 5,477 for the season, and Dallas drew 19,342 for their opener and their average attendance rose by 86 per cent. Fans were coming, and maybe that was in part thanks to the media coverage that some teams were given by the local press. The newspaper reports increased, and, while one match report or article isn't the be all and end all for teams in modern soccer, for the NASL back in the 70s, who were trying to establish a name for themselves, it was absolutely massive. The *New York Times*, who have been involved in writing about soccer since the golden age of the ASL, wrote this report from the 1973 NASL match between the New York Cosmos and the Philadelphia Atoms:

COSMOS AND ATOMS IN DEADLOCK

The New York Cosmos ran into a well-conditioned team in the Philadelphia Atoms at Veterans Stadium tonight and barely managed to gain a 1-1 tie before 9,168 fans.

The Atoms, an expansion team, did not look like one. With strong, fast and durable players, they dominated the Cosmos in the first half. They lacked one thing, however, and that was accuracy in their shooting at goal.

Al Miller, coach of the Atoms, has put together a machine that works flawlessly for 90 minutes. His fullbacks helped the halfbacks, and vice versa. Often the forwards displayed the ability to return to their defence and start a play by themselves.

It took the Cosmos a while to adjust to their play. Even when the New Yorkers, the defending North American Soccer League champions, settled down, the Atoms still showed their superiority in all phases of play in the first half. Despite their dominance, the Atoms were unable to score and the half ended without a goal.

In the second half, the Cosmos sent in Everald Cummings for Josef Jelinek and the Atoms used Stan Startzell for Lew Meehl. The change appeared to stimulate the Cosmos. The Atoms, however, scored first after 72 minutes of play.

In a play that Cosmos claimed afterwards was offside, Jim Fryatt got the ball from an opponent, and from outside the area lobbed it into the nets, over the outstretched hands of Jerry Sularz, the Cosmos goalkeeper.

Strangely enough, the Atoms did not keep on the pressure and the Cosmos took advantage of the lapse. Tibby Vigh, who had come on for Joe Fink earlier, gained a corner kick on the left side.

Jorge Siega took it with precision and the ball reached Len Renery, who blasted a shot past Bob Rigby, who had no chance to react. The goal was scored in the 77th minute.

This is what the NASL wanted – actual coverage of their games without the notion of the novelty that soccer may have possessed in America at the time, an accurate and well-written piece on the game itself. By all means it wasn't a feature in *Sports Illustrated*, but that was the end goal for written media. If they can have their own cultural icon like Mr NBA Logo himself Jerry West or Joe Di Maggio, the league would be thrilled, but this was still a good start. And the 1973 season did not disappoint either, with both the Cosmos and the Atoms impressing and playing some exciting soccer.

The crowds who attended these games certainly weren't disappointed, with the three leagues of three teams providing some excitement as the Philly Atoms captured the Eastern Division, the Toronto Metros won the Northern Division and the Dallas Tornado won the Southern Division with 111 points, ahead of closest challengers the St Louis Stars. The lowest average attendance for any team during the season was 3,317 with the Atlanta Apollos, who only managed to win three games all season, but many have since suggested that due to the likes of Philadelphia giving young Americans a chance, more casual fans were interested in watching and became more invested in the league. Dallas had the top scorer in the league, a rookie striker called Kyle Rote Jr, who would be the only American to ever win the NASL Golden Boot award when he got 10 goals and 10 assists, totalling 30 points, pipping Warren Archibald by one point. Gene Geimer of St Louis and Joey Fink, a draft pick for the Cosmos, all listed high on the scoring charts and were all products of American youth soccer, while the Cosmos had two American goalkeepers, with Shep Messing being the starting goalie and the reserve being a young man named Bruce Arena, who didn't play much for the Cosmos due to the performance of Messing, but he still made a lasting impression on the US game. A total of 42 Americans were listed on the rosters of the NASL clubs, with 30 of those being born in the US (Philly and St Louis had 23 US citizens between them, accounting for more than half of the total in the NASL). The growth in popularity of the NASL was not only down to the Americans getting their chance and becoming strong players in the league, but also the talent brought in from overseas to add to the quality. The Atoms built a team comprised mainly of eager Americans and experienced English veterans, and they had a run of 13 consecutive games without defeat, conceding just 14 goals in 19 games (0.62 goals per game), and had what was dubbed the 'No Goal Patrol', featuring Bobby Smith, Derek Travis, Chris Dunleavy and future Liverpool manager Roy Evans. Andy Provan, another Englishman brought in from Southport, provided the bulk of the attack as they romped to the Eastern Division title and smashed through Toronto in the play-off semi-finals 3-0 in front of a massive 18,766 fans at the Veterans Stadium.

Philly were looking like the team to beat in this championship race, but Dallas had other ideas as they dispatched of the Cosmos 1-0 with a Kyle Rote Jr goal, which was just enough to defeat the Cosmos, who had entered the play-offs as the 'wildcard' team from the regular season. Dallas had the better record throughout the season compared with their opponent Philadelphia, so they were allowed to pick the date of the game and had home field advantage. The date proved to be key for the fixture, as Dallas general manager Joe Echelle picked 25 August to play the game, which was the exact date when Southport, the team the Atoms borrowed their players from, were due back to start the English league season, meaning the Atoms would be without their two top scorers in Andy Provan and Jim Fryatt. Luckily a member of their defence, Dunleavy, was suspended for the fixture in England, so he was allowed to stay on to play the final. But it didn't all work to Dallas's advantage as they lost Ritchie Reynolds, Nick Jennings and John Collins, who were all on loan from Portsmouth.

With the Atoms's 'No Goal Patrol' still intact, they were more prepared than Dallas, who had their general manager to thank or blame for either a sheer lack of foresight or sheer amount of stupidity for picking that date to play the final. They had the best record in the league, and they were strong enough without the shenanigans anyway! Nevertheless, Atoms coach Al Miller gave the team a shake up to compensate for the departures of Provan and Fryatt, putting six Americans into the starting line-up. Some 18,824 fans showed up to watch the Atoms look more composed, more tactically astute and just straight-up the better team in the final, with Dunleavy man-marking Dallas striker Rote out of the game completely (or as it's known in the game today, Dunleavy had Rote in his back pocket). Philly knew they could beat Dallas. They let them have the ball in their own half and in the middle of the pitch because Miller knew that if they remained resolute and defensively strong, like they had done all season, Dallas didn't stand a chance. Hardly any shots were going towards Bob Rigby in the Atoms goal, with Rote not being able to have a sniff at a chance and Dallas not having any other primary goal threat, seeing as their two other strikers had to go back to England. Philadelphia took the lead around the 75-minute mark, when Dallas centre-back John Best tried to clear the ball away from danger but instead managed to somehow turn it into the back of the net. For all the pressing that Dallas wanted to do, it was ironic that the goal they conceded was from their own player. In the dying embers of the game, the Atoms sealed victory when Bill Straub, a defender who was placed up front and one of the Americans Miller had put into the starting 11, found himself with the chance to head the ball home, which he took without any further invitation to seal the win for the Atoms and seal the NASL championship for the expansion team. It was a big moment for the Atoms as Al Miller won Coach of the Year and goalkeeper Rigby was placed on the front cover of *Sports Illustrated*, marking the first time that the NASL *really* grabbed the headlines. The NASL was grabbing the attention of some fans across the country and, while Philadelphia were the champions, the west of America wanted a taste of the action. While the 1973 season set the standard for how franchises should approach soccer, 1974 would be the year of the second soccer boom in the 20th century as it went completely nationwide.

The momentum from the previous campaign allowed the NASL and Woosnam to expand the league and allow teams from elsewhere to join in with the fun. Woosnam wanted the west coast, but to get the west he needed to have four franchises. By August 1973 he had three in the form of the Seattle Sounders, the Vancouver Whitecaps and the Los Angeles Aztecs. All he needed was one more team and, ideally, he wanted it in San Francisco. The deadline to find that fourth team was edging ever closer, and when he found a buyer in future Portsmouth owner Milan Mandaric, Mandaric demanded that the team be in San Jose, which Woosnam accepted. Additionally, the NASL added teams from Denver, Boston, Washington and Baltimore and had a truly nationwide league for the first time since the days of the NPSL and USA. Split into four divisions (Northern, Eastern, Central and Western), the league moved on to the new season optimistic that soccer would continue to get more good press. There was an interesting new introduction that season – eliminating draws – which was designed for the American audience, to feed into the familiarity of the average American sports fan. The league assumed that American's couldn't fully appreciate a drawn match and decided to replace the draw with a penalty shootout, calling them a 'tie-win' in the standings, and teams were given three points for winning. There's no reasonable data to suggest that the penalty shootouts benefitted the league or attendances in any way, so there is no real way to determine whether or not it was a success, but some teams managed to find a way to master the shootouts, with the San Jose Earthquakes picking up eight 'tie-wins' and the Miami Toros gaining six. But what did manage to win the league some attention were two public appearances by some of its star names, but in two completely different arenas. Kyle Rote, the Dallas Tornado striker, was invited on to the ABC show *Superstars* (British readers may be familiar with this programme, as it's the American version of the show in which Kevin Keegan fell off a bike), where he would compete against other athletes to prove who was the best. It was a massive ratings success and Rote won the competition three times in four years, between 1974 and 1977; the only year he didn't win was 1975, which was won by OJ Simpson. Rote wasn't the only player to feature on the show, with Bob Rigby competing in the 1976 edition, finishing fourth. The NASL was getting some great attention, with players appearing on hugely popular television shows, but the more controversial of the appearances came from Shep Messing, the Comos goalkeeper, in a magazine called *Viva*. A soccer player appearing in a magazine? That seems normal and the standard thing, but *Viva* was an 'adult women's' magazine that paid him a few thousand dollars to pose nude. Messing was more than happy to take the money, claiming in his autobiography, 'I did more for the game by dropping my pants than the league did in five years of press releases.' *SBNATION* did a piece on Messing a while ago detailing his career, and this excerpt from the article explains how he was let go from the Cosmos shortly afterwards and how he kept his job as a teacher:

> He was joking – although probably not incorrect – but the Cosmos ownership concluded that they had enough of their eccentric, erratic backup goalkeeper. He played less than 10 games in 1973 and 1974 combined, and they played him on waivers, citing the morals clause in his contract. Incredibly, Messing kept his teaching gig after *Viva* hit the newsstand. He explained the story via email:

'When the girls from ninth grade to seniors went racing off to buy the magazine and piled into the girls' room to "read" it, I was summoned to the Superintendent's office. As I was being fired, both the principal and the wrestling coach came to my defence. The principal claimed that I was vital to the safety of the school because of my positive impact on tense race relations. The wrestling coach – I was his assistant coach – felt that our team would not recover if I were to be fired. I'm not sure which one had more influence, but I was warned instead of fired.' His mother did have him attend one of her sex ed classes at Nassau Community College. It is one of the few times Messing admits ever to being embarrassed, but 'What could I do? Say no to my mother?'

Nevertheless, the NASL was slowly becoming part of the American sports fans' consciousness. Whether they had seen someone from the league on *Superstars* or on the front cover of a different kind of magazine to one that sports stars are usually on, they were being seen and, rightly or wrongly, the league was getting the attention that it had craved. Mainstream media was paying attention and more fans were showing up to games, as the attendance figures showed once again. There was a vast increase of growth to 30.5 per cent from 1973, with over one million fans watching the 150 games played that season. Philly, San Jose, Seattle and Vancouver all averaged over 10,000 fans over the course of the season (San Jose had the most out of this group with 16,584, while Vancouver had the lowest with 10,979). The league was growing and the move out to the west was proving to be a genius move from Woosnam. But did the growth in attention correlate with what was on the field at the time? More games and more teams meant that the squads had to be deeper and the quality of the players had to be improved as a result. Anyone can put together a run of seven/eight or so impressive performances, and in the previous format that would have been enough to reach the play-offs, but with 20 games being played it meant there wasn't really time to slack off. In the 1974 season, the most wins a team had was 11, and they finished top of their group, so consistency had to be improved and for a large part of the league, it did. The Boston Minutemen, Miami Toros, Dallas Tornado and LA Aztecs (who were co-owned by Elton John for a period of time, although it must be stressed that he wasn't involved in anything to do with the franchise) all finished top of their divisions, with Baltimore and San Jose earning wildcard spots. Thanks to the scoring and penalty shootout expertise of Warren Archibald and Steve David, Miami ended the season with the joint-highest win percentage of any team in the NASL (with the Aztecs) and went 6-0 in shootouts, but perhaps the two biggest shocks came in Philadelphia and New York, where the Atoms failed to defend their title despite opening the season with a four-game winning streak and the Cosmos only managed to scrape together four wins all season and had to rely on a shootout win to avoid being the worst team in the NASL that season (the honour of that went to the Denver Dynamos, who won one game more than the Cosmos, but didn't win a single shootout). If anything, this goes to show how NASL franchises were influenced by the Atoms – so much so that the Atoms themselves couldn't match up with these new franchises. The top four players in the scoring charts, the best three goalkeepers, the MVP and Rookie of the Year all came from expansion teams as well as multiple All Stars. These new expansion franchises had learnt the lessons taught by the Atoms and used them to get the edge.

Moving on into the play-offs and the expansion teams were at it again, but some didn't fare as well as others. San Jose and Baltimore, the two wildcards, were knocked out in the first round against Dallas and fellow newcomer Boston respectively, which set up two ties of Miami vs Dallas and Los Angeles vs Boston (west vs east, expansion vs expansion). Miami dealt with Dallas easily enough by eliminating them 3-1 at home, while LA shut out the Minutemen 2-0 at home, leaving the NASL with a nice blend of Miami vs LA, two strong markets and the two best teams from the season, although one of the major positives for the championship final proved to be a bit of a controversial factor in it. As is the case with every NASL championship final, the team with the best record gets to pick the date and venue, but CBS, who bought the rights to broadcast the final and had an obligation to show the game live, had a hand in where the match would actually be played. CBS decided to play the game in Miami for mainly two reasons: 1) sports events were only primarily shown live when there was either a guarantee or strong possibility that it would be sold out so the television broadcast would look and sound incredible to so many fans (the Aztecs played their games at the Los Angeles Memorial Coliseum, which had a capacity of 94,500, and CBS felt that there was little to no chance whatsoever that the game would sell out) and 2) they wanted to capitalise on the prime east coast time slot. If the match was being played in Los Angeles, the kick-off time during Pacific Time would have to be 12:30pm, whereas if it was played on the east coast it would be played at 3:30pm so would be able to get as many audience members as possible from both sides. It also helped that CBS moved Miami's semi-final to a smaller venue called Tamiami Park in the event that if the Toros won their semi-final – which they did – the CBS crew would have an entire week to take equipment down from Tamiami Park and set it up for the final at the Orange Bowl Stadium. Would the home field advantage actually help Miami, or would LA put in a performance for the cameras and viewers at home? It may have only gotten a rating of 3.8 for CBS, and 15,507 fans were in attendance, but they were treated to a superb game. Miami took the lead after 17 minutes when Ralph Wright scored one of his five goals for his team, but LA were soon back level nine minutes later from the penalty spot. Ronnie Sharp missed from the penalty spot just after half-time in an incredible display of foreshadowing, while Ramon Moraldo made it 2-1 soon after. Miami looked like they were going to clinch the title in front of their own fans, but minutes after Moraldo scored LA hit back to make it 2-2. The Toros managed to grab one late goal in the 87th minute that looked, for all the money in the world, to be the decisive goal, but the Aztecs wouldn't go down without a fight as Doug

McMillan, that season's Rookie of the Year, levelled things up. The final went to penalties. The odds were stacked against LA as they were in the backyard of a team who won 6-0 in shootouts during the regular season. In a cruel twist of fate, the Toros missed one of their penalties – just like they did during the regular time – and Los Angeles went on to claim their first NASL championship in dramatic and incredible fashion.

Each year and each season there seemed to be a new landmark and achievement for the NASL, whether it was back-up goalkeepers on front covers of womens' magazines, CBS showcasing their championship final, *Sports Illustrated* and the *New York Times* caring enough to detail certain aspects of the league or hordes of eager fans waiting at the gates, anticipating what this sport might look like in real time. They had read about it, heard about it and they wanted to see it for themselves, as the numbers showed. Each year, the league grew. Each year the league learnt from its mistakes and each year the league got better. If 1973 was the first season considerable change was noticed, 1974 was the first season the league went nationwide and a sense of 'soccer fever' (not a real phrase, just something made up to try to bottle what was happening at the time) was taking over to some degree. Soccer was on the verge of going mainstream in America, which was no easy feat during the 1970s. Lew Alcindor (better known as the legendary Kareem Abdul-Jabbar) was just beginning his career in the NBA and was winning MVP awards, but still probably wouldn't be considered mainstream, while Nolan Ryan was making a name for himself in MLB but wasn't a worldwide star. The NASL and soccer just had one advantage over those sports. The NBA and MLB had to rely on the American college system as the Euroleagues and Japanese/Dominican markets hadn't been tapped into yet in either sport, whereas soccer was played all over the world. You're an American team who wants to sign a player from Peru? No problem, it can be done. Soccer had worldwide stars from almost every continent and the NASL had the chance to make their league a worldwide name. All they needed was that one player to take the leap of faith and join the NASL. If they could get that one big worldwide star the game would be changed completely, and the league knew it. Phil Woosnam knew it, Clive Toye knew it and, most importantly, the New York Cosmos knew it.

Edson Arantes do Nascimento, also known by millions across the globe as Pelé, became a New York Cosmos player on 10 June 1975 when he was unveiled to the world's media in the 21 Club bar on West 52nd Street in New York City (unlike many other famous soccer landmarks in New York, 21 Club is still alive and kicking and thankfully isn't a Duane Reades). Hordes of journalists, soccer writers and mainstream media outlets gathered around the table that Pelé occupied in order to get a glimpse of the most famous athlete on planet earth. 'COSMOS SIGN UP PELÉ FOR $4 MILLION' read the entire back page of the *Daily News*, and the Cosmos were *the* big news in New York City. Not the Yankees, not the Jets, not the Giants, not the Mets, not the Knicks, but the Cosmos. Soccer was mainstream news thanks to Pelé, but the arrival of Pelé in the Big Apple wasn't a spur of the moment, compulsive buy from the Cosmos, they had been planning and plotting this move since 1971. They wanted Pelé back then, they pushed to bring Pelé in every chance they could get and 1975 was the culmination of the work put in. The Cosmos, mainly Clive Toye, understood quite early on that to be a successful sporting franchise in New York you needed two things. First, you needed to win, and, second, you needed a superstar. Every other New York team had both. The Knicks won their only two NBA Championships during the 70s and had two stars in Walt 'Clyde' Frazier and Willis Reed, the Jets went into the decade fresh off a Super Bowl win in 1968 and had Joe Namath as their quarterback, the Mets – like the Jets – won the World Series in 1969 and were aided by the incredible pitching duo of Tom Seaver and Nolan Ryan, the Yankees won the World Series in 1977 with Thurman Munson, Reggie Jackson and Ron Guidry in their line-ups. Sport in New York was thriving, while the Cosmos had … nothing. They had no stars and one NASL championship, but the lack of mainstream stars hurt their appeal, regardless of how much they won. Toye chased Pelé around the world to try to sign him. Rome, Jamaica, Brazil, Belgium, wherever Pelé went Toye was their trying to get his signature. Pelé had offers from Juventus and Real Madrid at the time, but as Clive Toye says in the wonderfully made ESPN film *Once In A Lifetime,* 'Pelé could have won championships with Juventus and Real Madrid, but he could win an entire country with the Cosmos.'

Pelé was sold on the Cosmos and signed on the dotted line. There aren't many transfers in football that can shock enough to direct the attention of the entire world to a league that no one knew existed, and, ironically, the only transfer that comes close to Pelé and the Cosmos was David Beckham joining the LA Galaxy. The Cosmos knew what they were getting when they signed Pelé – a global icon – which is exactly why they brought in a man named Jim Trecker (a man who would work on World Cup '94 and develop the idea of a media mixed zone for journalists and broadcasters), a media relations guru who had worked closely with Jets quarterback Namath and had a love for soccer. Trecker's job was, to boil it down to simple terms, to make Pelé and the New York Cosmos the most recognisable and iconic sporting brand on the planet. Such was the magnitude of the transfer, George Best had to be moved from the Cosmos to another franchise (Best was the initial star signing for the Cosmos when those who ran the franchise felt like he was the best player they could sign). But, why not keep Best and Pelé on the same team? That would be a fan's dream to watch! Ideally the NASL would have let it happen but, whilst it was no secret that Pelé and Best were the two players Woosnam targeted to have as the main attractions of the entire league, it wouldn't have made much sense to have both on the same team. When the league thought Pelé wouldn't join, they made Best the primary star in their biggest market, New York, but once Pelé decided to join, Best was moved to the next biggest market in Los Angeles. The NASL needed both New York and Los Angeles to compete with the biggest names, and they managed to have their two targets in both markets. It was a dream come true for the league, and it quite literally ushered in a new era for the

NASL. Players saw the league as a viable option and a great opportunity to not only extend their playing careers but also earn a lot of money and try a new kind of lifestyle. The NASL was very forward thinking in this regard as not many players had considered a different lifestyle as a reason to move. It was always about winning and occasionally your pay cheque, but things were changing. Gone were the days of *Viva* magazine shoots, and enter the days of Andy Warhol taking photos of star players, Henry Kissinger and Mick Jagger lapping it up in Studio 54 with Ertegun, and when Trecker was asked about the attention he said, 'Were the Cosmos the Rolling Stones? Ahmet Ertegun went to the games in his own private jet. One day he attended the Cosmos games, the next day he lunched with Mick Jagger. For Pelé, it was very Hollywood: backdoors and entrances, exits to kitchens and hotels, but not for the others. Pelé created such mob scenes in the lobbies.' People wanted to be seen with Pelé and they wanted to be seen with Cosmos gear because, all of a sudden, it had become *cool*. Soccer being cool? That's the Pelé effect. Seemingly overnight, the world of soccer in the United States changed forever in a bar in Manhattan with a transfer that had been in the pipeline for five years, and all without a ball being kicked. It was a very 21st-century approach to soccer from the Cosmos, which is probably why the move worked so well for all parties.

But there was still soccer to be played, and for all the hard work in promoting the game off the field with Pelé, George Best and multiple new franchises, it had to be replicated on the field. You can have as many stars and teams as you wish, but if the quality is terrible fans will soon notice. Woosnam expanded the league even further to bump the numbers up to 20 franchises across four divisions (Northern, Eastern, Central and Western). He added the Hartford Bicentennials, Chicago Sting, San Antonio Thunder, Tampa Bay Rowdies and Portland Timbers to the mix. The NASL had finally become a 'major league' in Woosnam's eyes. Was his vision of major league sustainable at this point in time? He certainly thought so, and who could blame him. The NASL was bringing in the second golden age of US soccer and attendance numbers were through the roof. Logically, in the right markets, this could only grow the game further, and during the 1975 season it did. Best went to the Aztecs, former Tottenham defender Mike England, who was recognised as one of the game's finest defenders at the time, joined the Seattle Sounders, Peter Bonetti had fallen out of favour at Chelsea and joined the St Louis Stars, while the Boston Minutemen managed to pull off an amazing signing by bringing in Eusébio, once considered the second-best player in the world behind Pelé. Eusébio wasn't the same player who would light up Benfica, but Eusébio at 75 per cent was still better than the majority of players in the world. So the NASL had managed to expand further and bring in three bona fide juggernauts of world soccer, but it still remained that the soccer itself needed to be of a good standard and the fans needed to come in their masses and enjoy it. With expectations high in New York, the Cosmos were expected to win the NASL Championship. That was the bare minimum for such a squad (mainly because they had Pelé in their ranks), but they didn't make the NASL Championship game. They didn't even make the play-offs because they finished third in the Northern Division (mainly because they only had Pelé in their ranks). Now it must be noted that the official debut of Pelé didn't come until halfway through the season, but his impact on the crowds didn't correlate with his impact on the pitch, as, while he was by far and away the most talented player in the team (even at the age of 34), that was a glaring issue as much as it was a positive. A 34-year-old Pelé could not drag a team over the finishing line without some form of help, and other teams around the Cosmos like the Boston Minutemen and Toronto Metros-Croatia (that wasn't their official name because the league prohibited ethnic team names, but it was a nickname given to them because of the number of Yugoslavian players in their squad) had built teams instead of going for the big prize superstar. Pelé helped the Cosmos massively off the pitch, but he couldn't do it all the time on the pitch. His first game was on Randall's Island (nicknamed 'Vandall's Island' because, to put it nicely, the area was a complete mess – grass had to be spray-painted green to make it look healthier and it was directly underneath the Triborough Bridge) and brought 20,000 fans to watch him score and assist in a 2-2 draw with the Dallas Tornado in an exhibition match. This exhibition summed up the Cosmos in 1975. Thousands of fans arrived to watch Pelé, who put on a show and performed well, but the Cosmos hardly ever matched up with his levels. In fact, they lost more games than they won! But while the media and attention focus was almost solely on either the Cosmos or the Aztecs, the 1975 season proved to be a profitable one for most of the new expansion sides, with two of them winning their divisions at the first time of trying. Portland Timbers won the Western Division with 16 impressive wins, while the Aztecs, like the Cosmos, could only finish third with 12 wins and 10 losses. The Timbers, made up mainly of British imports, had the level-best win percentage in the entire NASL alongside another new franchise, the Tampa Bay Rowdies, who won the Eastern Division. New franchises were figuring out how to build sides to win, while everyone else was either caught in a quagmire of 'do we try to rebuild' or 'do we try to sign a superstar'? Only a few teams seemed to understand how to run their franchises to win games, and unsurprisingly these teams went on to have a strong play-off run.

Miami, who scored 23 goals from Steve David, made the play-offs alongside Tampa Bay, Portland, St Louis and Toronto, and it proved to be a good play-off season, even if there weren't as many 'stars' as the league and its fans would have hoped for. They would have wanted a Best or a Pelé in the post-season matches, but got neither, with Tampa Bay facing Portland in the 'Soccer Bowl' – this was Woosnam's way of rebranding the NASL Championship final, which had absolutely nothing to do with the Super Bowl and you're wrong if you think it did (okay, it was almost 100 per cent a copy of the Super Bowl because Woosnam had an obsession with American football). Tampa Bay became the third consecutive expansion team to win the NASL Championship, and while Pelé arrived and more people came to watch NASL matches than ever, it became quite clear that a lot of fans were there for Pelé whenever he came to town. That's natural, but when you see the figures it can be a bit concerning for the sport. When the Cosmos played the Philly Atoms, over 20,000 people went to see Pelé, even if he wasn't playing and just in his regular street wear. Washington set a new league record of 35,620 fans when Pelé and his Cosmos rode into town, and there were even riots when Boston refused people entry to watch the Cosmos vs Minutemen. It became clear early on that Pelé had taken the league to another level, which was to be expected, but more needed to be done to sustain the attention. One man can't carry a team, let alone carry a league. But what he did do was open the eyes of the world towards the United States, a country where it didn't seem viable to play soccer, let alone be considered as an option for professionals to earn a decent wage. He helped make the NASL look credible, and slowly but surely more professionals from abroad came over and the spread of stars that the league needed became a reality.

George Best officially became a Los Angeles Aztecs player, ending his period of limbo where he was a part of the franchise, but not officially registered to play for the team as he had been taken from the Cosmos to Los Angeles by the NASL before LA actually had an official team. All very confusing, but Best was in, Eusébio stayed in the NASL and moved to Toronto from Boston, and newcomers Geoff Hurst joined the Seattle Sounders, Rodney Marsh joined the Tampa Bay Rowdies from QPR and San Antonio made it three English stars in the league when they brought World Cup-winning captain Bobby Moore over. Suddenly, the NASL was starting to look the way we all recognise it retrospectively today. The stars, who had the skills, the charisma and flair, were in, and the league continued to grow as a result. Was it a fad, or was the NASL here to stay?

The 1976 season would go a very long way to answering that question because it showcased the very best of the NASL, while simultaneously showing the dangers of running a franchise in the NASL and how far the league had to go in order to, not only remain relevant and a force in America, but to change its image completely and become a respected league outside of Europe, something that was very rarely the case back in the 70s. If the NASL could break the boundaries down, they could be in for the long haul, but a lot hinged on that 1976 season.

With flair firmly engrained in the soccer culture of the NASL with the likes of Pelé, Best and Marsh strutting their stuff and with Best and Marsh having 'rock star' looks and playing like rock stars, it set the league alight. In fact, Marsh was adored in America, partially for the same reasons he was loathed (to a degree) in England – his confidence, his swagger and self-confidence which could be perceived as arrogance, depending on your view point – but his ability to play any tune with the ball being his instrument, he was the kind of player that was needed to counter Pelé. Pelé was a player that had verve, flair and world-class ability, but he didn't have the look that Marsh had. That's what set Marsh and Best apart. The two would join Fulham on loan in the NASL off-season, but during their season with the Rowdies and Aztecs, they brought a certain 'pizzazz' to the league. In England, they weren't always allowed to express themselves because during the 1960s and 1970s results come first and entertainment comes second, but what the duo had in the NASL was a platform to play their own game. This little excerpt from *Rock and Roll Soccer* by Ian Plenderith gives us a good indication of how Marsh played at the time:

> Rodney Marsh stopped the game, although referee Peter Johnson hadn't blown his whistle. The Tampa Bay Rowdies midfielder fell to his knees, stretched out his arms and gestured at the ball in his possession. 'Come and get it,' he was saying to the New York Cosmos, a team that was losing 4-0 and whose pivotal player, Pelé, was not having the greatest of days. 'Come on, come and get it – I know you can't, but try anyway.'

Rodney Marsh, formerly of Manchester City and Queens Park Rangers, was embarrassing World Cup-winner Pelé. And the crowd was loving it. The match was broadcast live on CBS and three million people witnessed this long, blond-haired attacking midfielder embarrass the greatest player to ever play the game. (CBS had come back into soccer once Pelé arrived and showed his debut for the Cosmos in that exhibition vs Detroit. Ten million people tuned in to see Pelé but missed his goal and assist because CBS went to commercials. At least the ref didn't stop the entire game this time.) The NASL didn't have to rely solely on Pelé after that game, they had Rodney Marsh in their ranks, who was called 'the White Pelé' by the Rowdies owner in his unveiling press conference, but Marsh himself corrected the owner saying, 'No, Pelé is known as the Black Rodney Marsh'. The arrogance consumed Marsh and it translated to the audience and the fans quicker than one could ever have imagined. In modern times Zlatan Ibrahimović is known as the arrogant showman who provides entertainment but always proves himself and finds a way to back up his claims, but Marsh was the first soccer player in America to have that act. He would perform back heels, dummies, no-look passes, Marsh was bringing the whole playbook out for the Cosmos match, and it worked. Marsh admitted that he didn't intend to become the trailblazer for American soccer, but he had no choice because any big-name European import was going to have that effect at the time, whether they liked it or not. His style of play was eaten up by the spectators, who wanted the flicks, the tricks and the arrogance, and, while some of his Tampa Bay team-mates probably weren't too keen on his style, it was good for the league at the time. Marsh had found his home following a rough spell with Manchester City, and even though he was wined and dined by Elton John in a bid to bring him to the LA Aztecs and team him up with George Best, as soon as Marsh got off the plane at Tampa Bay he felt at home. For Best, it was slightly different in Los Angeles. He decided that on some days he would miss training, and while Aztecs coach Terry Fisher had to tolerate his prized asset's ways, the rule was if he missed training twice he would be dropped. So, Best ended up missing training two days in a row, and thus was dropped. He missed training a third time and the club duly suspended him and the team went on to win their next two matches without him. They decided he wasn't worth the trouble, and off Best went to Fort Lauderdale, where he would flourish, but the tale of these two shows what the NASL could be like. The league and its teams had room for flair players who had world-class ability and perhaps relied on others to do their running for them, but as long as they put in the work and effort it would pay off. For Marsh it did, for Best it didn't. At least, not immediately.

However, while Marsh and Best went on to have very different seasons, it was the Cosmos who pulled off yet another blockbuster deal to sign the prolific Lazio forward Giorgio Chinaglia, whose story in getting to the Cosmos was incredible and probably could be a book on its own. Growing up in Wales from a young age, Chinaglia had always been destined to be a soccer player. He played for Swansea City and Serie C (Italian third division) before making the jump up to Lazio, where the star would really be born, scoring 122 goals in 246 matches and becoming known as one of the deadliest strikers in Italy, and perhaps Europe, at the time. It was during his time at Lazio that the seeds were sown for his move to America, when he purchased American real estate in 1972 while on a tour with Lazio. He then went on to buy a house in New Jersey in 1975. He met with Clive Toye and gave him two options: either he would be allowed to join the New York Cosmos, or he would buy his own franchise. He joined the Cosmos, and finally they had someone who could rival the other sporting teams in the city for making front- and back-page news just by opening his mouth. Chinaglia would wear silk robes to matches, he paid an artist to paint two portraits of him which he hung in his 22-room New Jersey mansion, he criticised Pelé when he felt like it was needed, he occasionally referred to himself in the third person. (There was a game in which Pelé wouldn't pass to Chinaglia because, no matter the angle, Chinaglia would shoot. Chinaglia, clearly offended by this, shouted, 'I AM CHINAGLIA! IF I SHOOT FROM A PLACE, IT'S BECAUSE CHINAGLIA CAN SCORE FROM THERE.') He was brash, he was arrogant, he probably had the biggest ego of any player in the entire league, he was powerful, he was confident, but most importantly he was a natural-born goalscorer. It didn't matter that he had an ego, because he would always score. With Marsh and Chinaglia providing incredible talent on the field and giving the NASL a huge presence off the field with their words, their lifestyle and their attitude, it was exactly what the league needed. Coupled with the Bicentennial Cup that was played to celebrate the 200th birthday of the United States (a competition that was played to promote soccer in the US and had a Team America featuring most of the NASL stars going up against famous soccer nations, with average audiences of 45,000 across the tournament and media coverage being beyond what was the usual for soccer at the time), soccer was climbing in the ranks of sports in America. It was still behind the big three, but the gap wasn't as wide as it once was. With well-known names who had character, passion and skill, people were able to relate to the NASL and be entertained by it, but the league itself provided fans with a few shocks in the 1976 season with a team taking home the championship that was perhaps unexpected.

Amid all the new arrivals into the NASL, one may be forgiven for forgetting the great Eusébio was now a member of the Toronto Metros following his time with Boston, and while the striker's body wasn't what it had been just a decade before, he still possessed the skill to win matches on his own. Finishing second in the Northern Division, Toronto made the NASL post-season matches alongside the New York Cosmos (who had two of the three top scorers in Chinaglia and Pelé), Tampa Bay (who had the second-top scorer in Derek Smethurst), the Rochester Lancers, Dallas Tornado, Los Angeles Aztecs, Chicago Sting, Washington Diplomats, Seattle Sounders, Minnesota Kicks, Vancouver Whitecaps and the San Jose Earthquakes. The new play-off system had a first round featuring teams who finished second and third in their respective divisions and the winners of those ties would move to the divisional championships to face the winners of their division; so, for example, the New York Cosmos finished second in the Eastern Division and faced the Washington Diplomats who finished third. The Cosmos beat Washington to face divisional winners Tampa Bay in the next round before moving into the Conference Championships, against whoever won the other divisional game from either the Pacific or Atlantic Conference. It was quite easy to get the hang of once you fully understood it, but the main reason it was implemented was to give more teams the opportunity to play post-season soccer. The Cosmos, despite their stacked roster of talent, were knocked out in the divisional rounds by Tampa Bay, who advanced to play Eusébio's Toronto in the Conference Championships. Pelé was out, meaning that Pelé vs Eusébio was off the cards, despite the fact that it probably would have drawn in a major audience, but Eusébio vs Marsh wasn't a bad alternative, even if a younger and fitter Marsh was probably favourite to triumph. The Minnesota Kicks defeated the Seattle Sounders in the Western divisional rounds and had to come up against San Jose for a chance to face either Eusébio's Toronto or Marsh's Rowdies in the final. Either way, CBS was going to have an interesting Soccer Bowl to televise! Toronto went on to upset everyone by beating Tampa Bay and then Minnesota 3-0 in the championship final – with Eusébio scoring the opening goal. While many considered the post-season to be somewhat of an anti-climax due to poor scheduling – fans wanted to see New York vs Tampa Bay deeper into the competition because they were the two big names in the league, had three genuine superstars playing for them and were statistically the best two teams in the entire league – but instead that was played in the divisional championships and fans were left unfulfilled. But it wasn't all doom and gloom, because league attendances were up once again (this time by 34 per cent) and European stars were looking at the NASL as a genuine league to express themselves without feeling any of the major pressures they felt back home. Stars flourished, fans enjoyed themselves and the league just kept growing and growing.

It was a strong year in 1976, and 1977 had to improve on that. The new season was set to be Pelé's last contracted with the Cosmos, and he still hadn't won the NASL championship, thus begging the question at the time whether he had been a success because he hadn't actually won anything. So the storyline for the season was set: could the Cosmos bring the NASL championship to Pelé before he retired? He had won everything at every level he played in, except the NASL. Despite Pelé, despite Chinaglia and despite the Warner dollars bankrolling the club, the Cosmos didn't really have an outstanding squad. They had two stars and a multitude of average-to-decent players and there was terrible infighting from the moment Pelé got to pre-season training, a week before the start of the season.

Pelé and Chinaglia, the two alpha males of the team, were fighting for every ball in training, trying to exert their dominance on the other, with Pelé looking more interested in what was going on off the field instead of on it. The team was made up of players from various countries who played different styles that didn't mix well, to the shock of literally no one. The Cosmos hadn't really planned out how to play, nor had they planned out who they had to bring in to the playing staff in order to get the best out of their star players. If you have Pelé, you don't sign Englishmen who only launch the ball long because that's all they've ever done in their career, while the South Americans only passed to Pelé and ignored Chinaglia, making matters all the more insufferable. There was no cohesion, no planning and this team was expected to win the championship for Pelé? Half of the team probably didn't even want him there! Pelé, realising that the end of his career was about to fade out with an embarrassing whimper, took over the team. He was the face of the team; he was the talisman and it was about time that he started acting like it, and with his band of superstars including himself, Chinaglia, Franz Beckenbauer (the German was signed in May that season and was reportedly shocked and disgusted at the infighting at the club), and Carlos Alberto, the Cosmos decided to show why they were tipped to go all the way. (Carlos Alberto was Pelé's Brazilian team-mate, who joined the Cosmos on the infamous 'New York blackout day' on 13 July. The blackout occurred when a lightning strike hit a substation on the Hudson River and eventually caused both JFK and LaGuardia Airports to shut down, subways to close and every store was looted. Meanwhile, Pelé and Beckenbauer had to find their way from Manhattan to Rochester for a game without being able to use an airport. Welcome to NYC, Carlos!) Win after win, goals flooded out in their droves, the Cosmos's record improved and it eventually led them to finish second in the Eastern Division, behind the Fort Lauderdale Strikers, with the fourth-best winning percentage in the league behind the Strikers, Dallas Tornado and Minnesota Kicks.

Pelé scored 13 (including a memorable hat-trick on Father's Day against Tampa Bay in New Jersey in front of 60,000-plus fans), while Los Angeles had Steve David and George Best (he finally bucked up his ideas once the club disciplined him, with Fort Lauderdale choosing to keep him on) who scored 37 goals between them, with Best getting a league-tying number of assists (18), but the lack of defence meant they only finished third. Chinaglia and Pelé, for all their issues, scored 28 between them but had to make do with the long run to the play-offs. It wasn't going to be easy for the Cosmos and Pelé to get his final championship, but at least they had made a step forward by qualifying for the play-offs instead of the backwards steps they had been making for the majority of the season (to be fair, it was probably harder not to qualify for the play-offs, but that's beside the point on this occasion).

In the division championship, the Rowdies and Rodney Marsh stood in the way of the Cosmos. A crowd of 57,828 saw Pelé and his band of superstars beat the Rowdies 3-0, followed by an 8-3 whooping of Fort Lauderdale and Gordon Banks in front of a record crowd of 77,691 in the divisional finals. At this stage, there was an air of invincibility to the Cosmos, even if other teams around them were playing extremely well too. Beckenbauer and Stephen Hunt scored the first two for New York before Chinaglia added a hat-trick to his goal from the divisional championship against Tampa Bay. Two rivals down, Rochester were next, and this time the Cosmos weren't affected by any kind of blackout as Chinaglia and Hunt both scored again in the first leg, before a Chinaglia double as well as a Pelé sealer meant the Cosmos won 4-1 and swept the series. On to the Soccer Bowl for one last hurrah for the greatest player of all time (arguably, just for the sake of debate). In Portland Oregon, the great Pelé would play his final professional game and he would make it his mission to go out on top.

Hunt opened the scoring after 19 minutes, only for Seattle to equalise four minutes later. To the surprise of absolutely no one, Giorgio Chinaglia came up clutch for the Cosmos with a powerful header after 77 minutes to win it for New York and for Pelé. They had done it. The first soccer superteam, assembled to raise the profile of soccer in the United States, who'd had money and fame thrown at them at every corner, had finally won the NASL Championship. It's by no means a stereotypical 'fairytale' story, not when you spend the money the Cosmos spent to win, but to win it in Pelé's final game must mean something in soccer history. Not only did Pelé get his title and his farewell in an exhibition against his former club Santos, but it meant that there was about to be a new era in US soccer. The Pelé days were gone, he was out the door, but with the likes of Chinaglia, Beckenbauer, Marsh and Best, the NASL was in a surprisingly good place still. It showed how far the NASL had come, when Pelé could retire and it wouldn't hugely affect attendances. Of course, the attendance average was down the following year, but more than 100 games extra was the reason, so not solely down to Pelé.

But what Pelé did bring to America was a new way of thinking. The stardom and attention that Pelé brought to the NASL was such a huge positive that it changed everything. Gone were the days of building a solid foundation of a franchise, establishing a core fanbase and perhaps building a team around one or two stars, most franchises skipped the first two parts and went straight to the stars because they saw what happened to the Cosmos and they wanted a slice of that Pelé pie, and who could blame them? The owners wanted to make money, the fans wanted to be wowed, that's why flair players worked in America. Deep down, however, this mindset completely crippled the league. People wanted something similar to what the Cosmos had in terms of media attention, and they were willing to bring in whoever they could at any price in order to obtain that notoriety. Marsh, Best, Chinaglia, Hurst, Moore, Banks, Beckenbauer, these players were signed with the objective of having as many paying fans come through the gates as possible, and the financial expenditure was outrageous, at least for franchises that had hardly any major financial backing or major market attention.

In 1978, a new strategy was put into practice. The NASL had a new philosophy that was known as 'the future is now', where teams spent more money than they had, putting their future on the line, to purchase the biggest names and to become popular as quickly as possible. They saw how much the Cosmos spent to the win the NASL championship and the crowds it brought in, so it obviously had to be the way forward (completely disregarding the years they didn't win and the fact that New Yorkers will pay attention to anything that is doing well and is fashionable). Developing young American talent went out of the window in favour of buying imports, and certain teams couldn't deal with the change in strategy and either fell behind or vanished. The St Louis Stars, a team that were synonymous with providing young Americans a chance to play NASL soccer, couldn't deal with the foreign players who were not only more experienced than their own players, but they were miles ahead of them in terms of ability.

Expansion fever struck the league again, and New England, Philadelphia, Detroit, Memphis, Houston and Colorado were added to the league, meaning the NASL had two conferences of three divisions and 24 teams. Most notable from these new teams was the Philadelphia Fury, who epitomised the new outlook from NASL franchises. Owned by a consortium of rock stars and musicians, such as keyboardist for the rock band Yes, Peter Frampton (who had his pig stolen from him in an episode of the Simpsons) and Paul Simon, the Fury decided that if you're owned by rock stars, you can't just buy any old players. Chelsea legend Peter Osgood, Johnny Giles, Alan Ball and Trevor Francis joined the team and were treated like superstars, which brought a great quote out of Francis:

> Every time I get the ball the commentator goes crazy and
> calls me Trevor Francis Superstar. I was interviewed by
> a woman journalist soon after I got here and one of the
> first things she wanted to know was how long I'd been a
> superstar. I said 'about three days'.

Trevor Francis – a man who would be voted Detroit's 'sexiest
athlete' during his time in the NASL – was the epitome of the
post-Pelé world and it wasn't even his fault. He was a very
good striker for Birmingham at the time and was a valuable
player to have, but with teams in search of their own superstar,
he was thrust into the limelight without being at the level of
Beckenbauer and Pelé. It summed up that the search for a
superstar was more important than actually running a healthy
franchise, which would prove to be a problem for the rest of
the season and for the foreseeable future. Attendances were
still high and playing surfaces were often dual-purpose ones
shared in larger NFL stadiums, while on the pitch it was more
of the same. The Cosmos romped to the Eastern Division win,
having an identical record to the Vancouver Whitecaps. Francis
and the Detroit Express won the Central Division, with Francis
finishing third in the scoring charts, while the play-offs looked
set to throw up some exciting fixtures, even if there were
probably too many teams in it. (The 1978 scoring charts were
a rather famous list in comparison to other years. Chinaglia
finished top with 34 goals and 11 assists, Mike Flanagan scored
30 goals with six assists, Francis had 22 goals and 10 assists,
Kevin Hector of Derby County fame scored 21 goals with 10
assists and Marsh had 18 goals and 16 assists.) Of the 24 teams,
16 made the play-offs, some with negative records too, and it
was more like an entirely new season instead of a play-off
round. The Conference Championships saw Tampa Bay face-off
against Fort Lauderdale and the Cosmos against the Timbers,
with both Tampa Bay and New York advancing to the Soccer
Bowl. A crowd of 74,901 packed into the Giants Stadium to see
the two sides go head to head, with Manchester City legend
Denis Tueart scoring twice for the Cosmos and Chinaglia

getting his obligatory goal to make it two NASL championships in a row. The NASL was looking like it was booming; it looked healthy with the stars on show, the television coverage was improving and the fans were coming in, but it was off the field that issues were arising. The expenditure of franchises wasn't being equalled by the income, and teams should've been feeling the heat ... but they didn't. Certain teams ignored the warning signs as 1979 rolled around and more stars were brought in for more money, such as Johan Cruyff at the Los Angeles Aztecs, Gerd Muller at Fort Lauderdale and Cruyff's Netherlands teammate Johan Neeskens joining the Cosmos. ABC picked up the rights for the NASL, and while it didn't draw as many ratings as they'd have hoped it was still a good sign of the improving times. But the question still remained, how long would these improving times last for? The 1979 season came as quickly as the 1978 season had ended. The NASL were looking to benefit from a number of new franchises, the star signings, and the new television broadcast deal with ABC to show nine games, including the Soccer Bowl. It may've only been nine matches, but it was a huge upgrade on the previous TVS deal (TVS being a sports syndicated channel). Of course, it wouldn't be soccer on television in America if there weren't constant reminders of what the rules were, commercial breaks during play and tape delays in certain matches (we will get to that at the end of the 1981 season, because it was a tape delay of a rather important match that was replaced by something completely different). Fans were excited because this was a sport that they had come to love, and those who loved the NASL *loved* soccer, mainly due to the fact it was something different, a sport that could probably only be compared to basketball in the non-stop, end-to-end action. When Atlanta got their Chiefs back from Colorado, the fans fell in love again and it energised the team completely, even if they did eventually finish bottom of the Central Division in the National Conference. The Cosmos were dominant yet again, with their 'United Nations' team looking unstoppable during the regular season, while Gerd Muller and his 19 league goals inspired the Fort Lauderdale Strikers to a play-off spot, although it was to be a play-off that would be rather long-winded, drawn out and considered somewhat of an anticlimax. You've got some of the best players in the world scoring goals for fun and controlling games, so how could it be an anticlimax? Well, Gerd Muller and his Fort Lauderdale Strikers went out in the Conference quarter-finals to the Chicago Sting, a team that was literally named after the 1973 film *The Sting,* starring Paul Newman and Robert Redford. So with Gerd Muller gone, what about NASL MVP Johan Cruyff over in Los Angeles? Thankfully, he managed to live up to his name with a win over the Washington Diplomats, and the fact the former Ajax and Barcelona legend was even in Los Angeles and the league was a major story. For Cruyff, the NASL proved to be a welcome distraction from the pressures he faced in his home country and provided him with a place to restart his life after a series of financial losses left the Dutch legend almost bankrupt. Cruyff insisted that after the horror of pulling out of the 1978 World Cup (he didn't want to play in a country – Argentina – that had such a vicious dictatorship) and ending his time at Barcelona on a sour note (it was later revealed that his family was held at gunpoint in his Spanish home), he was done playing football, including involvement in any capacity, for a period of time, but he was tempted to join the Aztecs to aide his financial woes and because he'd be playing under the man who brought his success and genius to the world. Under his mentor and one of the greatest managers of all time, Rinus Michels, Cruyff was named NASL MVP in his debut season, finishing with 13 goals and 16 assists, wowing American fans with his guile, vision and natural talent even if it was towards the twilight of his career.

However, the Los Angeles Aztecs fell in the Conference semi-finals to the Vancouver Whitecaps, meaning both Muller and Cruyff were gone by the end of the semis, but at least Marsh's Rowdies and the 'United Nations' of the Cosmos were still in the running, with the latter's post-season campaign seeming to have the momentum of a runaway freight train; however, the Cosmos train was about to come to an emergency halt against the Aztecs's foe, the Vancouver Whitecaps, in what was probably both the biggest shock of the entire season and the most exciting post-season series in 1979. The Whitecaps took game one, while the Cosmos took game two via a penalty shootout, and the deciding game was taken by the Whitecaps, with all three games combining to just under 100,000 spectators through the gates. It was a David vs Goliath kind of match, but this time Goliath was a multicultural juggernaut, whereas David was a plucky underdog who only had one top scorer on the leading scorers chart (Kevin Hector with 15 goals). The Whitecaps would face the Tampa Bay Rowdies in that season's Soccer Bowl after the Rowdies dispatched of the San Diego Sockers, with that series also going to a decider. If Tampa Bay didn't have enough motivation to win the championship anyway, it only added extra incentive when they knew it would be Rodney Marsh's last appearance as he was about to enter retirement. Could he do what Pelé had done and go out on a high? Could he, the swaggering Marsh, topple a team that had Kevin Hector, Alan Ball and Ray Lewington starting, with Bruce Grobbelaar on the bench? Well ... no, he couldn't. The Whitecaps won 2-1, with Trevor Whymark getting both goals, and Marsh trudged off after 79 minutes for Ivan Grnja, a Croatian who would depart the NASL after the final. Was it a fitting end for a genuine legend of the NASL? No, but it probably fit the story of Marsh better than if he had won it. He was a transformative player at a time when the NASL needed transforming, and he provided fans with the style, flair and excitement. Hardly anyone had his ability, hardly anyone had his arrogance, but the story of Rodney Marsh in the NASL wouldn't be the same if he'd actually won the NASL. He won't be seen as a failure because he didn't win a trophy, he was a success. A massive success. Why? Because he taught fans that you can enjoy watching beautiful football, and sometimes that's more important than silverware.

The end of the 70s for the NASL was prosperous on the field, with stars coming into their own, but off the field it was a different matter, which wasn't made public at the time. The financial constraints were taking their toll on some of the teams, who weren't able to continuously and consistently draw high crowd numbers, nor were they in a market to charge high ticket prices to boost revenue. No franchises moved or were renamed in the 1980 season, but only a handful of new stars were brought in, like Rob Rensenbrink, who joined the Portland Timbers, Wim Jansen, who joined up with his fellow Dutchman Johan Cruyff at the Washington Diplomats, and Ruud Krol, who went to the Vancouver Whitecaps. The new recruits were well equipped to make an impact in the league, but due to the already heavy cast of characters at the time the new signings didn't make as big an impact as perhaps they would have needed to a number of years ago. Why? Simply because the league was stacked with players who not only performed at a high level, but who were good enough to keep fans coming back. For example, Giorgio Chinaglia returned to his best that season with 32 goals and 13 assists, finishing top of the scoring charts with 77 points, while the Chicago Sting had Karl-Heinz Granitza in their ranks who scored 19 goals with 26 assists playing alongside Arno Steffenhagen, who scored 15 goals with 15 assists, as the Sting romped to the American Central Division win. Only seven teams had average attendance figures below 10,000 and eight had more than 15,000 fans regularly showing up, an all-time high for the NASL in total fans, average attendance and median attendance at this point in time (the records were broken the following season thanks to the addition of 24 more games). It looked like the league had finally established its core audience and a core fanbase, and the play-offs seemed like they would be better for the neutrals, or at least better than the previous season's. The Rowdies, Cosmos, Strikers, Sounders and Tornado made it through the first round with ease, while the Sting were stung out of the competition, losing to the San Diego Sockers, a team that had a .500 record (an above .500 record means they have more wins than losses and draws) in the regular season and only scored 53 goals. It was a shock to say the least because many had expected the Sting to carry on their impenetrable form from the regular season and were considered strong favourites to go all the way, but San Diego proved that their shock wasn't a fluke when they beat the Rowdies in a decider game before facing off against the Strikers in the Conference Championships, who themselves had beaten both the California Surf and Edmonton Drillers. The other two teams in the semis were the Cosmos and Aztecs, who both had to go through deciders to get to that position. The Cosmos breezed past Tulsa (winning the second game of the series 8-1) but needed a decider to fend off Dallas, while the Aztecs took the Diplomats to three games before advancing to face the Seattle Sounders, and required a penalty shootout in the deciding match to advance. On the face of it, the Cosmos were the favourites given their form in the regular season, and the goal machine that was Chinaglia didn't stop scoring, while the Aztecs had to go through two ties on deciders and were out on their feet, and it showed against New York. In Los Angeles, the Cosmos took the game 1-2, and in the second game at Giants Stadium in New Jersey the Cosmos completed the sweep with a 3-1 win, leaving them to see who they'd play between Fort Lauderdale and San Diego. The Strikers advanced to the Soccer Bowl and would pit perhaps the two best strikers in the league against each other: Giorgio Chinaglia and Gerd Muller. Not just that, but it had Franz Beckenbauer and Muller play against each other, despite the many years they spent playing together at Bayern Munich and in the German national team, in what would be Beckenbauer's last game for the Cosmos before returning to Germany with Hamburg. But the Muller vs Beckenbauer and Chinaglia storyline didn't play out the way that many had hoped, as the Cosmos completely dominated proceedings and ran out 3-0 winners, with Chinaglia getting a brace. An article and report from the *New York Evening News* from the game gave a review of the performances from both sides and playing conditions:

> Going into the championship game, Chinaglia had scored 16 goals in the play-offs to go with the 32 he had in the regular season. The Cosmos controlled the ball most

of the first half of the game, played in near 100 degree temperatures before a crowd of 50,768 at RFK Stadium, and they completely dominated the second half when the Strikers were without one of their foremost players, Gerd Muller, who left the game with an aggravated thigh injury with 5:33 remaining until the half-time break.

Both teams agreed that the turning point was the Cosmos goal by Julio Cesar Romero. Vladislav Bogicevic passed off to Chinaglia on a free kick, but the Italians 17-yard attempted goal was blocked by the defensive wall. The ball bounced toward Romero who easily beat Striker goalie Jon van Beveren with 2:55 gone in the second half.

'After the first goal, the Strikers went flat', said Chinaglia, who was named MVP of the play-offs. Van Beveren agreed. 'The first goal made the difference. In a game like this, it gave them confidence.'

'It was a lucky goal,' the goalie contended, 'but from there on out they had the advantage.'

The Cosmos's knowledge of how to win the big games, coupled with their striker being on blistering form, meant that they captured their third NASL Championship in four years and their fourth overall. On the pitch everything seemed rosy and like it was on the up and, to a degree, it was. However, the irony was that the league had never been more popular than it was in 1980, but certain teams' average attendances were dropping, including the Cosmos, who dropped from 49,000 to 42,000, even though they had won the championship. Some of the weaker sides, like the Philadelphia Fury, either had to sell their best players in order to stay afloat, or they just traded their best players for no reason other than the people at the top were so concerned about jumping on the bandwagon even though they had no idea what they were actually doing. The Fury sold their top three scorers before the start of the 1980 season and then were baffled as to why they couldn't win, why the fans weren't showing up anymore, why they finished third-bottom of the entire NASL and why they had the joint-second worst attack in the league. Certain teams weren't able to keep the charade up for much longer, and in the case of the historic Atlanta Chiefs franchise they were more or less confirmed as gone after the 1981 season, playing it out knowing it would be their last. That's it. Just gone, because they weren't willing to spend the money to compete with the big hitters. The league expansion meant that teams had to spend more to even sniff the post-season and some simply weren't able to do so and as a result they folded completely. The Houston Hurricane, Washington Diplomats and Rochester Lancers joined the Chiefs on the chopping block in November 1981, but while the Chiefs and Diplomats stuck around for one final season the other two folded immediately. The league couldn't hide it anymore. Finances were crippling some teams, and no one was making any money at all. The higher-paid players either stayed on and tried to make the league work or went back to Europe, with Gerd Muller, Franz Beckenbauer, Johan Cruyff, Ruud Krol, Alan Ball, Kevin Hector, Mark Hateley and Wim Jansen all leaving, so the NASL only had a handful of names that world soccer fans would recognise, let alone fans who were trying to get into the sport. Neeskens and Chinaglia stayed with the Cosmos, while Brian Kidd arrived in Atlanta as they finished top of the Southern Division in a valiant effort to end on a high, but they were eliminated in the first round of the play-offs. A young Peter Beardsley came to play at the Vancouver Whitecaps, but while we all know the legendary career he would go on to have with Liverpool, Everton and Newcastle United, he didn't have the desired effect immediately.

George Best was plying his trade in San Jose, while fellow British rockstar soccer player Frank Worthington was in Tampa Bay. Harry Redknapp's future assistant Kevin Bond was in Seattle, Duncan McKenzie, formerly of Brian Clough's Derby County and Leeds United sides, was in Tulsa and the NASL had regressed to a league that was the retirement home for talented players. Once again, the Cosmos and Sting ran riot in their respective divisions, tying for the best record, and once again having the two top scorers in Chinaglia and Granitza, with the Cosmos receiving a first-round play-off bye and the Sting defeating Seattle, Montreal and San Diego to reach the Soccer Bowl, the only game that ABC agreed to televise in the final year of their broadcast agreement due to low ratings. Atlanta would crash out in an upset against Jacksonville – who obtained their franchise from New England prior to the start of the season – and New York took the bye in their stride as they eliminated Tampa Bay and Frank Worthington in a decider game. To the shock of absolutely no one, the 1981 Soccer Bowl was contested between the two best sides, the Chicago Sting and the New York Cosmos, but neither fans in Chicago nor New York saw it live. Why? Remember that tape delay we mentioned earlier? Well, the Soccer Bowl was tape delayed in Chicago until late night because the network decided to show a rerun of the television show *Love Boat* instead.

What about New York? That wasn't shown live, nor was it on tape delay. In fact it wasn't even shown on the day of the match! If you wanted to watch the Chicago Sting vs New York Cosmos in New York, well you just had to wait until the very next day when you probably already knew the result from the newspapers. Chicago won via penalty shootout, which meant that the back-to-back dream for the Cosmos was over, but that was the least of the worries in the NASL. Finances were terrible for almost every franchise, television companies wanted nothing to do with them, and a new Major Indoor Soccer League (MISL) was making its way on to the scene and was proving rather popular, posing a legitimate threat to the NASL. Atlanta, Washington, Minnesota, Dallas, Los Angeles, California and Calgary all folded at the end of the 1981 season, leaving just Toronto as the only original franchise left. Fans didn't want to come to games anymore because players were leaving to go back to Europe, and owners knew they weren't going to make reasonable money so decided to pull out all together. The 1982 season saw more of the same, with the Cosmos winning the NASL Championship, Chinaglia and Granitza finishing the top two scorers and more players leaving the league, with Best and Worthington departing. Players departed and so did fans, as the average attendance dropped 6.6 per cent, from 14,084 to 13,155, with even the most popular soccer hotbeds like New York, Portland and Seattle all suffering from huge drops in attendance. During the 1982 season, the problems for the NASL were evident. There was no hiding behind big fan gates, superstar names or television contracts, the NASL was in a bleak position, with a brief yet bitter salary war ongoing, and the MISL signalling that change was needed. Perhaps they weren't as healthy as they had been beforehand, but a couple of changes could bring the league back to a healthy and sustainable position. The first change that was made? The sacking of Phil Woosnam as the league commissioner. A *New York Times* article explained how the league decided to move Woosnam on as commissioner:

NASL IS LIKELY TO OUST WOOSNAM

A majority of club owners in the North American Soccer League has voted to remove Phil Woosnam as commissioner of the league, according to executives who attended an owner's meeting in Chicago, March 16 when the decision was reached.

'Lack of leadership and loss of credibility,' is how one source summed up the owner's criticism of Woosnam. The consensus seemed to be that although Woosnam has been tireless about promoting the NASL, he has guided the league into several ill-advised business decisions, including the expansion to 24 teams in 1978. The league cut back to 21 teams last year and 14 this year. Woosnam has been intensely concerned with doing whatever was necessary to attract a network television contract (both CBS and ABC have televised NASL games). He pursued marketing policies similar to those used by the National Football League, policies that some owners regard as inappropriate for soccer.

The ownership representatives who attended the meeting were: Lee Stern of Chicago, Morgan McCammon of Montreal, Nesuhi Ertegun of New York, Elizabeth and

Tim Robbie of Fort Lauderdale, George Strawbridge of Tampa Bay, Derek Carroll of Jacksonville, Peter Pocklington of Edmonton, Herb Capozzi of Vancouver, Karston von Wersebe of Toronto, Rick Loewenherz of Tulsa, Bob Bell and Daley of San Diego and Milan Manderic of San Jose, who has since folded his franchise to another group.

And just like that, the man who helped bring about change to the NASL was gone by those who helped him in the expansion, because the same man who brought about change had done *too much*. A new era began in 1983 in the NASL, but it still only had 12 teams, with the Tulsa Roughnecks defeating the Toronto Blizzard in the Soccer Bowl, and the damage had been done. When you have a team called Team America in your league (a team based in Washington DC, filled with the best American national players, with the sole purpose of building up a strong USMNT for World Cups and other competitions, all the while getting paid to do it, and, to the shock of absolutely no one, they finished rock bottom of the NASL). Even though Franz Beckenbauer had returned to the Cosmos to finish his long career, it wasn't enough. Fans were still voting with their feet and attendances kept dropping, the television contract that the league needed never looked further away and the rise of indoor soccer meant that the NASL and major outdoor leagues were taking a back seat.

The Tulsa Roughnecks had to rely on a fundraiser to raise enough money to help the club meet its payroll. Seattle folded, and Robert St Louis, a representative of the club, said in the *Spokesman Review* in September 1983:

> I don't have the authority to fold anything because I just represent two of the stockholders, but in effect that's what we're going to do because we no longer are going to inject money into the club. Nobody, and that includes the players, is going to get paid from now on. I can't see why the employees would want to stay around.

Montreal and Team America, to the heartbreak of their legions of fans, folded too. San Diego, New York, Chicago and Fort Lauderdale (now in Minnesota due to the lack of indoor arenas in Florida) moved to the MISL, with plans for a 1985 season still on the cards, rather optimistically. But when only two teams put down funds to participate in the 1985 NASL season, the league decided enough was enough. They'd had enough of trying to convince teams to join their league, which at one point was one of the most talked about in the world, and with the rise of indoor soccer, the NASL officially shut down operations prior to their planned 1985 season. The sad end to what was a once bright and hopeful league was indicative of their own decision making, yet while the legacy of the end of the NASL will only bring about memories of over-expansion, mismanagement and dwindling attendance figures, the legacy and impact of the NASL during its prime should never be forgotten.

For millions of soccer fans in America, the NASL was as good as they could possibly have hoped for. Millions started playing soccer because of the NASL and, rather ironically, youth soccer had never been more popular when the NASL folded. Kids were playing soccer because either they loved it or it was the easiest sport to play with your friends. You didn't need a hoop, or a bat, or a helmet and shoulder pads, just a ball and two jumpers for goalposts, and in an instant you could be anyone you wanted to be. Would the rise in soccer have happened if Pelé hadn't joined the Cosmos? Probably not, most would agree, but without Pelé and the other stars would the league have folded in the financial ruin it did? Well, that's an impossible question.

Because of players like Pelé, Beckenbauer, Chinaglia, Best, Marsh and Cruyff, the league was able to grow and it could have been dead if they didn't have them, but did the clubs have to spend all the money they did on these players? No, but without these players you could argue that there wouldn't be any clubs in the league. The cultural impact the league had was huge for a period of time as well. As David Hirshey wrote on ESPN.com:

It was an extraordinary moment in time, when 'I'm with the Cosmos' carried as much weight as 'I'm with The Rolling Stones' – perhaps more, since even Mick Jagger wanted to be sprinkled with the stardust of New York's soccer demigods and its one supreme being.

Pelé helped change the perception of soccer, which was a sport known just as a game for immigrants and 'a game for commies', to something to be seen wearing or something to be seen around. Did Studio 54 let the Cosmos in because they were huge soccer fans? Probably not. Did they let them in because in a city like New York being cool and trendy is the most important thing? Absolutely! The more players that were like Pelé, Best and Marsh the league had, the cooler it became. Coupled with the unique kits and badges, it was a modern soccer league in a retro time. It's not all that different to how leagues and clubs work now. Signing a star player boosts your fanbase like Neymar at Paris Saint-Germain or Zlatan Ibrahimović at the LA Galaxy, and like PSG having partnerships with Air Jordan and BAPE, they're becoming trendy without people even watching them play. That's what the NASL wanted. They wanted teams and players to be trendy and then for fans to tune in. It didn't quite work like that, but you can't help but praise them for their effort and attempts at ingenuity, like with the offside line and various other ideas. For soccer purists, the NASL wasn't a good thing at all. It wasn't what they were used to, and to some people if they're not familiar with something it is immediately a negative to them.

But while the NASL fell down quicker than a game of Jenga at a New Year's Eve party, it has to be praised for what it did during it's time. The Seattle Sounders, Portland Timbers and Vancouver Whitecaps all used the NASL and their previous encounters to build a history in their current form in the MLS, hanging on to their fanbase from all those years ago. Atlanta has a strong soccer culture that perhaps started with the Chiefs at the very beginning of this chapter and even New York had a culture for it. The NASL provides US soccer fans now with a way to look at its history in their own country without having to look abroad to Mexico, Europe or South America, they had it in their own backyard. Sure, the NASL was managed terribly towards the end, and for some owners it was nothing more than a cash grab and a way to benefit from a craze, but it did leave a legacy for some. NASL video collectors are still active today, historians look at it intensely to remember a time when perhaps they got hooked on soccer, and modern reporters and fans look back on it with a sense of intrigue, like it was a league from the future. You can't go far in the United States without seeing a soccer field or a soccer shirt from any country. The television coverage is more respectable now than perhaps ever, with broadcasters and fans taking both the men's and women's games extremely seriously. That's part of the legacy the NASL left behind. There would be no MLS without the NASL, or a thriving soccer community that needed to be let out to breathe in the mid-90s. The superstars left a legacy, the teams left a legacy, and while it was poorly run despite its high ambitions, you cannot argue that the North American Soccer League did not leave a legacy.

Chapter Six

The USMNT History from the 1930 World Cup to the 1994 World Cup

AT international level, how do you quantify success? Is it by winning whatever competition is on offer to you? Is it simply just qualifying for a World Cup? Is it continuously developing top-level talent and earning respect as a nation across the world? It's different ideas and different goals for different nations, and it has been for as long as the World Cup and the Olympics have been hosting tournaments, but for certain countries they are still at a crossroads of how to get to their goals. For a young country, do you just build and build across a number of tournaments, trying to find an identity and a way to play at all ages, then implement it for years to come, like they have done in Spain and Germany? If you're a nation like Brazil, Argentina or France, that have a pedigree in winning titles, developing players and entertaining fans, it's all about winning. For the Dutch, Belgians and English, it's more about trying to take the next step in building a foundation around top-class players and eventually winning a competition, but for a nation that has a huge population, a population that has a youth sports scene dominated by soccer players, what should their goal be? When you have 325 million people in your country, with millions addicted to sports and nearly as many playing soccer, what is your goal? Is it to develop? Is it to win? Is it to establish a history and a culture? For the United States of America, none of these things should be an issue. At least, on paper they shouldn't be an issue. They've developed tons of very talented and accomplished players, they should have a winning mentality and they've had a style of play that quite clearly worked for them and a history in international soccer. Yes, the United States Men's National Team has a long history in soccer that goes beyond almost every country that has won a World Cup or won a tournament. But no one knows, no one understands, that in correlation with leagues such as the American Soccer League and the North American Soccer League, the USMNT has been active and playing. In fact, it's a little-known fact that the first international game that was played outside of the United Kingdom in 1885 was in the United States when they hosted Canada in Newark, New Jersey. While it wasn't officially recognised by a governing body, it's recognised in the record books as a 'friendly' match, which is close to official considering it pre-dated FIFA, the Canadian soccer federation and the American soccer federation, and there was a match report in an early edition of the *New York Times*, which read:

CANADIANS THE VICTORS
THE PICKED AMERICAN FOOTBALL TEAM BEATEN
Some rough and a small score – the Stevens Institute
Boys defeat the Brooklyn Hill Club.
　　The football match yesterday between the champion elevens of Canada and of the United States, playing according to the American Association rules, on the grounds of the O.N.T Athletic Association, at East Newark, was one of the best contested games ever seen in

this neighbourhood. The Canadians won, but only after a hard fight. The play was very rough at times, so much so that the referee had to intervene several times. Once, two players indulged in a regular fist fight. The home team had been well selected and played well together, considering they had no practice as a team. About 2,000 people were present, some 60 of whom were ladies.

The ball was kicked off by the home team punctually at 3 o'clock. Both sides played up well and no advantage was scored until A. Gibson, of the Canadian team, got the ball near the touchline and dribbled it up to the goal posts and shot through. Several times after this the Canadians' goal was saved by McKendrick, who was ably assisted by Brubacher and Holden. The forwards of the mixed team did good service towards the latter part of the game but were unable to get the goal. The Canadians at the call of time having scored the only goal made. The two teams were as follows:

Canada – Goal – J. J McKendrick. Full-backs – A. Bowman, S. Brubacher. Half-backs – H. B Fraser, W. Malcolm. Forwards, Left-wings – J. M Palmer, W. A Lamporte. Right-wings – W. P Thomson, A. Gibson. Centres – T. Gibson, D. Forsyth (captain)

United States – Goal – Hughes. Full-backs – Holden, Lennox. Half-backs – Hood, Joseph Swithenby – Forwards, Left-wings – W. Turner, McGurck. Right-wings – Young, John Swithenby (captain). Centres – A. Turner, Lucas

Another newspaper, the *Toronto Globe,* said that 'the balance of the game was simply an exhibition of reckless kicking and rough and tumble play'. To make it more entertaining, a fistfight broke out during the game between players, and there were probably more punches thrown than shots at goal, but that's neither here nor there, the point is that the USMNT had made their start, although unofficially, in the world of soccer. Canada obviously won this slugfest of a match 1-0 in Newark, so a year later they decided to have a rematch in the same place, with the same teams and in front of (they'd hope) 2,000 more fans. The official scoreline varies depending on which historical report you read, with some claiming that the US won 1-0 and another claiming they won 3-2 with goals from McGurck, Chapman and John Gray (only John Gray was listed with a full name on one match report, with only five of the starting 11 being given full names). Either way, the US won. They had two games under their belt, with a win and a loss against the same opposition, and it could have been a good starting point to maybe have a few friendlies a year to boost support for a national team. Instead, the USMNT didn't play for another 30 years. Or at least that's what the records show, because their next game came against Sweden in 1916, just three years after the formation of the United States Soccer Federation.

The USMNT went on a short tour of Sweden and Norway in 1916 to boost awareness of soccer in the United States, and faced off against an All Star team in Stockholm, the Swedish national team and the Norwegian national side. The first game against the Stockholm All Stars finished 1-1 in front of 20,000 fans, before the USMNT embarked on their first fully recognised international match against a Sweden side selected by the Swedish Federation, with around 21,000 spectators believed to be in attendance, one of whom was King Gustav V, the King of Sweden, who died on the throne in 1950, 43 years after first being gifted the crown. It was pouring down with rain as the Americans' fast, strong and attacking style of play featured heavily in a 3-2 win, with goals from Thomas Swords, Charlie Ellis and a wonderful solo goal from Harry Cooper (you can tell it's professional, the players have full names now!), and so the official record for the USMNT in 1916 read: Played: 1, Won: 1. A 100 per cent record, even if technically that wasn't the case, but in professional and officially recognised games the USMNT were unbeaten. Two more exhibition games between the USMNT and All Star teams followed, with the USMNT losing one and winning one before moving their tour towards Norway to play their second official game. They travelled over to Kristiania – a place we now know as Oslo – on 3 September to face a Norway national side that had never actually won an international match (a year later the Norwegians would go on to lose 12-0 against Denmark, still their heaviest defeat to this day). The Americans lost a number of players due to injury and, without substitutions back then they just had to make do with a few less players , but nevertheless they kept the Norwegians at bay and managed to hold on to a 1-1 draw before setting sail back over to Sweden for one more exhibition match. For the USMNT, this would prove to be their final competitive fixture of the 1910s, with no more official matches played until the 1924 Paris Olympics, when the United States entered alongside 21 other nations to form the soccer tournament of that Olympics and the largest soccer competition until the 1982 World Cup, which hosted 24 nations.

One must remember that during this time period the ASL was into its third season and was slowly building a following in the United States, and both the ASL and governing USFA saw the 1924 Olympics as a great opportunity to show the world that they were treating the game with respect in regards to forming a competitive league, but also in producing the players capable of showcasing their talents and giving the ASL and American soccer a positive look on a grander, more notable, stage. Unlike most Olympic squads that America have put forward for Olympic soccer events, this 1924 squad was made up entirely of non-college players and all amateurs from the ASL. Four were playing for Fleischer Yarn at the time, five others were from Pennsylvania and three were from new Jersey, with five other states represented as well. While the majority of the squad hailed from the United States, a handful of players were born outside the country, with Irving Davis from Stourport-on-Severn in England, Arthur Rudd from Widnes in England, Carl Johnson from Gävleborg, Sweden, William Findlay from Musselburgh, Scotland, and Andy Straden from Bothwell in Scotland. Now, the ratio of American-born players in the 1924 Olympic squad was much higher than the 1930 World Cup, but perhaps one might argue that the ratio could explain why the team was so distinctly average in the tournament, despite getting off to a good start in their opening game against Estonia.

On 25 May 1924 the USMNT began their Olympic campaign against Estonia at Stade Pershing in Paris (the running track at Stade Pershing is still there today – at least it isn't a Duane Reades – and is just a 26-minute drive from the Eiffel Tower, if you were wondering) in front of 8,110 fans, and within the opening 15 minutes of play, the US took the lead through Straden from the penalty spot. Future 1930 World Cup member Jimmy Douglas was named man of the match in this round of 32 games, as Estonia peppered the US goal, but to no avail as the US ran out victors, albeit with a helping hand from their own rough tactics that clearly stuck by them from their clashes against Canada all those years ago. The victory meant that the USMNT would go on to face Uruguay in the next round of 16 games, a side who had just finished demolishing Yugoslavia 7-0, so the Americans were considered underdogs and rightly so judging by the scorelines. In front of 10,455 fans at the Stade Bergeyre (a stadium no longer in Paris, after it was knocked down in place of housing in 1926), could the Americans shock the Uruguayans with a win? They were in the lead for a matter of 10 minutes, but three first-half goals from the South Americans were enough to send them through and the Americans packing, but it wasn't all a negative for the Americans considering that Uruguay went on to win the 1924 Olympics – and the 1928 Olympics and the 1930 World Cup – and would only score fewer than three goals in one other game, so they did themselves proud when you consider they were all amateurs and were drafted into this makeshift squad with no practice or structure and the nation hadn't actually played a game for the past eight years. In fact, if that happened in modern soccer now, not only would it be impossible to qualify for a tournament without winning a game, but it would also be an incredible achievement. A bunch of amateurs won a game at an Olympics and weren't embarrassed by the eventual world champions. It was a platform to build on and with the addition of the ASL blossoming and the influx of cash that was being poured in, could this bring in new recruits who would be able to play for the national side? The 1924 Olympic team head coach, George Collins, pleaded with the USFA to introduce a fully fledged national team that would practice together and play exhibition matches, so they would be prepared for future tournaments. It must be noted that Collins was completely in love with soccer, as was most of the squad at the time, with Michael Lewis writing this in *The Guardian* about Collins:

> Collins, who wrote soccer columns in the Boston Globe, was named manager. He was soccer crazy himself. Once after breaking his leg, he played under the name George Mathews so his wife wouldn't worry about him.

Collins's pleas did nothing, as the USFA rejected his request of a full national squad, so they continued to play the odd friendly here and there, including a brief mini-tour of Europe following the Olympics when they would beat Poland 3-2 in Warsaw in June 1924, before falling to the Irish 3-1 in Dublin.

It would be almost a year before the USMNT would join up again and continue their regular series of games against Canada, with the first of two games in 1925 being another 1-0 victory in favour of the Canadians in Montreal. Ed McLaine grabbed the only goal of the game, but at the end of 1925 the US had the last laugh between the two, putting in a wonderful record-breaking performance in Brooklyn, New York. Five goals from Archie Stark – another member of the 1930 World Cup squad – helped the USMNT defeat Canada 6-1, which to this day remains one of their biggest and most dominant victories in their history. It would be another full year before the USMNT would meet up again, and once more it would be against Canada, their great rivals, this time in Ebbets Field, Brooklyn (for the sake of continuity, Ebbets Field does not exist anymore as a stadium, but the site is now an apartment complex – it's just a stone's throw away from Prospect Park and it definitely isn't a Duane Reades), where they battered the Canadians once again by a 6-2 scoreline. The Americans were improving and looking like a much more accomplished side, albeit playing against the same opposition and only playing five friendly games between the 1924 and 1928 Olympic Games, which wasn't an ideal situation, but it was all they could make do with without travelling to Europe or South America for tours. In fact, the lack of games and lack of different opposition didn't stand the Americans in good stead heading into the 1928 Games, and actually their slapdash approach with regards to forming a squad was, quite frankly, embarrassing. The USFA did not want to miss any major international tournaments after feeling that the 1924 Olympics had provided them with a good base to push soccer forward, and it provided them with a victory and, perhaps most importantly, a good reason to carry on with a USMNT. With FIFA still not fully creating the World Cup yet, the 1928 Olympic Games in Amsterdam were the only opportunity that the US had to show how far they had come in four years and decided that instead of picking the squad of players that had triumphed magnificently over Canada in the past few years and had chemistry from either playing with each other at club level in the ASL or with the national team itself, they would pick a younger cast of players. Perhaps adhering to the college/younger players ruling, the USFA picked a squad that ranged from a 19-year-old forward named Rudolph Kuntner to two 27-year-olds, Raymond Littley and John Lyons. Now, it's very likely that these 27 year olds weren't going to college, but a lot of the younger players were playing for youth clubs or at ASL clubs, while the older players were plying their skills down in the lower leagues of the American soccer pyramids and weren't considered ready for the Olympics. Now, that might be harsh to say of players who were selected for such a prestigious event, and it would be harsh if the selection process was worthy of a prestigious event, but it wasn't. It was terribly run by the USFA, and was met with criticism from those who advised the organisation on how to send a squad to the Olympics and actually told them not to throw a random team together at the last minute and to actually consider their selection. The USFA decided not to listen to any of the advice given to them and threw together a team at the last minute based on two trial sessions. There were no full team practices, or any games played in preparation, the team was just selected based on two very quick trial days and sent off to the Netherlands to play. Just as simple as that. No thought was put in to it, no training was done, they didn't even know if the members of the squad actually got along with each other and no one knew if they could play cohesively as a team! Of course, why on earth would planning and preparation matter when you have to play a strong nation such as Argentina in your first game, a team who were almost fully professional and very knowledgeable in the ways of how to win soccer matches. So, what could possibly go wrong? An unprepared US side facing an Argentina side who had the quality and capability to win the entire Games, what's the worst that could happen? It all culminated in one big pile of embarrassment for the United States as Argentina smashed 11 past them, and they could only muster up two goals (the first US goal was scored when Argentina were 6-0 up, the second was scored when the score was 10-1). To put it lightly, it was a complete and utter thrashing, and it was the least of what the US deserved for not taking the tournament seriously. The loss didn't gain all that much traction in the US, with the *Washington Evening Star* only publishing a short article on the matter in their May 30 edition:

US TEAM ELIMINATED FROM OLYMPIC SOCCER
Youth and inexperience, as represented by the United States soccer team, proved no match for the veteran Argentina eleven and the Americans fell easy victims to the South American champions, 11 to 2 yesterday. The United States were thus eliminated from the Olympic competition.

All it took was one game. One game for the USMNT to be eliminated from the Olympics, one game to be humiliated, one game for the federation to realise that they had made a huge error with their squad selection. One game that should have opened the eyes of the Americans to the fact that perhaps they weren't as good as they thought. Nevertheless, it was cause for reflection, which the USFA combated by sending the USMNT on a mini-tour of Europe, facing a bunch of clubs and Poland in a game that finished 3-3 in front of a figure believed to be around 10,000. With the domestic leagues in America slowly eating themselves alive with the Soccer Wars in the middle of its melting point, the USMNT was inactive in 1929, but the inactivity wasn't an issue, on the whole, as just a year on the 1930 World Cup was introduced and the United States was invited to travel down to Uruguay to compete, doing incredibly well to finish in third place (go back to chapter three if you want to recap that tournament before carrying on). The semi-final success for the USMNT remains the best finish by any CONCACAF (Confederation of North American and Caribbean Association Football) nation in any World Cup and the only time that a nation from outside Europe or South America has finished in the top three, which, given the talent that some parts of the world are blessed with, is still an amazing accomplishment. The nation was on the soccer map worldwide, and for a brief time other prominent nations started to keep an eye on the US. Perhaps they weren't going to win a World Cup in the near future, given the state their domestic system was in, but they had the ability to compete and could give anyone a game, which was all it took in international tournaments. If you remain competitive and put in the maximum effort alongside the talent that players such as Billy Goncalves had, the US were somewhat of a threat. Their follow-up friendly after the 1930 World Cup was against Brazil, which ended 4-3, but it epitomised what the Americans were all about. They never gave up and with Goncalves getting one and Bert Patenaude grabbing the other two, they had enough quality and worked hard enough to trouble Brazil. Of course, this wasn't the Brazil that would go on to dominate world football for years to come, but it certainly wasn't like the Americans were playing minnows from a far-off land, they were playing some of the most technically gifted players South America had to offer.

With no matches played in 1931 and no soccer tournament at the 1932 Olympics (the Los Angeles Olympic Committee decided against having soccer a few years prior, inspiring the formation and creation of the World Cup) and the Great Depression hitting soccer in the United States hard, the national team didn't play a single game until 1934 when the World Cup was played in Italy. Only this time the US had to play in a play-off game to earn qualification, with a match against Mexico played to determine who would enter the tournament as North American champions. With both nations arriving in Rome to play the game, many weren't sure how it would pan out. The Mexicans were technically better players, but the USMNT had kept a lot of their 1930 squad together and were faster, fitter and stronger. One player who was drafted into the squad primarily as a reserve but raised eyebrows in the training sessions was Aldo 'Buff' Donelli, who played for the Curry Silver Tops. 'Buff' was so good that Goncalves told the USMNT manager that if he wasn't put into the starting 11, he simply would not play. Being an amateur amongst a group of professionals, 'Buff' had to work that little bit harder to get noticed as he was shunned on the pitch and stuck out wide, unable to get the ball too often. However, the inclusion of 'Buff' would prove to be a masterstroke as a strong and experienced US side dispatched of the Mexicans in Rome 4-2, after he scored all four goals. Every goal was a sign of the talent he had, with his pace, shot power, trickery and spacial awareness all coming in to play to fool the Mexican defenders, with one defender getting sent off for trying to stop him. The USMNT had made it to their second consecutive World Cup and their fourth straight international soccer tournament, and all signs pointed towards this one being extremely positive, building on their impressive qualifying match and the third-place finish in 1930, but in rather controversial and occasionally hostile settings it wouldn't be the success that the United States had hoped for.

The 1934 World Cup was not without its controversies. From a sporting standpoint, it remains the only World Cup in history where the host nation had to qualify. From a political and reality standpoint, it had much larger implications and was a much more sinister World Cup than perhaps many realised. The fact of the matter is sport and politics are so heavily intertwined that many either do not see the link or refuse to see it. Certain clubs are linked with certain political parties, even though players and staff may not have a specific party they support, because of the area where that club is. For instance, Liverpool – the north-west of England has always been known as a working-class area of the country and some places wear that working-class tag as a badge of honour, something to be proud of, and Liverpool is no different, so Liverpool Football Club are primarily known as a Labour-supporting club. But, ironically enough, Liverpool FC was founded by a man by the name of John Houlding, who was a Conservative. Now, the point of relaying that story is that in the history of one of the most prestigious clubs in English soccer, politics played a huge part, although some fans may not realise this, or at least may not have as much knowledge about it as others, and the same goes for the 1934 World Cup in Italy, as most people are aware of the kind of regime Benito Mussolini ran in Italy at the time, but many aren't aware of what he did to promote his fascism during the World Cup. Italy was an uncertain place at the time of this World Cup and Mussolini wanted to show how dominant a team of Italians could be in a period when he was creating grand unity within his own country, and to essentially build an all-Italian empire was Mussolini's goal for the tournament. As Greg Lea says in the piece titled 'The Relationship Between Mussolini and Calcio' for *These Football Times,* it was more than just a game:

> Few have understood the power of football more than Benito Mussolini, the fascist leader of Italy between 1922 and 1943. Post-First World War Italy was an uncertain place; the economy, relatively slow to industrialise, was hit hard by the four-year conflict, and the transition towards a unified nation from the country's previous

existence as a patchwork of independent city-states still felt incomplete.

Mussolini's grand ambitions to make Italy a great power by restoring the grandeur associated with Ancient Rome and creating an empire that exhibited strength and significance on the world stage thus relied upon the construction of internal unity, and the dictator soon realised that football was the ideal vehicle to secure popular support for his nationalistic movement.

Mussolini understood the significance of hosting a world event, and just like Nazi Germany did in the 1936 Olympics, he used it as a vehicle to push his way of thinking and promote his line of fascism to the world. Mussolini had his stage, the biggest stage in the biggest sport on the planet, and he had his country at the forefront of it all. The Italian side actually had some world-class talent at the time, headlined by the famous and iconic Giuseppe Meazza – the very same Giuseppe Meazza who would have a stadium in Milan named after him, more commonly known as the San Siro – and were tipped to be one of the front-runners for the World Cup crown due to not only the talents of Meazza but also due to the home advantage. Normally home advantage just means the majority of the crowd are your fans or they travel with you extensively to cities you're more familiar with, but with allegations of corruption and rigging towards match officials in the quarter-final and semi-final in favour of the Italians, it gave 'home advantage' a new meaning. But while the Italians were expected to be front-runners and expected to essentially destroy all who came before them, who were the lucky 11 who were tasked with heading into Rome in front of a fascist leader and a team who were ready to be the best in the world? That's right, the amateurs from the United States of America! A team that was built primarily from amateurs and remaining 1930 stars such as Archie Stark (who scored a hat-trick against the USMNT in a warm up game for an ASL All Star team) were to go up against an Italian side that was expected to win, and win they did. Handsomely. The scoring was opened after just 18 minutes when Angelo Schiavio scored the first of his three goals before Raymundo Orsi scored two minutes later for the first of his double. At half-time the US were 3-0 down and looked like they had no chance of scoring, let alone getting a result out of the match, but surprisingly enough the first goal of the second half came from Aldo 'Buff' Donelli. Would it be the lifeline the US needed to get back into the game? Nope, because within 12 minutes of Donelli's goal, Italy were 6-1 up. Meazza added a seventh in the dying embers of the game to send the USA home after just one match, with their tails tucked firmly between their legs and their heads dropped to the floor. Another competitive soccer tournament, another embarrassing defeat. Was this the norm? Was the success in 1930 an anomaly? Was the US that far behind the rest of the world or was it down to poor planning from the USFA once again? Whatever the reason for this loss, it was another disappointing end to a competition even if they had deservedly lost to a far superior side, who would eventually go on a win the competition (although claims of match-fixing would stick around the Italians' victory for years and years), but in more ways than one this World Cup was a lesson to the US. Firstly, they learned that they had to pick their best professional players, or as close to professional as they could get as their leagues were disintegrating, and, secondly, it prepared them for the 1936 Berlin Olympic Games in more ways than one. It prepared them for the soccer tournament – with 1935 only having the USMNT play two games the entire year, both against Scotland in May and June, and both resulting in losses for the USA (1-5 in the first game, 1-4 in the second). It also allowed the amateurs to assemble for yet another trial game in Brooklyn, knowing this could be their chance to shine, but it also prepared the US for yet another political storm, one that would be remembered in history forever at the height of fascism and Nazism in Germany at the time.

Like Mussolini in the World Cup, Adolf Hitler wanted to use the Olympics as a platform to promote his anti-Semitic views and as a propaganda tool for his Nazi government, and many across the world who planned on sending their athletes to the games thought twice about attending, with the United States being one of them. Hitler had made it clear, via the Nazi's official newspaper *Volkishcer Beobachter,* that he did not want Jews or black athletes to compete. When he learnt about nations pulling out due to his comments, Hitler pulled back on his stance, and in an attempt to 'clean up' their look, many signs that read 'No Jews Wanted' were taken down from landmarks across the host city, although the German Ministry of Interior ordered the arrests of every Romani Gypsy prior to the games, with around 800 in total being arrested.

Avery Brundage, then a member of the United States Olympic Committee, was against a boycott, feeling that Jewish athletes were being treated fairly and believed that there was a 'Jewish-Communist conspiracy' implemented to keep the United States from entering the Games (Brundage went to Germany in 1934 to try to see whether or not Jews were being treated fairly, and found no evidence of their mistreatment, or so he was told by his Nazi translators, and he was said to have spoken with the Germans about his involvement with a sports club in Chicago that did not allow entry to those of the Jewish faith). Brundage found opposition from Jeremiah Mahoney, the president of the Amateur Athletics Union, who wanted to boycott the Games, claiming that the racial discrimination was against Olympic rules and regulations and that participation in the Games in Berlin would be akin to supporting the Third Reich. The United States eventually did not boycott the games, and when President Roosevelt didn't get involved with the debate, in keeping with a tradition of letting the Olympic Committee operate without outside influence, despite warnings from those around him that the Games were being used for Nazi propaganda, the Games were not boycotted and for the United States it actually proved to be quite a successful Olympics in terms of medals, finishing second in the medals table behind Germany. But while the boycott talks and debates were ongoing, the USMNT were still waiting to see whether they would compete at the Games. The governing body was struggling to raise enough funds to send the squad over to Berlin, but they did raise enough eventually, once the US had confirmed that they were going. Elmer Schroeder was appointed manager after his impressive work with the Philadelphia German-Americans (Schroeder was also against the boycott of the games and was eventually given a special award from the Reich for his efforts in not supporting a boycott). So while history will obviously tell us how important the 1936 Olympic Games was for the US and the entire world, how did the soccer team get on amongst yet another tournament overshadowed by fascism and political issues?

Drawn to play world champions and former World Cup opponents (and eventual winners of the 1936 Games) Italy, the US had the chance to inflict revenge on the side that had humiliated them to such a huge degree in the last World Cup. It was always going to be a tough game for the Americans, but despite falling to a 1-0 loss, it was a much better performance given the previous result and the fact they were playing the world champions. With seven of Schroeder's German-American's in the starting line-up, the Italians were made to wait until the 58th minute when Annibale Frossi, a midfielder who could play as a forward and registered over 120 games for Inter Milan from 1936 to 1942, scored the only goal of the game. One interesting point of the match was the sending off of Italian defender Pietro Rava, with various reports giving different accounts of what actually happened. The Italian almanac of soccer, known as *Illustrato Almanancco Del Calcio* reported that Rava was sent off in the 53rd minute, but the *New York Times* ran a report by the Associated Press that went along the lines of the following:

> Fiedler suffered torn ligaments in his knee when pushed roughly by Piccini of the rival team. Weingartner [the referee] 'put the thumb' on the Italian, ordering him from the game. Three times he tried to get Piccini to leave but finally gave up. A half dozen Italian players swarmed over the referee, pinning his hands to his side and clamping hands over his mouth. The game was formally finished with Piccini still in the line-up.

No one was really sure who was still on the pitch or if anyone got sent off at all, but one thing that was for certain in every report was the final scoreline, which was only brought about because of a mistake by the US. Charles Altemose made an error from a falling ball when he misjudged his own pass on the wet and damp surface, with goalscorer Frossi anticipating the mistake and taking full advantage of it. But the fact that the US lost wasn't as much of a negative as perhaps you'd have expected because, despite their early exit, their ability to take the game to a bunch of Italian players who were either very young Serie A players or just very good Serie A players and to take them to half-time at level pegging was a vast improvement from their last meeting. While the 1936 Olympic Games ended in an early disappointment for the Americans, it should have been cause for optimism. Once again, hard work and determination was favoured by the Americans over technical ability and flair, but it served them better than perhaps any other nation. Was it pretty? No. Was it efficient and effective? Absolutely (to a degree), which is why it suited the Americans. They weren't blessed with the talents that Italy and Uruguay had, but they were able to bridge the gap between the teams via their different style of play. But the efforts at the 1936 World Cup were in vain because of what was to follow.

The perfect opportunity to build the game of soccer in America had passed through the 20s and was about to pass through the 30s without any improvements made. Sure, the USMNT managed to reach a few World Cups and Olympics but with the exception of 1930 they never pulled up any serious trees. Losing just 1-0 to world champions Italy was a good result, but it wasn't anything to write home about, certainly not if you consider yourself to be a top soccer nation. The following year the US played Mexico in an unofficial friendly series, with the Mexicans winning four games out of four, scoring 22 goals in the process and conceding just eight. This was an embarrassment for the US, and little did they know that their 5-1 loss to Mexico in Mexico City would be their final game for a decade, until they next played Mexico again in Havana, when they lost 5-0 and played worse after 10 years without a game. Of course, the outbreak of the Second World War prevented any nation from fully competing, but you can't help but feel that the USMNT was on a downward spiral due to the condition of its own domestic league. The ASL had reformed at amateur level, meaning the United States did not have a professional soccer league. In fact, they would not have a professionally recognised league until the NASL in the 1960s, meaning there was a 30-year gap for the USA to bridge in order to become a soccer nation. England had multiple professional leagues in their Football League system, France had just implemented its own professional system and introduced Ligue 1 in 1932, 1929 saw the creation of La Liga in Spain, and Serie A in Italy was officially formed as a regional group system in 1898, but changed to the system we know today in 1929, meaning that three top nations had established first divisions at a professional level at the same time that the US's own pro league was disintegrating (just for further note, the Argentine Primera Division was formed in 1891, so when they played the US in these tournaments, they had years upon years of experiences as professionals). While US soccer was an anomaly in a time when soccer was flourishing across the globe, it was hardly failing through its own fault, as Dave Wagerin says in his book *Soccer in a Football World:*

> If, as some claim, the 1920s had produced American soccer's golden age, the 1930s represented an age of balsa wood: flimsy, fragile and not much to look at. But it had hardly been the sport to struggle through the penury of the decade. Baseball's attendances did not fully recover from the effects of the Depression until after the Second World War. Babe Ruth retired in 1935 and proved irreplaceable as an icon. Player salaries dropped to levels last seen in the early 1920s and poorer clubs from smaller cities flirted with bankruptcy. All manner of innovations were introduced in an effort to drum up interest. Some – the All Star game, floodlights and a

Hall of Fame – endured, though as late as 1934 radio broadcasts were still banned at certain clubs.

Professional football, still an uncertain prospect in the 1930s, also suffered badly, its image still tarnished in relation to the theoretically simon-pure collegiates. The Heisman Trophy, awarded annually to the nation's top college player, was instituted in 1936, but its first five winners all declined to turn professional. Very few NFL franchises made money, and the Depression all but wiped out the small-town teams (save for Green Bay, Wisconsin, whose Packers grew into a formidable success). The NFL, too, staged an All Star Game, pitting its league champions against a selection of top collegiates in an exhibition which often proved the biggest draw of the season. Attitudes began to change during the war, but it wasn't until the late 1950s that pro football seriously began to rival baseball for attention.

So while soccer was shooting itself in the foot with petty squabbling, poor performances and a lack of structure, at least it could take solace in the fact that it wasn't the only sport suffering. But regardless of what the other sports were doing, the fact of the matter was that soccer had officially left its golden age behind and was in serious need of improvements to the standard of its game, both domestically and internationally, if they were to become a force. After their 5-0 loss against Mexico in Havana and their 5-2 loss against Cuba (both fixtures played in the North American Nations Cup, a competition that only had four tournaments between 1947 and 1991, with America failing to win one against Cuba, Mexico and Canada), the Americans had to prepare for the 1948 Olympics in London, being drawn up against Italy. Again. With many grounds such as White Hart Lane, Highbury, Wembley, Selhurst Park, Craven Cottage and Griffin Park used in London to host the soccer tournament, it would be the latter of the venues that would play host to Italy vs America in Brentford, West London, and they would be treated to a far different affair from the 1-0 meeting the last time. It wouldn't be as tight a game, nor would it be as competitive, because the nine goals in the game would all go into one net. The Americans' net. The game finished 9-0 to the Italians, and it was still more of the same story. The team was formed via trials and training sessions, once again not having a full practice session as a squad. Originally, the US were due to play Poland in the opener, but with the Europeans pulling out at the last minute it meant that Italy were drafted in as their opponents in either a flash of dumb luck or fate. The Americans managed to keep it level for two whole minutes when Francesco Pernigo opened the scoring, the first of his four goals on the day. Adone Stellin scored a penalty a quarter of an hour before the second-half onslaught began. Angelo Turconi and Emilio Caprile ended with a goal apiece, while Emidio Cavigioli scored twice in the 72nd and 87th minute, before four goals in the final three minutes ended what was an embarrassment of a match for the USMNT. Losing is one thing, losing to world champions is one thing too, but to lose 9-0? The USMNT were a bunch of amateurs, and the scoreline showed it; however, the USSFA didn't quite see it that way. Actually, they were quite proud of the Olympic showing, as this statement shows:

> Naturally, that 9-0 score is discouraging, but the USSFA should be proud of the US Olympic soccer team. All of them conducted themselves as gentlemen and sportsmen and made many friends for the United States in London and the other places they visited ... If at all possible, the US Olympic team should be assembled several weeks prior to sailing so that combination play could be developed. Our team can compete on an equal basis with most of the countries entered in the Olympics but we must give the team a chance to practice as a unit.

On one hand, it's a positive that they recognised the need to actually train as a team and prepare like professionals, on the other hand it's incredible that they can draw any positives from being battered 9-0. It would be a landmark moment in some regards for the US, because it was one of three games that will be remembered in the history books in US soccer. The 9-0 loss against Italy was game number one, the one where it became blatantly obvious that things needed to change and the way the organisation operated needed change in order to bring the US to prominence in world soccer. Game number two came just a few days after the Italian defeat and the game is, as of 2018, still the heaviest defeat the USMNT have ever suffered. The 9-0 was bad, but when Norway defeated the US 11-0 in Oslo it was a disaster. In front of 25,000 fans in the Norwegian capital, Gunnar Thoresen grabbed a hat-trick and the wonderfully named Odd Wang Sorensen went two better than his compatriot and scored five, with a double from Jan Sordahl and the solitary Gunnar Dahlen goal wrapping up proceedings. The US were at the bottom of the barrel at this point, having not won a game since 17 July 1930, which was their 3-0 victory over Paraguay in the World Cup. A 14-game winless run spanned 18 years (albeit the Second World War intervened), with multiple hammerings and first-round exits in competitions. Another loss against Northern Ireland followed (just 5-0 this time), but three wins against Israel ended their losing streak, although only one of the wins was declared official (26 September 1948 at the New York Polo Grounds). A 3-2 win against Israel ended the USMNT's adventures in 1948 before they started their attempt at qualification for the 1950 World Cup, although an unofficial friendly against Scotland didn't fill anyone with confidence after a 4-0 drubbing on Randall's Island. If that didn't fill the fans and players with confidence, then a 6-0 defeat against Mexico in a World Cup qualifier certainly didn't, but the 1-1 draw with Cuba in Mexico City at least gave the US some hope heading into their final two games. First up was another game against Mexico, and this time the US actually scored. Twice, in fact. The only problem was, they conceded six again. One game down, one more to go, and the task was simple. They had to beat Cuba. If they didn't beat Cuba, they'd miss out on their first World Cup (side note: the US didn't compete at the 1938 World Cup, but withdrew during the qualification process, along with every other Americas nation other than Cuba, so technically the 1950 World Cup would have been the first World Cup the US would have missed while actually trying to qualify for it). So with the pressure on, could the US do it? Absolutely they could, beating Cuba 5-2 and officially booking their place in the 1950 World Cup. This World Cup was the first post-Second World War World Cup and was bound to throw up controversies and historical moments, but not even the most optimistic of soccer fans, players or governing bodies could have imagined what was about to happen to the United States. While various opponents across Europe and South America didn't attend the tournament for different reasons, there was still low expectation on the shoulders of the Americans. Germany was still occupied by the allied forces at this time and they weren't readmitted into FIFA until September 1950, as was the case with Japan (East Germany wasn't admitted into FIFA until 1952, meaning no part of Germany was entered). Italy qualified as champions, although there were some question marks over their participation due to their involvement with the Nazi's in the Second World War, and likewise with Austria, but both were allowed to participate. The Soviet Union, Czechoslovakia and Hungary did not enter, while outside of Europe, Argentina, Ecuador and Peru did not enter. India cited lack of funds to travel to Brazil and the prioritisation of the Olympics over the World Cup as their reason not to go, while France also cited the amount of travelling as a reason to pull out after the group-stage draw, leaving just two groups of four, one group of three and one group of two. Of all the nations involved, only one was making its debut in the competition: England. Crucially, the home nations of England, Scotland, Wales and Ireland were invited by FIFA, with England committing to playing in the tournament even if they finished second in the home nations group, but Scotland insisted on only competing if they won the home nations. As fate would have it, the Scots finished second, and despite attempted persuasion from England star Billy Wright Scotland stayed at home and England were the only home nation at the World Cup that year. England, perhaps the nation who could rightly be considered the most traditional of soccer nations at this World Cup, were considered favourites due to the talent they had amongst their ranks. Led by their big three of captain Billy Wright, Tom Finney and Stanley Matthews, England had others players like future England manager Alf Ramsey, future Tottenham Hotspur manager Bill Nicholson, Newcastle legend Jackie Milburn, Matthews's partner-in-crime at Blackpool Stan Mortensen and many more. England were the favourites even if it was their first crack at a World Cup. In the group-stage draw they were handed a group that some would have considered 'easy', which included Spain, Chile and ... the United States. Finally, the US had avoided the dreaded Italians, but they'd been drawn against the favourites instead! It just wasn't meant to be, because there was surely no way that the Americans, filled with amateurs, could defeat a star-studded England line-up? Well, this time was different for the United States. Yes, they may have been amateurs with other jobs and other life commitments, but the USSFA had learnt from last time, and they made adequate changes. Many of the players in the World Cup squad played in the qualification campaign, while training sessions were organised to improve team chemistry and matches were played against select-XIs to improve game management and performance. They had the right planning, they kept a core group of players together and were heading into the World Cup as a unit. It was like someone at the USSFA had actually had that lightbulb moment in understanding how soccer works, and while they weren't expected to win every game, one win would be enough (and a drastic improvement in performances) to consider the 1950 World Cup a success.

First up for the US was Spain, a powerful outfit who were expected to romp through with ease, but they were dealt a shock when the USMNT took the lead via Gino Pariani when he shot past a couple of Spanish defenders to give them an advantage. They were so, so close to winning the game as well, but with ten minutes to go a dreadful mistake from Charlie Colombo allowed Spain to counter and equalise. After the equaliser, the

American backline crumbled and Spain scored two more to make it 3-1, but the scoreline was deceiving. The Americans may have suffered a heart-breaking loss, but nevertheless it was an improvement. In all honesty, no one expected a win or a good performance for their next game against England, but what happened next would turn out to be not only the greatest win in the US's World Cup history, or the most embarrassing defeat in England's World Cup history, but one of the most iconic moments in the entire history of international football.

The game was played on 29 June 1950 in Belo Horizonte, Brazil. England, dubbed the 'Kings of Football' across the world, were expected to roll through Brazil and win the entire World Cup at the first time of asking, such was the sheer strength of their squad. In their first game, England breezed past Chile with a comfortable 2-0 win, all without their star man Stanley Matthews, who was on a 'goodwill' tour of Canada at the time of the tournament and plans were arranged to have Matthews fly to Brazil in time for the second group game against the Americans. Ultimately Matthews made it back in time, but, despite the pleas from England manager Walter Winterbottom, the selection committee decided not to pick Matthews for the second game, citing their idea that a winning team should never be changed as the reason. England, who weren't used to cramped changing rooms and felt that the game against the US would be similar to the Chile match, decided to rest a few players in order to keep the squad fresh for the later rounds, obviously playing under the assumption that they would easily qualify once the US game was said and done. The Americans, on the other hand, were the total opposite. Many expected them to not only lose, but to lose heavily, including the local fans who showed up wanting to see barrels of goals. The group of amateurs played to win and had a fighting mindset after the opening game against Spain, and they were prepared to give everything they had to England, even if it meant going down in defeat. 'We were still really feeling pretty good about ourselves because we had really scared the hell out of Spain,' said Harry Keough, a member of the USMNT 1950 World Cup squad. 'Then we had another two and a half days in between to play England, so we certainly didn't entertain any ideas that we were going to beat them! But we figured we could give them a battle for the win.'

Even the Americans thought that while they were prepared to fight until they couldn't fight any more, there was no chance they could actually beat England. With reported odds of 500/1 to win the entire tournament, not many people gave the US a chance to even get a draw at the World Cup, and the players were under no illusions. It's not that they expected to get thrashed, but they certainly didn't expect to win. The thought process of both sides didn't change much, even after kick-off and a few chances. The USA were defending for their lives, the English were creating chance after chance, and shots went wide, over or were saved by American goalkeeper Frank Borghi, who had the game of his career. The fans soon started to realise that even if the English kept pressing, the US were not going to roll over and let England win. But the course of the game completely changed in the 37th minute when Walter Bahr's shot was met by the glancing head of the Haitian-born New Yorker playing up front for the Americans, Joe Gaetjens. The US had taken the lead. They had not only scored, but they had taken the lead. At the half-time break they went in ahead and thought that England would eventually score. They always score. Chance after chance, miss after miss, let-off after let-off for the US, who hung on bravely to shock the world and steal a famous, incredulous and incredible 1-0 victory over the World Cup favourites. The United States, who had a mailman, hearse driver, dishwasher, a teacher and a knitting machinist in their ranks, had done the impossible in Brazil, in perhaps the most 'Hollywood' World Cup match you're ever likely to see (more fittingly, the most 'Hollywood' World Cup match you'll hear about because while the match was filmed from behind one goal, Gaetjens's goal wasn't recorded on film, nor were any clear pictures taken. Even more fittingly, a novel and film was made about this game called *The Game of their Lives,* starring Gerard Butler and Patrick Stewart). The *Daily Express* wrote at the time that 'it would be to give the US three goals of a start', such was the unlikely nature of them even scoring, let alone winning. When listeners of BBC radio heard the full-time result on a bulletin the next morning, most assumed it was a mistake and went about their lives thinking that England had won. The *New York Times* had received a wire report of the result but just ignored it because they thought it was a hoax, that someone was lying for a headline. The English reacted well, according to Keough and Bahr, with the latter saying in an interview with *The Guardian,* 'I admired the players. They shook our hands. They did not say anything like "you lucky bastards". The dream of a World Cup run soon ended for both teams after this result as England crashed out embarrassed against Spain, while Chile defeated the US, but the headlines were already about the US and how they managed to pull off the biggest upset the World Cup has ever seen. This quote from Bahr in *The Guardian* perhaps sums up the match and situation more than anything else could:

> The perfect game is to win and to play well. We won, but we certainly did not outplay England. It was one of those games where the best team does not win. I am proud of it, because we had a decent team. But if we played England 10 times, they would have won nine of them.

He was right. They had improved, but no one knew then that this would be the last time the United States would appear in a World Cup until 40 years later at Italia '90. The desired effect of the 1950 World Cup did not pan out quite as many had expected. The *New York Times* dedicated just two paragraphs to the win, whereas in this day and age it would take up entire back pages of sports sections and would be all over social media and television, but that was the nature of the beast that soccer was up against. A bunch of amateurs had just beaten perhaps the best team in the world and no one cared, or at least no one in the media cared. The team's results didn't improve much after that, with just one win in the four years following the

Astor Place, New York City. The building in Manhattan where the ASL was formed

US team group: (back row, l-r) coach Bob Millar, unknown, Jimmy Gallagher, Alexander Wood, Jimmy Douglas, George Moorhouse, Ralph Tracy, Andy Auld, unknown; (front row, l-r) Jim Brown, Billy Gonsalves, Bert Patenaude, Tom Florie, Bart McGhee

1930 World Cup. Photographers race across the pitch to get pictures of the US team as they form a huddle

(Left-right) Belgium's Nicolas Hoydonckx is challenged by the US's Bert Patenaude in the 1930 World Cup

Pele officially signs for the Cosmos amid a media frenzy

Pele always loved New York, and enjoyed walking around Central Park, even in his own jersey

Pele and President Gerald Ford – when you can get the President of the United States doing keepie-uppies, you know you've done something good

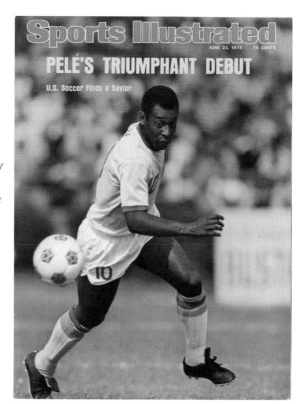

Sports Illustrated very rarely put soccer stars on their front cover, but couldn't resist the fame of a certain Brazilian in New York

New York Cosmos line up. One of the most formidable line-ups in US soccer history with Pele front and centre, Giorgio Chinaglia behind and Franz Beckenbauer lurking at the back

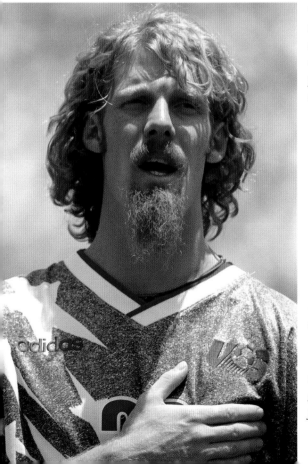

George Best always brings a certain amount of celebrity to wherever he goes, never missing a photo opportunity with soccer-mad Elton John

One of the most iconic things to come out of USA '94 was the denim US kit and the wild-looking Alexi Lalas, giving us an iconic look for the ages

Romario was arguably the best player in the world at the time, Lalas had never played a professional game of soccer before the World Cup. Here they are battling for the same ball in USA '94

Perhaps the most iconic image in all of Women's soccer, Brandi Chastain lets out all of her emotion as she wins the 1999 women's World Cup on penalty kicks

Perhaps the moment that changed MLS forever, David Beckham holding up his LA Galaxy shirt on his unveiling, a moment that beamed across the world

Landon Donovan in tears as he scores the last-minute winner in the final group game of the 2010 World Cup to send the US top of their group ahead of England

Proving that they are the dominant force in women's soccer yet again, the USWNT hold the 2015 World Cup aloft, with this being their third triumph

Welcome to Zlatan. Zlatan Ibrahimovic after scoring an incredible volley on his Galaxy debut in the first LA derby against newly-formed LAFC

A moment in US soccer history. Columbus Crew fans starting their 'SaveTheCrew' movement against Toronto FC, a movement which successfully prevented the culture of team relocations entering into modern day MLS

England win, with two wins coming in two days against Haiti in 1954. After those two wins, the US didn't win again until March 1965 against Honduras, beating them by the familiar scoreline of 1-0. The barren days of US soccer had hit the national team hard, and despite their best efforts in 1950 it could not save the sport from the downward spiral it was on. No major professional league meant there was no concrete pipeline for better players, meaning results suffered massively. They consistently faced off against better opposition in Mexico and occasionally Canada in CONCACAF qualification, which, at the time, only had one spot open that usually went to Mexico, but on one occasion went to Haiti in 1974. Multiple friendlies were played, multiple friendlies were lost and most of the losses were by heavy scorelines.

Mexico beat them 6-0 and 7-2 in the space of 21 days in 1957, while England inflicted a terrible 8-1 defeat on them in 1959, which included a hat-trick from Bobby Charlton, who was on his road to full recovery just one year after the tragic Munich air crash that took the lives of many of Charlton's team-mates at Manchester United. The Americans actually took the lead in this game after eight minutes when Eddie Murphy (no, not *that* Eddie Murphy) opened the scoring, but the lead only lasted until 35 minutes in, and with the scores level at half-time it looked to be a positive result until England turned on the style. England once again turned on the style against the US in May 1964 when they went even better and won 10-0, with Liverpool legend Roger Hunt scoring four goals and Blackburn's Fred Pickering getting a hat-trick (Pickering only earned three caps for England, but scored five goals, with the majority of them coming in this game). Four years prior to this game the US had managed to get a draw with Mexico, 3-3, in a World Cup qualifying match, which had ended a run of six defeats that spanned over six years.

Their 1-0 win against Honduras in 1965 was their first win since 1954 and their first clean sheet since the same game against Haiti, and whereas their next win against the Haitians came in 1968 in a friendly, it would be the same nation that would block the US's path to reaching the 1970 World Cup Finals, their best chance in an entire generation. Coached by the familiar face of Phil Woosnam, the USSFA allowed him to pick the squad, and he was the first coach to do so after the selection committee took a step back. With the NASL slowly growing around the same time as the 1970 World Cup qualifiers began, there was a period of renewed optimism surrounding the national team. Mexico had already qualified due to the host nation rule, so the US had one less opponent to get through – which just happened to be the one team they couldn't beat – and they had a coach who had been successful with the Atlanta Chiefs and was allowed to pick his own teams. With no Mexico to face, the task was simple. Beat Bermuda and Canada (who were in the US's group) and you'll more than likely reach the World Cup Finals. The campaign began with a disappointing 4-2 loss north of the border against Canada, which immediately set the USMNT on the wrong path. Canada had opened their campaign with a 4-0 win over Bermuda, which saw them unbeaten at the top of the group, but a surprising 0-0 between Canada and Bermuda allowed the US a chance to grab a foothold back in the group, and they did just that when a goal from German-born Dietrich Albrecht was enough to give America all three points and the chance to finish top of the group with two wins over Bermuda.

Two games, two wins. That's all they needed to reach the qualifying play-off, and two wins was exactly what they delivered. A 6-2 win on 2 November 1968 in Kansas City was soon followed by a comfortable 2-0 win away from home, leaving the Americans with one team left to face to earn the right to compete at their first World Cup since 1950. That team? Haiti. In their past five meetings, the US had won three and had the slight upper hand heading into the play-off games, but the upper hand that the US had was almost immediately stripped from them when rumours of discontent and dissent from the squad emanated following dissatisfaction over payments and, the biggest shock of all, the departure of Woosnam as manager, who was leaving the team to focus on saving and popularising the NASL. All the confusion and upheaval left the US team confused and disorientated, like a boxer who had been hit by a sucker punch that no one had anticipated. Just like the boxer, the team knew what they had to do and they knew they could do it, but because of the unexpected sucker punch they were thrown off their own game plan. The Haitians took full advantage of the confusion and won both ties 2-0 and 1-0, and in what seemed like the blink of an eye the best chance the United States had to qualify for a World Cup was gone. They had done so well to get into the play-off position in the first place but, through no fault of their own, it was all undone over two games. Could it have been a turning point in US soccer? Almost certainly, because the 1970 World Cup would prove to be iconic.

It was the first World Cup televised in colour and it grasped the imagination of millions of fans, young and old. Imagine if the US had qualified and pulled off another shock victory like they had done in 1950? The win against England was considered iconic yet no one has ever seen the goal because it wasn't filmed, now imagine the reaction if people watched it live in vibrant colours and were able to see it with their own eyes instead of just reading about it the newspaper. The effect it could have had on the sport was huge, but instead of improving soccer in the United States, the play-off loss seemed to really get the USMNT down in a funk, because that second leg against Haiti in 1969 was their last game until 1972, when they played Canada in another World Cup qualifier (they lost 3-2 and finished bottom of their group with one point). Another World Cup was missed but the USSFA decided to show that they had improved their planning and strategy, introducing an intensive friendly schedule in 1973, with 12 games played. But like most things in the United States at the time, it didn't quite go to plan. Most of the players didn't know each other, they lost their opening three games, the ASL and other amateur leagues had to lend them players because the NASL refused to send players out, the players who joined up for the first wave of friendlies were drastically unfit because the outdoor season hadn't officially started yet, and the manager, Walt Czychowycz, publicly complained to the media that selecting squads on a few days' notice with only largely amateur players available was 'no way to prepare for international matches.' However, they won their first-ever game on Canadian soil thanks to another goal from Albrecht. Czychowycz was asked to take only half the squad to California to face Poland, so players based there had to take up some of the spots, meaning he had half a squad of players he'd never met before (Poland won 4-0, unsurprisingly). They then beat Bermuda before losing to Mexico, Haiti and Israel, and they lost Czychowycz as manager because he dared to suggest the idea of having a full-time coach for the national team instead of a part-time one from the NASL (the federation sacked poor Walt in favour of Gordon Bradley, the Cosmos manager who would be in charge for the final three losses). Sound simple enough? Well, all of this mess made a 3-0-9 record in the many friendlies, but what was gained out of all of this? Well, people realised that despite thinking they were good at preparation, the USSFA was not good at it at all.

They needed a new manager once Bradley went back to the Cosmos and appointed Dettmar Cramer, a German coach who had built a reputation for being able to outthink any opposing manager after his Japan side defeated Argentina in the Tokyo Olympics, and he was one of the assistant managers for West Germany in the 1966 World Cup. Cramer was only in charge of the US for two games, which they lost, both against Mexico, and subsequently left to return home to Germany, managing Bayer Munich to two European Cups and earning the praise of Franz Beckenbauer, who referred to him as 'The Footballing Professor'. So 1974 ended as it had begun, under a cloud of disappointment, a culture of losing and no way forward. The next positive result came in 1976 in a World Cup qualifying game against Canada (a 1-1 draw) and then again in October of the same year, once again against Canada (2-0). Between September 1976 and November 1976, the USMNT only lost once (against Mexico, of course), but while it would be easy to twist that as a huge positive, they could only manage one win in that whole run, and that 2-0 win against Canada wasn't just the only win, it was also the only two goals they scored in the entire run! Eventually, as Al Miller was moved out of the role as full-time manager of the national team, the now USSF (United States Soccer Federation) decided to follow the lead set by the NASL and tried to lure a world-class, big-name foreign coach to take on the job. No one was surprised when they failed in this task, so they reappointed former boss and the man who was sacked for suggesting that they even have a permanent manager in the first place, Walt Czychowycz, and he was tasked with qualifying for the 1978 World Cup. Of course, they failed to qualify and broke their unfortunate streak of attending soccer competitions hosted by dictatorships.

Fixtures against more prominent nations were how the US ended the 1970s, with games against Switzerland, Portugal, France and the Republic of Ireland coming up against the likes of Michel Platini, Chris Hughton and Steve Heighway. After missing out on a place at the 1978 World Cup, the US had three issues on their agenda heading into 1979 and later into the 1980s. Firstly, they had to qualify for the 1980 Olympics, then the 1979 Pan-American Games and prepare for the 1982 World Cup in Spain. Starting off with Olympic qualification, it was all for nothing as a boycott of the Games in the Soviet Union led to the US teams not taking part in the competition, so while the Olympics were out of the window (mainly for political reasons more than anything sporting, as it was a tense time in the Cold War) the Pan-American Games gave the US a good opportunity to test themselves. The Pan-American Games, colloquially known as the Pan-Am, served as preparation for the Olympics as nations from North, Central and South America would compete against each other in the year before an Olympic Games, with the 1979 edition pitting the United States up against the likes of Brazil, reigning world champions Argentina, and Cuba. The United States had to field the youngest team of the tournament (average age of 20 years) due to the NASL's lack of co-operation by not allowing players to be released for the competition. With their band of youth amateurs, the US won group C after beating both Puerto Rico and the Dominican Republic, but finished bottom of their second-round group, losing to Cuba and Argentina (they conceded nine goals and scored a whopping zero). Rather than play their fifth-place match against Puerto Rico, the US just abandoned the tournament and set their sights on the 1982 World Cup. So, their agenda of the Olympics, Pan-Am Games and the 1982 World Cup was slowly going down the pan, with just one target left to aim for.

The Olympics was out of the USMNT's control, and the Pan-Am tournament could've been much, much worse, so hopes were somewhat high for their 1982 qualification group. But with the same format as the last World Cup qualifying campaign, the US knew what they needed to do: finish second and you'll reach the play-off, lose and you'll be out once again. The campaign didn't start as they had hoped, drawing 0-0 with Canada before two losses in a row against Canada again and then Mexico, leaving them in a perilous position. The US needed Canada to beat Mexico then beat Mexico themselves to be in with a chance of qualifying, but when Canada and Mexico could only draw against each other, the US were out. Their eventual 2-1 win against Mexico, their first against their rivals since 1934, was for nothing, and another chance to test themselves had gone. Nevertheless, while they struck out with their three targets from 1979 to 1982, the 1986 World Cup was going to be *the* time that the United States made a World Cup. The USSF had finally implemented a strong strategy of giving the USMNT friendlies to test themselves and to train together in preparation for big games, such as the 1986 qualifiers, but what made this World Cup so special? Well, Mexico had been brought in to host the competition after Colombia's withdrawal, meaning that the US didn't have the face their rivals, just like in 1970. Interestingly enough, the United States could actually have hosted the tournament themselves. The *New York Times* ran a piece about the new host nation, and the following extract shows they thought the United States had a chance at hosting:

COLOMBIA WON'T BE CUP HOST

The Colombian government dropped out yesterday as the host country for the 1986 international soccer tournament, the World Cup, thus opening the door for the United States, Canada or Brazil to take over the championship ... Brazil is viewed as the leading competitor of the United States for the World Cup nomination, and the current president of FIFA, Joao Havelange, is a Brazilian. The difficulties of the North American Soccer League are also viewed as a mark against any United States efforts. The NASL has dropped from 24 clubs to 12 clubs, with attendance no longer growing.

With rising tension in the NASL and the league suffering from growing expenses and over-expansion, the United States wasn't seen to have as strong a soccer 'heritage' as Brazil or other South American countries, but they had the infrastructure to host the competition and had US Secretary of State Henry Kissinger involved in the bidding process alongside New York Cosmos head honcho Steve Ross – who had gained support from his Cosmos stars Pelé and Franz Beckenbauer – but it would all fall on deaf ears because FIFA President Havelange selected Mexico to host the competition. Some suggested that due to FIFA's ties with Mexican media giant *Televisa* they had swayed the FIFA voting with various monetary offers. Mexico, United States and Canada were the final three nations, and despite Kissinger gaining support from President Ronald Reagan and Congress, despite Havelange admitting that the US and Canada had better presentations, and despite an official claiming that the Mexican bid was 'a joke', Mexico became the first team to host two World Cups, but while the US didn't get the World Cup, it allowed them to plan thoroughly and effectively for future World Cup bids.

Nevertheless, with Mexico out of the qualification picture, it was down to Canada and the US to fight it out again for that one CONCACAF spot. Such was the climate of soccer in the United

States at the time, it's not unfair to suggest that the future of the game rested on the shoulders of the USMNT. The NASL had folded and the MISL was just starting, but with a very small following, while the World Cup had become the largest sporting event on the planet and an appearance would've almost certainly boosted the scene in the country. Maybe not by much, but hypothetically it could have been massive. The campaign really started as the NASL's Team America, which was a complete disaster, but the official World Cup qualifying campaign started with a two-leg affair with the Dutch Antilles in 1984, coming out with a 0-0 draw and a 4-0 win. Fast forward a few months to May 1985, and the US followed up with two wins against Trinidad and Tobago and a draw away against Costa Rica, meaning that the United States needed just one win at home against Costa Rica and a play-off win to qualify. On paper, it seemed like an easy task. Get the job done at home like you had done against Trinidad and Tobago, and you'll be one step away and will be heroes to the soccer fans, who needed an injection of inspiration. But with a squad made up almost entirely of indoor soccer players, and a huge Costa Rican following in the States, America failed. Another heart-breaking 1-0 defeat meant that the United States were out and had failed to make the grade once again.

But with failure comes lessons, and the lessons were learnt by the Americans, who immediately set about planning how to reach the next World Cup in 1990. Between the two World Cup qualifying campaigns, the US played nearly 20 games and only won three times, but the 1990 qualifiers would change US soccer on the international stage in a positive way for the first time since either 1930 or 1950 (pick whichever one you like). With the US entering the campaign with a first-round bye (Canada, Honduras, El Salvador and Mexico also received byes due to their FIFA standings), meaning their two wins against Jamaica put them in the final group stage, finishing second to Costa Rica. They lost just once in their eight games (against Costa Rica, of all teams) and seemingly perfected the art of winning games by the odd goal or so, with their wins being

1-0, 2-1, 1-0, 1-0 (even their draws were low scoring, with their three draws being 1-1, 0-0 and 0-0). Exciting perhaps wasn't the right word to describe this US team, but they tapped into exactly what their successful predecessors had done in the past – they played with passion, they worked harder than the opposition and they never gave up. Were they always going to blow teams away with impressive soccer in 4-0 wins? No, but they always got the job done and had managed to make history doing it that way. The United States were finally going to the World Cup and, in somewhat ironic fashion, it was in Italy, the one nation who always had America's number in the early days of the USMNT.

Italia '90 became *the* World Cup for an entire generation of fans, and the United States had picked the perfect time to improve as a national team. To add to the irony, the US were drawn against hosts Italy, and with a squad of young, emerging players like goalkeeper Tony Meola, John Harkes, Tab Ramos, Peter Vermes, Eric Wynalda and Kasey Keller to name just a few, and with the oldest player in the squad being 27, it was a team looking towards the future. And in the nicest way possible, this was the most relevant soccer had been in America since the NASL days of Pelé, and, while not many expected much from such a young team, it brought modern soccer into modern America at a time when Larry Bird and Magic Johnson took the NBA to a whole new level, baseball had stars like Ken Griffey Jr making his debut, Don Mattingly was the Yankees captain and *The Simpsons* episode 'Homer at the Bat' was being made (it had a huge cultural effect on MLB and the show). Joe Montana had just beaten John Elway in Super Bowl XXIV, and sport was dominating the headlines, but soccer only had one shot to even come close to reaching those heights and Italia '90 was it. Led by Bob Gansler, the US headed into their first match against the Czechoslovakians with mixed feelings. As Peter Vermes said in an interview on MLS.com:

> ... we were all very excited to be there, but the makeup of the group was not 'happy to be there' type of guys. The

makeup of the group was very much in line with seeing
if we could upset the apple cart, if you will.

And while the attempt to upset was there, maybe it was a
tournament too soon for this particular set of players. Tab
Ramos, who was 23 at the time of the 1990 World Cup, said in
the same interview:

> I think we were, in general, so naive at the time, that
> we were just going to play the games. I mean, we didn't
> necessarily think we were going to lose the games. We
> were just there to compete and sort of see what happens.
> I know personally – I can't speak for all the guys on the
> team – but for me personally, I was in awe of the players
> that I was playing against. Here I was playing against
> guys that I used to see on TV. That, for me, was a treat.

The first game showed those mixed feelings and uneasy
thoughts, because the United States got taught a tough lesson.
Perhaps they underestimated quite how intense the tournament
was going to be (a fair assessment given their lack of competitive
fixtures at a high level for both club and country), or they were
just simply outclassed, and there isn't much more to it, but
when you lose 5-1 in your opening game, it's going to hurt. You
can find a highlights package on YouTube of the game, and
throughout the 1 minute 52 second clip you can see where the
US went wrong. The Czechs were always one step quicker than
them, knew how to exploit a wide-open defence and took their
chances, although Paul Caligiuri's goal was a good example of
an efficient counter-attack, even if it was a case of too little, too
late with the score being 3-0, and America being down to 10
men, courtesy of Wynalda's sending off, when he pulled one
back. It was a 5-1 drubbing because the US were outclassed,
but, as this group of players had done in recent years, they
learnt from it and understood what needed to change for their
next match against hosts and undoubted favourites Italy, who
were loaded with stars such as Gianluca Vialli, Carlo Ancelotti,

Roberto Mancini, Roberto Donadoni, Walter Zenga, top scorer of the tournament Salvatore 'Toto' Schillaci, Ciro Ferrara, Giuseppe Bergomi, Paolo Maldini, Franco Baresi and led by their curly haired diamond Roberto Baggio, one of the biggest stars in world soccer at the time.

Yes, the Americans were there to enjoy themselves, but they were there to compete and to put in a performance or two that they could be proud of, and when they played the Italians it was a far better showing than they had shown the game before. Granted, it wasn't a million miles better defensively – as shown by the Italy goal and penalty that was missed – but overall it was better. If not for a magnificent save from Zenga, the US might have stolen a point from this game and could have had the shock of the tournament, but when an Italian side takes a 1-0 lead early on, it's nigh on impossible to get a foothold back in the game. While the Americans may have been knocked out with that loss to Italy, they certainly weren't downhearted because they had kept the Italians to just one goal, and it was by another one-goal margin that they lost by in their final group game against Austria, as the Austrians took the win in group A's dead-rubber game. Again, when you watch parts of the game back you realise just how quick the Austrians were to loose balls, demonstrated by Andreas Ogris's opener when he ran half the length of the field like a 100m runner and dinked the ball over Meola, and again by Gerhard Rodax's goal when Austria took advantage of poor midfield play by the Americans to break away and almost kill the game off. The US showed their ability to score on the break when Bruce Murray scored, but the game would mark the end of Italia '90 for the United States, but they were heading home with experience of how to play against top-class internationals, how to set your team up tactically in a high-pressure situation and understanding just how good the opposition can be. But, nevertheless, Italia '90 would prove to be just the starting point of the new modern era of soccer in the United States because they managed to qualify for their second consecutive World Cup (the first time that had happened since 1930 and 1934) without even kicking a ball. In fact, they managed to qualify for the 1994 World Cup before they had even qualified for the 1990 World Cup. After trying to host the 1986 World Cup, the United States had finally gotten their wish. On 4 July 1988 (of all dates), FIFA officially awarded the United States of America the rights to host the 1994 edition of the FIFA World Cup. The new USSF administration had learnt from the mistakes of the old administration with their 1986 bid and decided to do it right for 1994, creating an application that cost $500,000 to compile and was 381 pages long. They got it right, much to the surprise of everyone, who was shocked that the United States had an interest in soccer, let alone had an interest in actually playing/hosting it. This time, the country was determined to get it spot on at every corner. If they didn't, the consequences could have been huge: soccer in America could fade away due to the sheer amount of money spent and teams wouldn't take the US and its newly formed MLS seriously (MLS had to be formed once the bid was confirmed by FIFA as every host nation had to have a fully operational professional league). Thankfully, 1994 proved to be a turning point of US soccer. The World Cup in 1994, one might say, saved soccer in the United States of America.

Chapter Seven

The 1994 World Cup and the USMNT from 1994

IN 1994 Manchester United won the Premier League and FA Cup double, their first of three before the close of the millennium. The MLB season ended abruptly as a players' strike saw 948 games cancelled and it was the first time there wasn't a World Series since 1904. Arnold Palmer played his final round of golf at the US Open at the age of 64, his first Open in 11 years, finishing with a +16 score. The New York Rangers won the NHL's Stanley Cup, the fourth in their history and their first since 1940, ending the city of New York's wait for a champion in ice hockey, and they became the first New York team to win a championship since the 1987 New York Giants Super Bowl champions. Michael Jordan had left the NBA to start up a career in baseball, making his debut for both the Birmingham Barons and Scottsdale Scorpions in '94. The Houston Rockets and New York Knicks went head to head in the battle of the centres as Patrick Ewing and Hakeem Olajuwon would face off against one another, with Hakeem's Houston Rockets looking to win their first ever NBA Championship and Ewing's Knicks looking to win their first Championship since the days of Frazier and King in the 1970s. Perhaps most infamously, OJ Simpson and his white Ford Bronco drove down the Los Angeles highway to flee the LAPD, with an estimated 95 million people tuning in to news networks to watch the chase (some stations even interrupted the Rockets vs Knicks game to broadcast it live, with the chase relegating the basketball to a little mini-box in the corner of the screen), an incident that changed how we, as a society, viewed celebrities and how we viewed the news. But the biggest sporting moment of the year – at least from a purely sporting perspective (except for one incident) – was the 1994 World Cup, hosted in the United States of America. In a year when basketball, hockey, golf and even real-life stories tried to steal the headlines, the only true headline act was soccer, the biggest sporting event on earth, and it was coming to the US in a pivotal moment in the history of the sport in the country. It was not only a chance to show the world that the United States cared about soccer, but it was also a chance to showcase the game to Americans who were waiting for a car chase to finish on the news or to those who were in between Game 5, Game 6 and Game 7 of the NBA finals. The NASL had been given a smaller audience to work with and brought in a cult following, but America, a nation still without a fully functioning professional league at the time, were thrusted into the world's gaze thanks to this World Cup and they promised that this World Cup would be different to any before it.

It would be different to any other World Cup because being different was ingrained into the culture of the US, like we saw with the NASL. From the over-the-top nature of their production and presentation, to the cheesy and outdated music videos (the official song of the tournament, 'Gloryland', was sung by Daryl Hall and the Sound of Blackness and eventually had a video released with it, and a second official song was 'We Are the Champions'), everything about USA '94 was going to different, not out of choice but mainly because the US didn't know any better! When you host a tournament of this size, you *have* to go OTT, and it changed how the World Cup was hosted in the future. It had been nearly a decade since the fall of the NASL and the USMNT rarely had games televised, but the World Cup was on every day and more eyes than ever could potentially see a soccer game in America, not that many people were sold on the idea. On Channel 4's website you can find a short video of a news report on USA '94 before the opening game, where thoughts range from:

'What's soccer?', 'What's the World Cup?', 'Do I care about how America will do? Of course, because we are America and we're the best,' with Los Angeles Dodgers coach Tommy Lasorda screaming, 'Don't ever come to me and tell me that America does not have a chance to win the World Soccer Tournament! They have a chance and I predict that the United States will win it.'

There was no basis for Lasorda's belief that the United States would win it, but the sheer confidence (or arrogance, depending on how you look at it) that the United States was able to put on the best show on earth despite not having a clue what they were hosting was indicative of USA '94. Did regular sports fans and citizens quite understand what was happening? You'd wager that they probably didn't, but to those who did know, this was the ultimate chance to change the perception of sport not only in their own country but across the world.

The opening ceremony was about as American as American could get, with the sun blazing over Chicago's Soldier Field, the host stadium, and Oprah Winfrey introducing Diana Ross to perform 'I'm Coming Out' (apparently Oprah fell down a hole and fell off the stage during the ceremony), which led to the infamous Ross penalty miss where she stuttered her run (an immediate retake in the modern game and something that would be a bit of foreshadowing for the last kick of the entire tournament) and missed the goal before the goal exploded because her penalty was meant to be so powerful that the goal would 'break' in half (duh). With President Bill Clinton in the stands, it promised to be one of the most memorable opening ceremonies in World Cup history without a ball being kicked (apart from Ross, of course), and it summed up what the tournament would be remembered for. Pure carnage, a lot of fun and moments that would live in infamy. We should have known what USA '94 would be like when Franz Beckenbauer, Evander Holyfield and Robin Williams did the World Cup group draw in Las Vegas, with James Brown providing some entertainment (the Robin Williams section of the draw is on YouTube and is a definitely worth a watch – he's brilliant, and Sepp Blatter doesn't quite know how to react to wit and actual charisma).

The tournament officially began once Oprah got up off the deck and Diana Ross cleared up her dancers from the pitch in Chicago as holders Germany, armed with Jürgen Klinsmann, Lothar Matthäus, Andreas Brehme, Rudi Völler, Thomas Hässler, Steffan Effenberg and a young, uncapped Oliver Kahn faced off against Bolivia on 17 June, with Klinsmann scoring the only goal in a game that was deemed to be just a side note compared with the Simpson Ford Bronco chase, but the big event for the United States came just a day later when the USMNT kicked off their campaign against a Switzerland side led by future Liverpool, Fulham, Inter Milan and England boss Roy Hodgson. Players like Tim Meola, Tab Ramos and Eric Wynalda added their experience from Italia '90 and the new blood injected by the likes of Earnie Stewart, Cobi Jones and the instantly recognisable and iconic look of central defender Alexi Lalas, whose long red hair and beard combo – as well as the equally iconic denim USMNT kit – made him stand out from almost anyone else in the tournament. The story of Lalas has been forgotten thanks to his media career and this World Cup in particular, but before 1994 he hadn't ever played professionally, only at Rutgers University, as he described in an article with *FourFourTwo* magazine:

> I was fortunate that I went to Rutgers University. That was the first exposure I had to high-level soccer, in an area that was known for it. I got picked for the 1992 Olympic team and was immediately put into the residency

program. It wasn't at all with an eye to becoming a pro – it just seemed like a cool adventure at the time.

By the time I got to the World Cup in 1994, I was standing on the field in Detroit in front of a billion people – and I had never played a professional game in my life. We really didn't have any opportunities; we were living in between the NASL and MLS and no one would give American players a chance.

Such was the state of US soccer at the time that they had to pick players, like Lalas, who'd never played pro before, but they didn't look out of place in their 1-1 draw with the Swiss. Georges Bregy gave the Swiss the lead from a free kick on the edge of the box, but Wynalda – who had now moved to Germany to play with Bochum and Saarbrücken – curled in a perfect free kick at the Pontiac Silverdome. The term 'postage stamp' (when you curl a shot perfectly between the right angle of the cross bar and post) is rarely used these days, but Wynalda's free kick was textbook postage stamp, making up for his red card from the last World Cup. More than 73,000 people saw the US as the underdogs going into this game, which ended with a draw against a highly ranked Swiss team, with Wynalda describing the goal as 'the goal of his life', and it probably changed US soccer forever. If they had lost that game, the stench of disappointment could have stunk out the rest of the tournament, and people mightn't have been bothered about a bunch of losers, like what happened in 1990, but this team was different and the next game against Colombia gave the US one of its most important victories and gave the world one of the most infamous sporting stories ever. A crowd of 93,869 fans were crammed into the Pasadena Rose Bowl on 22 June to see the United States pick up their first World Cup victory since 1950, and it gave them a brilliant chance to actually qualify for the knockout rounds, where they would have the chance to play the likes of Brazil. But standing up against them would be Colombia, a tricky team of South Americans captained by the frizzy-haired Carlos Valderrama, with Tino Asprilla in attack, but it would be a defender who would have the biggest impact in front of goal and would dominate discussions of the World Cup.

Andrés Escobar was nicknamed 'the gentleman' for his calmness on the ball and his ability to never falter when the pressure was on. If you needed someone to hold your backline, to not make a mistake and to play with comfort and confidence, Escobar was the man for you. He was assured and the most reliable defender you could ask for, yet it was he who made a mistake for Colombia against the US that would not only make a huge difference in the individual game, as the Americans went on to win 2-1, but it also proved to be fatal after Colombia's elimination from the World Cup when Escobar was gunned down beside his car in an empty car park, with some people suggesting it was due to his own goal in this game, but many have also suggested that it was simply a case of being in the wrong place at the wrong time.

Escobar had flown back to Colombia following their elimination and was in his car in El Indio when three men appeared and began to argue with him. Two of the men pulled out guns and one of them shot Escobar, shouting 'Gol!' after every shot emulating the commentator during the US vs Colombia match. The three men fled the scene and Escobar was left to bleed to death, dying just 45 minutes later. It tarnished the reputation of Colombia across the world at a time when drug cartels were making headlines for all the wrong reasons. The ESPN *30 for 30* series made a film called *The Two Escobars* that analyses the murder and suggests that had Pablo Escobar still been alive (not related to Andrés) then perhaps the murder would not have been committed seeing as Pablo was a huge supporter of the Colombian national team. The events that happened in Colombia cast a shadow over the entire World Cup, and it's important to highlight it because it played such a big part in the competition both on and off the field. As captain of the Colombian team, Andrés wrote a short excerpt in the national newspaper following the elimination prior to his death as a timely reminder that soccer isn't a matter of life or death:

Life does not end here. We have to go on. Life cannot end here. No matter how difficult, we must stand back up. We only have two options: either allow anger to paralyse us and the violence continues, or we overcome it and try our best to help others. It's our choice. Let us please maintain respect. My warmest regards to everyone. It's been a most amazing and rare experience. We'll see each other again soon because life does not end here.

Getting back to the soccer, and the infamous victory against Colombia meant that the US were more or less through to the next round, regardless of what happened in the Colombia vs Switzerland game. One win, one loss and one draw was enough to see the US advance due to the best third-placed system that was brought in for this tournament, and their final group game against Group A winners Romania – captained by the legendary Gheorghe Hagi – which may have resulted in a 1-0 loss, but to the US it didn't matter. They eventually went through as one of the third-placed teams along with Italy, Belgium and Argentina (the latter were Diego Maradona-less for the rest of the tournament following his drug suspension). The World Cup shattered attendance records and seemingly gripped the nation and introduced them to how great the sport can be thanks to the ability of players, the presentation of the tournament on television and some of the biggest, most iconic players of a generation. Keeping on the topic of iconic players, the US had to face the Brazilians in the next round, who had perhaps the second-best player at the tournament, Romario, in their ranks. It wasn't a typical Brazil side, with this incarnation being particularly strong in defence and not taking too many risks, yet they possessed enough talent with Romario, Bebeto and Leonardo to win any game (they also had a young duo of Cafu and Ronaldo on the bench). It took 72 minutes for Brazil to take the lead and score the only goal when Bebeto rolled past Meola, but the US handled themselves well. They weren't embarrassed and they gave Brazil a good game, having chances of their own, but they ultimately fell short, which wasn't too bad considering that Brazil would go on to win the tournament. The US were out, but they certainly were not failures. With no expectation on them heading into the tournament, they bowed out with their heads held high. Amidst a cacophony of other sporting highlights during the summer of 1994, the World Cup left an indelible mark on almost anyone who watched, aided by its iconic moments. Whether that was the irony of the tournament's best player Roberto Baggio skying his penalty in the final against Brazil to hand over the trophy, or the kits, or Yordan Letchkov's bald head and Hristo Stoichkov sending Bulgaria to the semi-finals. Kits always play a big part, with multiple memorable ones on show. If you go to Ireland, Sweden, Bulgaria, the United States, or even Nigeria they will remember this World Cup fondly because it provided so many memories. England not being at the tournament is perhaps why USA '94 doesn't always get the recognition it deserves on these shores, but across the world many viewed it as the perfect gateway from the drab, dull and meticulous Italia '90 into the new generation of soccer, where personalities took over, the game got quicker and image and marketing became just as important as what you could actually do with the ball at your feet.

The USMNT were role models and heroes for many future generations of soccer players, and they started to show signs of more and more improvement as they had done in the 1993 Gold Cup – where they lost 4-0 to Mexico in the final – and then in the 1995 Copa America where they reached the third-placed play-off before losing to Colombia 4-1, meaning they finished fourth behind World Cup 1994 opponents Colombia and Brazil and eventual winners Uruguay, so all in all it wasn't too bad a period considering the teams that they came up against, and, in the case of Copa America, the fantastic 3-0 defeat of Argentina, where Eric Wynalda had Diego Simeone up against the wall as the pair cursed each other in Spanish and a team of Gabriel 'Batigol' Batistuta, Ariel Ortega, Roberto Ayala and Hugo Perez were unable to stop Wynalda, Lalas and Frank Klopas from scoring, meaning the Americans topped their group and sent Argentina to play Brazil in the next round. The US prevailed in the quarter-finals against Mexico on penalties but were eventually knocked out, once again, by Brazil, and Aldair's solitary goal saw the Seleção advance. Two more Gold Cups were played prior to the 1998 World Cup in France, with Brazil once again proving to be the American's kryptonite in the first one when a much-changed Brazil side defeated them in the semi-finals courtesy of a Marcelo Balboa own goal. However in the next Gold Cup, in the early months of 1998, the USMNT would finally get the better of the Seleção, as Preki, a Yugoslavian-born midfielder, scored the only goal, but then the US lost to Mexico 1-0 in the final. Progression was evident in the USMNT camp, and ahead of the 1998 World Cup spirits were high. They had the experience of playing in tournaments against world-class opposition and were ready to test themselves once again in France. Before the 1998 World Cup, the US had experienced the 1990 World Cup, a World Cup in their own backyard, a win in the 1991 Gold Cup on penalties against Honduras, a loss in the 1993 final, third placed in the 1996 Gold Cup, another 1-0 loss against Mexico in the 1998 Gold Cup Final and two Copa America tournaments. For a country that didn't have a professional league for most of the decade and had to essentially change their entire system and structure in the matter of a few years, this was great progress.

The World Cups were getting better as each edition was played, and Gold Cup success was to be expected given the nations they were up against (with the exception of Mexico), so in theory the 1998 World Cup *should* have been the stepping stone to reach the next level of international soccer. Instead, it was the opposite. They crashed out of the 1998 World Cup at the very first hurdle after three losses against Germany (2-0), Iran (2-1) and Yugoslavia (1-0) and were sent packing. Germany, filled with stars and captained by Klinsmann, dispatched of the Americans with ease, as did a Yugoslavia side led by the likes of Siniša Mihajlović, Slaviša Jokanović and Dejan Stanković, but the biggest story of the tournament for perhaps both the US and the world was the second group game against Iran, with reality and soccer mixing once again.

For years, the relationship between Iran and the United States had been fractious and controversial, with the Iranian Revolution in 1979 ousting the pro-American government and heightening tensions between the two countries, something that was felt during the 1998 World Cup and the build-up to the game. When the two had been drawn in the same group, the world waited with anticipation to see what would transpire and how each team would fair in the fixture, with even the pre-match handshakes being a point of discussion. 'One of the first problems was that Iran were team B and the US were team A,' explained Mehrdad Masoudi in an interview with *FourFourTwo*, who was the Iranian-born FIFA media officer for this game, 'and according to FIFA regulations, team B should walk towards team A for the pre-match handshakes, but Iran's Supreme Leader Khamenei gave express orders that the Iranian team must not walk towards the Americans.' Masoudi would eventually have the Americans walk towards the Iranians, but that wasn't the end of the off-field issues as 7,000 tickets were purchased by a terrorist organisation called Mujahdin Khalq, who were funded by Saddam Hussein and who were planning to stage a protest during the game on social issues and against the Iranian regime at the time.

Camera operators were given pictures of certain people and banners to avoid during the match. The television cameras missed what happened in the stands, but protesters still managed to smuggle in a few banners, although only those people at the game saw them. Security at the Stade Gerland stadium in Lyon was on high alert as plan B for the group was a pitch invasion, but the action on the pitch itself gave a different message altogether. The Iranians and Americans got together for the joint team photo, with both sets of players linked arm over shoulder, and the Iran team handing over white roses, the symbol of peace in their country. The game didn't go in the favour of the Americans, but while the loss eliminated the US and gave Iran their very first World Cup victory, everyone involved was well aware that they had just played potentially the most politically charged World Cup game in history. Jeff

Agoos, one of the US's defenders on the day, said, 'We did more in 90 minutes than the politicians had done in 20 years,' and he was right. The World Cup provided the two nations with a chance to show that peace was an option and that everyone could get along. The 1998 World Cup ended on a sour note for the US – going home without a win – but it was all irrelevant compared to what had happened during that Iran game. It was a massive moment and both sides, even though they were desperate to win, made a huge impact off the field.

But while the 1998 World Cup was initially deemed a failure, it impacted the future of the USMNT in more ways than many imagined at the time. The 1998 squad was getting on in years, with the likes of Tab Ramos, Preki and team captain Thomas Dooley all 31 or older and other players like Alexi Lalas, Eric Wynalda, Earnie Stewart and Kasey Keller all 28 and above, but the more youthful members of the squad like Frankie Hejduk, who earned a move to Bayer Leverkusen following his performances at the tournament, Claudio Reyna, who was already in Germany with Leverkusen and Wolfsburg but was to join Glasgow Rangers just a year later, and Brian McBride, of the Columbus Crew, all providing a platform to build the team around. With Brad Friedel being 27 years old at the time and with Liverpool, the spine of the team was set with Friedel/Keller (goalkeepers age differently to outfield players, so while Keller was 28 that's still relatively 'young' in goalkeeping years) in goal, Hejduk in defence, Reyna in midfield and McBride up front. Was this the front line for the future? Not entirely, because the US had other pieces that were developing behind the scenes that were ready to burst into life following the turn of the millennium. Their final win of the 20th century was against Saudi Arabia in the 1999 Confederations Cup. The third-placed play-off match meant that the Americans performed admirably with McBride finishing with two goals in the tournament. Managed by Bruce Arena, the US added the likes of Ben Olsen and Gregg Berhalter to the mix to add depth to their squad, but this was from far the finished product. A friendly win over Argentina (containing the likes of Mauricio Pochettino, Pablo

Aimar, Roberto Ayala, Diego Simeone and Javier Zanetti) and a win in the Confederations Cup against Germany (with Lothar Matthäus, Jens Lehmann, Thomas Linke, Christian Wörns and Oliver Neuville all playing) meant that the future looked bright for the USMNT as the 21st century dawned on the world. The road to South Korea/Japan 2002 (the first World Cup to be jointly hosted by multiple nations, and the only one until 2026 when the US, Mexico and Canada will host) was navigated by Arena through unnecessarily troubled waters given the ease in which this group of players should have qualified. The CONCACAF system worked in two stages, where the winners and runners-up of three groups of four would qualify for the final round, which consisted of one group of six. The USMNT won the first group stage, but only by a hair as they finished ahead of runners-up Costa Rica on goal difference and ahead of Guatemala by just one point.

A 7-0 drubbing of Barbados and a 4-0 win over the same opponents meant that the superior goal difference sent the US through as group winners, although they once again only qualified from the final round by three points. Ten games played, five games won, two drawn and three lost were the final results for the USMNT, with losses against Costa Rica and Honduras denying them six extra points that would have seen them finish top of the group. The final results did not matter though, because Costa Rica, Mexico and the USMNT all qualified for the competition and were drawn up against Portugal, Poland and hosts South Korea. Using the Gold Cup in 2002 as practice, the US romped to their second Gold Cup triumph, and with a mixture of positive results from friendlies against the Netherlands (lost 2-0), Mexico (won 1-0), Germany (lost 4-2) and Uruguay (won 2-1), the team felt confident. The US had nothing to lose; manager Bruce Arena said about the tournament:

> We're not going to win [the World Cup] because we're not a good enough team. I don't think anyone is going to be damaged by us saying that. I mean, how many countries

have won it? If we can get a point in the first game, it will put the whole group in chaos.

But a Portugal side featuring Luis Figo, Rui Costa, Pauleta and Baia were considered dark horses for the tournament. They had the 2000 Ballon D'or winner and FIFA World Player of the Year in Figo, so with that comes obvious expectation, but the US had their own star in the making at this point playing up front alongside McBride – a young 20-year-old who had departed the States to join Bayer Leverkusen but returned on loan to the San Jose Earthquakes in MLS, who went by the name of Landon Donovan. Donovan was born in California and joined the IMG Academy in 1999 (the IMG Academy, to put it simply, was a boarding sporting school where you learned like a regular school but had supplemented sports programmes too) and seemed destined to have a career in soccer. After being spotted by their sporting director at a soccer tournament in Europe, Bayer Leverkusen tied Donovan down to a six-year deal, but while the American starlet was busy in the reserves and at youth tournaments, first-team opportunities were looking few and far between at Leverkusen. Despite his reputation as one of soccer's rising stars and as the US's next great hope, Donovan was kept out of the Leverkusen first team as they chased silverware, coming agonisingly close to winning the Bundesliga, and midfielders like Michael Ballack, Zé Roberto, Bernd Schneider, Carsten Ramelow and even fellow American Frankie Hejduk were in the path of Donovan. With these experienced and top-class players ahead of him, the American needed a change of scenery to get minutes under his belt, and a two-year loan to San Jose Earthquakes marked the next chapter in his career as he won the 2001 MLS Cup with San Jose, scoring in the Conference semi-final and the MLS Cup Final. The victory led him perfectly into the 2002 World Cup as one of the young players to look out for and one of the players who had a point to prove after departing Europe so early. He, alongside fellow IMG Academy graduate DeMarcus Beasley, were touted as being part of a bright American future, and the game against Portugal was the perfect chance to show what they had to offer. In one of the shocks of the tournament, the US raced into a 3-0 lead courtesy of goals from John O'Brien, an own goal from Jorge Costa and one from Brian McBride, which gave the Portuguese a massive fright and it took the US just 36 minutes to score more in one game than they had done in the entire World Cup '98. Despite Portugal grabbing one back before the half-time break, and some absolutely terrifying American defending, the US managed to hold on for a 3-2 win, an historic victory to kick-start what would be the most successful tournament since 1930. A 1-1 draw with South Korea and a 3-1 loss to Poland meant that the US advanced to the next round to face Mexico, which would produce another upset. After being heavy underdogs for the fixture, the US defeated the Mexican side 2-0 with more goals from McBride and Donovan, as a disappointing Mexico fell by the wayside, swept out by an American team that was determined to win. Perhaps for the first time, the US had exceeded expectations in this World Cup. In 1994, there had been expectation, but it was a different kind because when you're hosting the World Cup many believe you should go far because of that advantage, but in 2002 it was a different kind of success. This squad had players who either had high potential or were established players at big European clubs, and they were extremely talented. The goals they scored in the game against Mexico weren't smash and grab goals, they were good goals. Claudio Reyna's run for the opener was outstanding, as was the positional awareness of McBride, to be in the right place at the right time to smash home, and Donovan for the second. It's easy to say that he was just in the right place, but he lost his marker to head home perfectly from Eddie Lewis's cross. It wasn't just sheer luck, this win was by design, and Bruce Arena had designed his team's game plan perfectly. Absorb the pressure and make your chances count on the break; this was how the USMNT played and in 2002 it worked perfectly, with the team advancing to face Germany in the quarter-finals. This has been a World Cup where the veterans from 1998 were meant to be weaned out of the squad in place of the youth, more specifically the youth from the under-17 team, but they had exceeded expectations even before a ball had been kicked in the quarter-final. As Arena said at the beginning of the tournament, they were never going to win it, but the performances were a step in the right direction. A repeat of 1998 would have been a hammer blow for the soccer scene, but in the build-up to the match against Germany there was once again this feeling that the team had nothing to lose. There is no shame in going out to Germany, especially when you're the underdog, but the US were there to make a fight of it, like they always did. This Germany side were littered with stars, from captain Oliver Kahn, Christoph Metzelder, Torsten Frings, Didi Hamann, Sebastian Kehl, Christian Ziege, Oliver Neuville, Miroslav Klose and Bayer Leverkusen duo (and two players who blocked Landon Donovan's path into the first team) Bernd Schneider and Michael Ballack, and it was going to take a lot for the US to beat them ... and they nearly did it.

One goal was all it took for Germany to sneak past the US, and on a different day we'd be sat here discussing how the USMNT reached the semi-finals of the 2002 World Cup, if only Oli Kahn, Michael Ballack and a missed penalty call on Torsten Frings didn't exist. (Gregg Berhalter's header was saved by Kahn and rebounded up on to Frings's hand. He didn't mean to handball it, but if he hadn't been there it would have been a goal.) If the US could get past Kahn and if someone had beaten Ballack to his header, it would have been a much different story.

They had gone into this tournament as huge underdogs and managed to get within a penalty and a goalpost from a semi-final against group rivals South Korea. A young core was breaking through and forming its own team, while veterans were adding experience at every tournament. Was there a long way to go in terms of building a sufficient team that could challenge for world honours? Of course, but it was a huge step in the right direction. The USMNT had shown that they had the right tools to build a good team, but now the 2006 World Cup was the target to take the next giant leap to becoming a serious contender at the top.

With the 2005 Gold Cup in the winner's cabinet (their third overall), the US were feeling like they could make an impact in Germany, the hosts for the 2006 World Cup. Drawn against Italy, Ghana and the Czech Republic, there was a strong possibility that the US could qualify for the knockout rounds, and it didn't seem too far-fetched when you consider a number of factors: they had a perfect mix of youth and experience, with Eddie Johnson, Bobby Convey, Clint Dempsey, DeMarcus Beasley, Oguchi Oneywu and Landon Donovan all 24 or younger, and they had Kasey Keller, Brian McBride, Claudio Reyna and Gregg Berhalter all reaching the end of their respective careers with multiple World Cups' worth of experience under their belts. The expectation in US soccer had changed from 'will they qualify for the World Cup?' to 'what will they achieve when they get to the World Cup?' They had shown before that they were dangerous, and this time they went in with a different mentality, as this quote from Landon Donovan in the *New York Times* suggested:

> You cannot go into a World Cup timid and shy, thinking 'I'm happy to be here.' We're there to win. Everyone has to be on the same page and willing to take responsibility.

And he was right too. Everyone had to be in the same frame of mind, and given that many of the players had played together for years there was a strong possibility that they *were* on the same page. It's just a shame that it didn't fully translate on to the pitch. The US crashed out losing two of their three group games and getting a draw in the other, ironically against eventual winners Italy in a game that saw three red cards (two for the United States) and no goals for an American (Christian Zaccardo scored an own goal), which meant the US went home without a single victory to their name. The Ghana game was perhaps the more heart-breaking because, despite needing a win and having arguably the better side (at least on paper), the US weren't as attacking as they should have been and a contentious penalty decision in favour of Ghana was what settled the game and ultimately decided the fate of the US, but it wasn't the only factor. Despite the mentality Donovan spoke of, it was rather disappointing that the US were out so early and were so flat and boring in the group stage. With the exception of Italy, the US could have easily qualified, or at least won a game. The early exit from the World Cup prompted a quick look at the playing side of the operation, and manager Bruce Arena's future was brought into question. The former goalkeeper's contract was up in the six months after the tournament anyway, but a lot of the blame from this tournament was placed on his shoulders in the immediate aftermath. There was criticism of his 4-4-2/4-5-1 formation, suggesting it lacked creativity and imagination, his constant loyalty to out-of-form players that hindered the team – mainly DeMarcus Beasley, who some were calling to be dropped – and his inability to find matching partnerships across the field, with Claudio Reyna and Landon Donovan not gelling quite as well as they should have. Newly appointed USSF president Sunil Gulati wanted a 'fresh approach' to the USMNT following the failure and replaced Arena – who departed the set-up with the best US World Cup performance since 1930 and two Gold Cup wins – with Bob Bradley, who had made a name for himself in the late 1990s for winning the 1998 MLS Cup with Chicago Fire, the first-ever expansion team to win the MLS Cup (more on that in two chapters' time). In short, Bradley was brought in to take the USMNT to the next level, which was ultimately why Arena was let go.

Bradley was brought in to usher the new generation of talent into the first team and consistently make the US a better nation at world competitions. The Gold Cup was a tournament they'd always be in contention for because, in the grand scheme of things, the US and Mexico held a stranglehold over the rest of CONCACAF, and the Confederations Cup didn't really hold much in the way of prestige, so the World Cup was the main goal. Qualification was easy enough, finishing top of the hexagonal (the name given to the CONCACAF World Cup qualifying stage because only six teams play in it), and they went into pot two of the 2010 draw. The group they were drawn into wasn't particular hard either, with England, Algeria and Slovenia the opposition. Only England were a real threat, led by Fabio Capello and with one of the best players in the world at the time – Wayne Rooney – up front). Realistically, the US were in a very strong position to qualify. They might not finish top of the group because England were considered one of the favourites, but the US were almost favourites to finish second. Why almost? Because no one could quite wipe away the memory of 2006. Sure, they had the Confederations Cup match against Brazil when they threw away a 2-0 lead to lose 3-2, and the 5-0 thrashing handed to them by Mexico in the Gold Cup Final that didn't help matters either, but the fact remained that this group of young players, led by their manager – who was about to experience his first-ever World Cup – were somehow underdogs to qualify. Carlos Bocanegra was captain, Landon Donovan was emerging as the team's primary star alongside fellow midfielder Michael Bradley, son of boss Bob, who was just 22 at the time, and they had forward talents like Clint Dempsey, who had started to perform with regular consistency at Fulham, and Jozy Altidore, who spent the 2009/10 season with Hull City. The spine of the team was perhaps the strongest it had ever been at this point, with the key players performing at a high standard and the supporting cast delivering too, and that showed in the opener against group favourites England. While in England the game is remembered for three things: 1) the howler from Rob Green that gifted Dempsey US's equaliser, 2) the ITV feed cutting to an advert for Hyundai right as Steven Gerrard opened the scoring, meaning millions of fans missed the only England goal and 3) the *New York Post* headline who went with, 'US Wins 1-1', with many English pundits and writers missing the point of the headline, which was intended to mean that the result was much more important to the US than England. The USMNT didn't play poorly in that game, not at all, but if they'd had a lethal frontman to finish off some of the chances, they could easily have gotten the win. Another cause for concern was the slow start, with the US only really kicking into gear once England had taken the lead, almost as if the Gerrard goal was the shot in the arm they needed to think 'hang on, we're at the WORLD CUP'. A 1-1 draw against a team that was filled with as many top players as England wasn't a bad thing at all, but the real business started in the follow-up game against Slovenia. The draw against England was a bonus, and the US knew that to qualify the next two games were must-wins. Slovenia and Algeria were two sides that the US could beat, but once again a slow start punished Bradley's side. Slovenia went 2-0 up at half-time when Valter Birsa and Zlatan Ljubijankić scored, but the resilience of the US showed once again when Donovan halved the deficit just after half-time and Dempsey rescued a point in the 82nd minute. It was a poor first half made up for by a spirited second half, and the US escaped with their future still intact. Donovan took the game over in the second half and was awarded the man of the match, and he performed like many had expected him to, but while the US escaped with a point and their future still to play for, the final game against Algeria was a do-or-die situation. Win and you qualify (you may even finish top after England's drab 0-0 against Algeria), lose and you're out. It was as simple as that. There were no permutations about how many goals were needed, or relying on other results, they knew their task. Just win.

The game started off with Algeria hitting the crossbar. An early warning sign for the Americans and a massive let-off. It could have been yet another slow start, but they got away with one here. Clint Dempsey thought he had opened the scoring after 'pinball in the box' following Hercules Gomez's saved shot, but he was flagged for offside in a very, very tight call. Landon Donovan and Jozy Altidore – a duo who only had one goal between them before this game at the tournament – got in each other's way and both managed to blaze the ball over the bar. The early let-off for the United States was a chance to take the game over, and to some degree they did. They just couldn't put the ball in the back of the net (without the offside flag going up). At half-time the USMNT was on the verge of crashing out at the group stage for the second consecutive World Cup. England had taken the lead against Slovenia thanks to Jermain Defoe, which meant that the US would finish third if results stayed the same. And until the 90th minute the results did stay the same. England won, so they qualified but there was still a minute left in the US game. They weren't out just yet, but if they planned on getting through, they were cutting it very close. The board went up and showed the number four. Four minutes to save their campaign. An Algerian header was caught with ease by Tim Howard, who rolled the ball out as quickly as he could to Donovan on the wing, who carried the ball to just outside the Algerian 18-yard box. The ball found its way to Altidore, who tried to get the ball into Dempsey's path, but Raïs M'Bolhi in the Algerian goal parried the ball away ... but Donovan kept running and he was the only man near the ball, he had an empty net to shoot into and he did! Landon Donovan scored in the dying seconds to save the United States from elimination, to save their World Cup campaign, to potentially save the future of international soccer in the US and to help the United States finish top of Group C for the first time since 1930. A teary eyed Donovan composed himself in the post-match press conference, and Bill Clinton even got in on the act saying, 'All great contests at some point become head games. Athletic contests, elections, wars. I like people who don't quit though.' (I'm not quite sure it was fair to compare a full-out war to a last-minute winner, but you do you, Bill). The Americans were through and had avoided Germany in the next round, instead facing the surprise package of the tournament, Ghana. Ghana, containing the likes of Asamoah Gyan and Kevin Prince Boateng, were no slouches and had finished second in Group D alongside Germany – who would go on to thrash England in the knock-out round and reach the semi-finals – and the Ghana vs US match was somewhat of a dark horse face-off. Both sides had players who the common soccer fan recognised, but at the same time both sides had almost reached a point where they had exceeded their expectations. Neither side were to be underestimated because they both had the talent to win the game in an instant, but it would promise to be a close and cagey affair.

Naturally, the US conceded first when Boateng opened the scoring after just five minutes. It was a well-taken goal, but not the start that the US had in mind, and it took them until the second half to get back into it when Dempsey was brought down, giving Donovan the chance to level the scores. He stepped up for his penalty and dispatched it with ease, but with the game entering extra time, and with Bill Clinton and Mick Jagger in the crowd, one long ball set Gyan up to score the winner and knock the Americans out of the tournament. One long, dreadful defending hoof up the field was all it took, and the World Cup was done for the USMNT, but it wasn't the end of the world and here's why. Firstly, it was an improvement from 2006, which is what Bradley was brought in to do. Secondly, Bradley was also brought in to further the talents of the younger members of the squad. Jozy Altidore looked like he could have been a good support striker to Clint Dempsey, and Michael Bradley looked like an absolute star at times. Thirdly, it gave everyone in the squad a good balance of experience and youth for the future. The younger players got valuable experience and (in theory) their ability improved, while the older players either had enough left in the tank for one more World Cup or were able to hand over the reins to the middle-aged players from 2010. It could have been better for the Americans because that Ghana team they faced certainly weren't invincible, but the entire tournament was a positive. They finished top of their group and introduced a new bunch of younger players into the system, something that only improved as the years went on.

In 2011, with the Gold Cup in full swing, Bradley decided to use the tournament to try out younger players. Forwards Juan Agudelo and the infamous teenage sensation Freddy Adu were introduced into the team, Eric Lichaj, Tim Ream, Robbie Rogers, Alejandro Bedoya, Sacha Kljestan, Chris Wondolowski and Jermaine Jones were also brought into the squad, with the overall depth improving, even if the US managed to throw away a two-goal lead in the Gold Cup Final against Mexico. This loss was the straw that broke the camel's back for Bob Bradley, who was sacked as head coach immediately after the tournament –

despite signing a new extension in 2010 after reported interest from Aston Villa – because many felt that the USMNT were stagnating following the 2010 World Cup despite the injection of newer players into the team. The rumours of a replacement started even before Bradley was shown the door, with former Germany and Bayern Munich boss Jürgen Klinsmann at the very top of the USSF's shortlist. Some felt that Bradley was a bland manager, some felt that he should have stayed on as boss, some felt that Klinsmann's experience was a step forward, and some felt that the manager needed to be an American, but despite Klinsmann turning down the job in 2006 (citing that he needed more control over proceedings from the federation, something that Arena and Bradley didn't totally have), he was officially appointed manager July 2011. It was the start of a new, exciting era and one in which people felt that they truly had a chance to make a difference at a World Cup. Not just turn up, cause a few shocks and ultimately get sent home after a loss in extra time, but actually challenge and become a team that no one wanted to face.

Losing to Ghana in 2010 was a body blow because it was somewhat of a missed opportunity, but Klinsmann's appointment as well as the fresh look of the USMNT meant that fans were excited for the future. The German guided the team to the 2014 World Cup with ease and won the 2013 Gold Cup with just as much ease, if not more, winning every game, scoring 20 and conceding just four. The US had not just won the Gold Cup, they had dominated it, but this was only the first step of the Klinsmann revolution. The 2014 World Cup and the build-up to the tournament was perhaps going to be the most important period in the USMNT's recent history. The sport had grown in ways that had hardly been seen before. It wasn't quite the Pelé hype of the NASL era, but it was a different kind of hype, because rather than just flocking to a match to see one star player, not really invested in the final score, the spectators and fans were incredibly passionate about how the team did. The American Outlaws – the supporters group for the USMNT formed in 2007 – were growing in numbers seemingly every year (meaning more people were singing 'I believe that we will win'), and optimism was growing. A near-perfect qualifying campaign and a perfect Gold Cup victory meant, heading into the 2014 World Cup, the USMNT were firmly considered dark horses to do well. Klinsmann's impact had been noticeable from afar, but the preliminary squad for the tournament would be the very first point of major contention for the German as he looked to firmly assert his authority not only on the USMNT, but also men's soccer in the United States as well.

Klinsmann had been a huge advocate of letting young American players go overseas and play in leagues like the Premier League or the Bundesliga in order to gain the most experience from a higher level of play. Klinsmann was rather dismissive of MLS, and unless you were an outstanding talent or showed outstanding levels of ability over the course of a season he hardly picked any MLS players for his squads, and his 2014 World Cup squad showed this in its full glory. Of course, MLS had some great players at the time who made it into the squad like mainstays Michael Bradley and Clint Dempsey, who were still there after moving to Toronto and Seattle Sounders respectively, while Dempsey's club team-mate DeAndre Yedlin – just 20 years old at the time – was called up. Graham Zusi and Matt Besler of Sporting Kansas City got called up, as did Real Salt Lake duo Kyle Beckerman and Nick Rimando, but outside of MLS most of the players came from Europe, and in particular England and Germany. A young core of German-Americans arrived on the scene with John Brooks, Julian Green, Fabian Johnson and Timothy Chandler all making the squad in Klinsmann's attempts to change the culture of soccer in the US, but one huge name was left off the full 23-man list and that was Landon Donovan. Rumours had been circulating about his future in the USMNT set up since Klinsmann's arrival, with Donovan saying, 'In 2006 and 2010 I knew, for the most part – unless I was awful – that I was going to make the team. This time is more similar to '02, to where I wasn't sure. I have to prove that and I have to earn it,' but Klinsmann, who did include Donovan in his preliminary squad, had questioned Donovan's commitment to the sport because of his three-month sabbatical after averaging nearly a game every eight days for an entire decade. Older players, such as Donovan, were cut from the squad and younger players, like Yedlin, were brought in despite near enough no international experience at all, but it seemed clear that Klinsmann was looking ahead to building a steady team for the 2018 World Cup in Russia and was using this tournament as practice. While this seemed entirely plausible, the 2014 World Cup was one in which the US went into the competition not entirely filled with hope, but not entirely filled with dread either. More of a sense of trepidation and uncertainty as to what might happen to them, but the feeling of dread re-emerged once the groups were drawn, mainly because the United States had been drawn in the toughest group alongside 2006 and 2010 opponents Ghana, 2002 opponents Portugal and 2002 opponents and Klinsmann's home nation Germany, who were one of the favourites. Just their luck. But while it didn't seem luck was on their side, they were still ready to go to battle with the determination and the will to win that they had become synonymous with. It also seemed rather fitting that in order for the United States to progress and further themselves as a soccer nation, they had to face-off against teams that had played significant parts in their recent history, starting with Ghana.

The Ghana game would not only prove to be cathartic but also historic in many senses, including the Clint Dempsey opener after just 30 seconds which was the fastest goal scored by an American at a World Cup and the fifth-fastest in World Cup history, and what a goal it was too. He received a pass from Jermaine Jones and Dempsey danced his way through a few Ghanaian defenders to fire the US into the lead. DeMarcus Beasley – who started the game at left-back – became the first US player to play at four separate World Cups, but the veteran couldn't prevent the Ghana striker Andre Ayew equalising in the final ten minutes with what looked like a goal that would condemn the US to another draw, but John Brooks, one of Klinsmann's German-Americans, came off the bench for

Matt Besler and headed home the winner just moments later, becoming the first American substitute to score at a World Cup. The final whistle blew and the US had exacted their revenge and had gotten off to the perfect start. One game, one win and up next was Portugal. The US, while not exactly gifted with the same level of talent as the Europeans, ran them very close in the group stage game. Despite having Cristiano Ronaldo, Nani, Raul Meireles and João Moutinho in their side, Portugal relied on an 95th-minute equaliser to prevent the US from making it two wins out of two, after they'd had to fight back from a 5th-minute Nani opener to go 2-1 up until the final seconds. Jermaine Jones scored a peach of a strike just after the hour mark before Dempsey thought he had scored what looked to be the winner, but the point wasn't the worst result, even if it was grasped from the claws of defeat. A rampant Germany were up next, who looked in fine form following their 4-0 defeat of Portugal and their 2-2 draw against Ghana, with both the Germans and the US only needing a point to qualify. As luck would have it, Germany won 1-0 and the US still qualified on goal difference after Portugal could only muster up a 2-1 win against Ghana. In his first attempt, Klinsmann managed to guide his side out of the group and into a last-16 tie against Belgium, a game that has gone down in legend in US soccer history for good and bad reasons. Regardless of the final score, it was a game that no one will ever forget.

The difference between the US and a quarter-final place and going home was inches. Their opponents, Belgium, who were coming into their own golden generation period with the likes of Eden Hazard, Kevin de Bruyne, Romelu Lukaku, Jan Vertonghen, Toby Alderweireld, Thibaut Courtois and many others, were heavy favourites and throughout the knock-out game they battered the United States. This group of Belgians had their own history to make. If they defeated the Americans, they would reach their first World Cup quarter-final for 28 years and potentially kick-start a team that would challenge for honours in the future. These two sides had the same goal in mind – to become a force on the international stage – but they were lightyears away from each other, as this game showed. Just looking at the stats alone, Belgium had 39 shots on goal compared to the US's 17. Putting that into a bit more context, Belgium had 17 shots on target while the US had just five. Fifteen of those Belgium shots on target were saved by Tim Howard, a World Cup record for most saves in a single game, but why was the difference for the US just a matter of inches? They were outshot and outplayed at times, but they had perhaps the best chance of the entire 90 minutes through Chris Wondolowski, who, nine times out of ten, given the exact same chance in the exact same position, would score. It was just his luck that his one miss would come when it truly mattered. With the goal seemingly at his mercy, all the striker, affectionately known as 'Wondo', had to do was keep his shot down. If he kept his shot down, the US would win and advance to the quarter final, but one tiny bobble before his boot made contact with the ball changed the trajectory of the shot. It would have been a snatch-and-grab win, but a win nonetheless, but the game wasn't over. There was still extra time to be played, and with the superior Belgian side fresher with the addition of Romelu Lukaku and Dries Mertens, their dominance eventually showed. Kevin de Bruyne managed to slot past Howard, as did Lukaku, but a fightback was on the cards when Julian Green pulled one back just two minutes later; however, the story was written and the show was over. Despite their determination, their resilience and their attitude, the United States were out, beaten by the better side. There could be no complaints on the balance of play, because Belgium had the majority of the key chances, but you cannot help but wonder what if Wondo had scored? If he scored that chance, a tie against Lionel Messi's Argentina awaited them, but it wasn't to be. The US had given everything they had and, while they may have been knocked out in cruel circumstances, no one was upset. No one was mad, no one was angry at the players or the manager, they were proud. The 2014 World Cup was a success – to a degree, of course – and it was a tournament to be proud of, and a great way to introduce new blood into the team ahead of their campaign to get to Russia

2018. The majority of the squad would likely still be available in 2018, along with other young players breaking on to the scene. Post-2014 was set to be the most exciting time in USMNT history, with so much to look forward to, and a bright future under a coach who wanted change in US soccer. They were becoming a team that no other nation wanted to face because it was never an easy tie, and that was something to be proud of and something to wear as some kind of badge of honour. All they had to do was integrate young stars into this line-up, qualify for Russia 2018 and go even further than they had done before.

Except ... it didn't quite go to plan.

In fact, it went so horribly off plan that it took them until 2018/19 to get themselves back on plan. If the 2014 World Cup was the peak time, then the following five years were perhaps the worst it's been in the modern era. Sure, there have been times where they have been worse, when they've not had any wins over a prolonged period of time, but the years between the 2014 World Cup and Russia 2018 had a lot more riding on them than ever before. Jürgen Klinsmann had made the US into a team that were tough to beat, and their reputation was growing, but while it was growing at a steady rate, the nation had to strike while the iron was hot. They were coming off the back of a World Cup that captured the imagination of so many American citizens, which meant the only possible way for this team to go was, seemingly, upwards. A fourth-place finish in the 2015 Gold Cup was somewhat of a red flag that no one picked up on, mainly because there was still a Copa America to host and World Cup hexagonal hadn't started yet. The Copa America was a huge test for the Americans and a good chance to show how they can play up against top opposition, and they reached the semi-final before getting beaten 4-0 by Argentina and finishing fourth after losing the play-off match to Colombia, but it was a positive sign in some ways. But it was after this very same tournament that everything fell to pieces and the entire system started to crumble. The first game of the hex resulted in a 2-1 loss at home against Mexico, with Rafael Márquez scoring an 88th-minute winner, and it was the USMNT's first home loss in the hex for 15 years (also, in reality, this game took place just a number of days after the 2016 US Election, so there was probably a bit more attention on it than usual). One loss isn't the end of the world. It was a poor result, but it was salvageable, but losing 4-0 to Costa Rica was downright embarrassing and left the US with an 0-2 record, leaving Klinsmann's job in the balance and the USSF – mainly Sunil Gulati – rushing into a decision. On 21 November Jürgen Klinsmann was sacked. The USSF put out a statement that said:

> Today we made the difficult decision of parting ways with Jürgen Klinsmann. There were considerable achievements along the way ... but there were also lesser publicised efforts behind the scenes. He challenged everyone in the US soccer community to think about things in new ways, and thanks to his efforts we have grown as an organisation and expect there will be benefits from his work for years to come.
>
> While we remain confident that we have quality players to help us advance to Russia 2018, the form and growth of the team up to this point left us convinced that we need to go in a different direction.

The USSF rehired Bruce Arena to take charge of the team for the remainder of the hexagonal and for the 2017 Gold Cup, with a view to extend his contract until the end of the 2018 World Cup, provided they got there. Some suggested that this was a 'safety-first' appointment from the USSF, who were fearful of missing out on the World Cup for the first time since 1986, while some argued that if Bob Bradley hadn't taken the Swansea City job a month earlier it would have been Bradley who'd have gotten the job and not Arena. Either way, the team had a new manager and had to wait until March 2017 to get back to playing in the hex, resulting in a win against Honduras and a draw against Panama. Another win against Trinidad and Tobago and a draw in June put the USMNT in a much healthier position to at least get into the top-three places of the hex (the top three qualify for the World Cup instead of just one, and fourth place goes into play-off). The form continued into the Gold Cup and the US won with ease, beating Jamaica in Santa Clara for their sixth title. The form of the side and the new talent in the team, like Christian Pulisic, Gyasi Zardes, Darlington Nagbe, Kellyn Acosta and Bobby Wood, meant that the team had a good mix of youth and experience and at the very least had enough quality to make it into the top three teams in the hex. The USMNT had four games after the Gold Cup to make sure of their place in Russia 2018.

First up was a home game against Costa Rica, a side that inflicted the 4-0 defeat that summoned the end of the Klinsmann era, and they dealt an even bigger blow to the Bruce Arena 2.0 era with a shocking 2-0 win. It was a terrible defensive display, with the team shape all over the place and no cohesion whatsoever. A draw against Honduras didn't help matters at all and left the USMNT in the dangerous position they had appointed Arena to avoid. They had two very winnable games against Panama and Trinidad left – and they just had to win. They beat Panama comfortably, an impressive 4-0 thrashing that made everyone feel like a win in Trinidad was a formality. But it wasn't. Far from it. Somehow, they lost. They didn't even draw, they just lost, 2-1, and the dream was over. The worst-case scenario had become the only scenario. The USMNT would miss out on Russia 2018 thanks to an own goal from Omar Gonzalez. It was a disaster, and inquiries were made even before the final whistle had blown. Fans wanted Arena and Gulati out of the system, and an entire overhaul of how soccer is taught and played was called into question. Alexi Lalas's quote of, 'Are you going to continue to be a bunch of soft, underperforming, tattooed millionaires? You are a soccer generation that has been given everything; you are a soccer generation who's on the verge of squandering everything,' and Taylor Twellman shouting, 'WHAT ARE WE DOING?' on ESPN went viral, and never has the USMNT been more embarrassed. They couldn't even beat Trinidad, which is a far cry from what was meant to be happening after the 2014 World Cup. Arena and Gulati eventually stepped down from their respective positions, and with interim coach Dave Sarachan involved in the set-up, younger players like Zack Steffen, Weston McKennie, Tyler Adams and Shaq Moore got game time and started the next cycle of development. A few friendlies were played with no real notable results, but it became startlingly clear from the outset that whoever took over as boss needed to find a way to bleed youth into the team and erase some of the players from the squad who played Trinidad. Given that it took the USSF a few days to hire Bruce Arena after the sacking of Klinsmann, it came as a surprise (or not, depending on your view on the competency of the USSF) that it took them a year to announce Gregg Berhalter from the Columbus Crew as the new manager.

The future under Berhalter is unclear because anything can happen at any given time, but while hopes may not be high for the USMNT at the end of 2018 and start of 2019, it cannot get much worse from here. Changes have been made, perhaps not the right ones in some fans' eyes, but they are changes nevertheless. From hosting the 1994 World Cup and being proud of a nation that shocked the likes of Portugal and came agonisingly close to beating Germany and Belgium, it's a shame that it's all been reduced back to square one. Yet another rebuilding job for a nation that seemingly lacks a cohesive soccer structure at national level and one that is unsure on its main objective, but with the level of talent that is emerging, surely the only way is up? Stop me if you've heard that one before ...

Chapter Eight

The Introduction of the Women's Game and the Success of the USWNT

UP until this point in the book, the history of soccer in the United States has been dominated by men. It's been about the men's leagues, the men's World Cup, the male players, and that's not due to a case of ignoring anyone else, it's just because up until 1985 that's all that was played at a professional level. The United States Women's National Team (USWNT) was formed and played their first-ever game in 1985. But while the men's game has undoubtedly been around for much longer and, in the case of the respective leagues, gets more worldwide coverage than the women's league, there is no doubt in anyone's mind that the men's national team aren't the most successful national team in the United States. Without a shadow of a doubt, the USWNT is the more successful of the two, and the case could certainly be made that they are *the* most successful national team ever. Some may argue that the USWNT have been more influential in soccer than the USMNT or any MLS/NASL side, which is a fair statement because they started a revolution of the women's game in 1999 and it completely changed how people would view their side of the sport. While many arguments about US soccer say that the entire system is in transition or the entire system needs an overhaul, that simply isn't true. The USMNT may need an overhaul, but the USWNT continue to be a success, they continue to create world-class soccer superstars that are successful on the international stage and are talented enough to play for the biggest clubs in Europe and win all kinds of team and individual honours.

The women's game has benefitted more from grass roots than most people realise, it's inspired generations of young girls to take up soccer in order to be like their heroes from the Women's World Cup, and when Pelé did his 'FIFA 100' list in 2004, he only included two American soccer players. One was Michelle Akers, the other was Mia Hamm. Two women. The only two Americans on the list were the only two females on the list, and if that doesn't tell you the talent and importance of these players, don't worry, because once you finish this chapter you'll understand how important these players were, how talented they were (and are in modern soccer) and how they dominated world soccer. You can't look at the history of soccer in the United States without giving the USWNT a fair shake and a platform on which to showcase their achievements, because it's a massively important part of the growth of soccer in the US. And back in 1985, not many people were prepared or expecting the next few decades of dominance that were to proceed the inaugural match, and they certainly wouldn't have expected the dominance after they lost the game.

Jesolo, Italy, a town just 45 minutes away from Venice, was where women's soccer in the United States started, or at the very least where women's soccer played its first game. On 18 August 1985 the USWNT lined up to face Italy in the Mundialito Cup (Mundialito translates in Spanish to 'Little World Cup') and while the score was 1-0 in favour of the Azzurri, the Italian fans started to cheer for the US, with USWNT left-back Stacey Enos saying, 'They were chanting "OOOSA, OOOSA" and it took us a while to figure out that it was "USA, USA".' It's still not fully clear why the Italian fans started to chant for the US – maybe they were just cheering for the underdog and the crowd was more neutral – but the *OOOSA* chants have stuck around, and it's now a tradition for the USWNT players and fans to chant it. Even though the result was a negative one, it was more a case of showing how far women's soccer in America had come. Women's leagues in the US had existed since the 1930s, although never pro like the ASL at the time or NASL in the future. Women's soccer was mainly confined to schools and all-female colleges, without any sign of it forming into professional teams or leagues, let alone a fully fledged national side, with the exception of the Craig Girls' Soccer League, which formed in 1951, consisted of just four teams and lasted for two seasons. The game would stay largely in schools and colleges, but thanks to the Educational Amendments of 1972 (a bill that allowed for a few changes in the Education Act of 1965), which allowed more equality in schools across the United States for equal access and equal spending on athletic programmes, the US saw a boom in female participation in soccer. By 1981, there were almost 100 varsity programmes for NCAA women's soccer, along with another group called AIAW (Association for Intercollegiate Athletics for Women), a female counter part of the NCAA that set up an informal championship in 1980. While the two organisations battled it out for supremacy, it was the NCAA that came out on top and established a fully fledged female soccer championship.

With the introduction of amateur leagues that were stable, and a rapid growth in participation, the natural next step was to form a national team. In 1985, with seemingly no preparation, little practice, harsh travel conditions and next to zero media attention, the USWNT was flying to Jesolo to start a new chapter of history. Whereas the men's game in the United States started with little pockets of booms in certain areas of the country, the women's game spread everywhere thanks to the college system and the partnership with the NCAA. It allowed the game to spread out more than perhaps it would have otherwise, and allowed the USWNT to fill the team up with players who were playing regularly and were young enough to build a core around.

The core of the first USWNT squad was made up primarily of players who were on the college scene, and very few stuck around for the following years. The results certainly didn't reflect too kindly on the USWNT either. Managed by Dublin-born Mike Ryan – a man who was later said to have been 'one of – if not the – principal pioneer for soccer in Seattle' upon his passing in 2012 – the team registered three losses and one draw, scoring just three goals and letting in seven, but while the stats of the tournament didn't really matter all that much in the long term, the scorer of their first-ever goal in the 2-2 draw against Denmark was an historically important one, because it started the career of one of women's soccer's most integral players and perhaps one of its most legendary figures ... or, at least that's what was believed for many years afterwards. On the official scoresheet against Denmark, the first goalscorer for the United States was Michelle Akers and the second goalscorer was Emily Pickering, thus making Akers (who would become the key figure of women's soccer in the coming years) the very first scorer, but in an interview with the *Los Angeles Times*, coach Ryan thought otherwise:

> [Akers] didn't really score the first goal. It was a girl named Emily Pickering. She got the first goal on a free kick and put it right in the corner. The Danes were flabbergasted.

While Ryan thought Pickering got the goal, Pickering herself wasn't all too sure, saying:

> That seems to be the big debate as to whether Michelle Akers or I scored the first goal for the national team. I know Mike Ryan said I did, but I'm pretty certain I was feeling somewhat vindicated because I scored the tying goal and for me it was disappointing because I didn't get to play in that first game.

No one was quite sure who actually got the first goal, but a match report from a *Gazzetta Dello Sport* (one of the main soccer newspapers in Italy) stated that Denmark took the lead before Akers levelled it up for the Americans, and Pickering put the US in front. So, with good authority, we can say that it was Michelle Akers, and she also scored the third in the loss against England not long after, but while the tournament was a disappointment for the women, it was a building block. Building blocks are a big theme in the US national teams, and this had been a big step because they now had a new national team that they could focus their entire college programmes on. The women would have a lot of things to overcome in the future, and setting up a functioning team was just one of them, but with a new manager appointed in 1986 things were about to get a whole lot different. A new manager was brought in to replace Ryan by the name of Anson Dorrance, a man once described by Chuck Blazer (who was acting as USSF vice-president at the time) as 'an abrasive combination of politically incorrect and noisy'. (Side note – and this is rather important – Blazer was caught out in the 2015 FIFA bribery scandal and became an informant for the FBI and IRS. He also paid $6,000 a month for a room in Trump Tower just for his cats.) Dorrance was an absolute women's soccer coaching machine, winning 13 out of 14 NCAA championships with his North Carolina team, and he looked like the perfect fit to take them forward and pursue domination. Dorrance's goal was to topple Canada and become the premium North American women's side before eyeing up the rest of the world, and he wasn't prepared to carry any passengers for the ride, once writing in a letter to the squad, 'If you do not come in fit, I will cut you!' Thanks to his years of college knowledge and scouting in the NCAA, Dorrance knew pretty much everything he needed to know about the players available to him, and he knew the potential strengths and weaknesses of every player. Tactics improved, physical fitness improved and the USWNT improved as a whole.

In 1986 the USSF invited the Canadian Federation over to play in the North American Cup – the first games on US soil for the USWNT and the first-ever games for the Canadian women – for a three-game series. At the Blaine Soccer Complex in Blaine, Minnesota, the two were about to make more history. The Canadians brought over 16 provincial players who had only practised for two days before taking the 20-hour bus journey to Minnesota, while Dorrance and the USWNT were more prepared but hadn't been able to fully scout their opposition, with the manager saying:

> None of us knew how good anybody was [for Canada]. The first time I got a sense of how good Canada was, was in the first couple minutes of the first game. It was a brave new world for all of us.

While the US weren't too sure of the Canadians' quality, they were able to win the first match on 9 July in a game that was historic for being the first win, the first shutout (the USWNT won 2-0), the first cap for April Heinrichs – who would go on to be the captain – and the first goals at international level for Marcia McDermott and Joan Dunlap-Seivold. The first match went to the US, the second went to Canada, before the third and final match was won by the US (although it was never recognised as an official match because it only lasted 60 minutes), and it showed that both teams were capable of being competitive in any game and that they had long-term futures as viable national teams with the talent to make a mark on the world game, which they intended to do when they were invited back to the 1986 edition of the Mundialito Cup, with big wins against the likes of Japan, Brazil and China. The 1986 tournament marked an improvement, but Dorrance looked further into the future the following year when he started to scout the under-19 talent pool with an eye to the 1991 Women's World Cup (which was named the Women's World Championship for the inaugural tournament). A camp in Marquette, Michigan, led Dorrance to the talents of two 16-year-olds called Julie Foudy and Kristine Lilly, and an invitation to a youth tournament in Louisiana guided him to a player named Mia Hamm, a 14-year-old who Dorrance said, upon the first time of seeing her, 'the team kicks off, a girl passes it to the right about 30 yards and I see this skinny brunette take off like she had been shot from a cannon'.

Without huge competitive tournaments within the US, Dorrance felt that his team needed tours to keep up with the likes of China and Norway – both of whom were considered the top nations in women's soccer. Wins against those two countries did come in 1987, but with tours in China and Taiwan, as well as a four-game series back in Blaine, the schedule took its toll on the players. Both 1988 and 1989 were transitional years for the USSF, who needed to change how the women's game worked. They had amazing players on their books but rarely met up, and because of the poor planning from the USSF (hastily assembled squads, lack of training camps, no real objective) it looked as if a generation of women's soccer players would pass the country by. However, in 1991, thanks to FIFA, the USWNT came into their own and actually had an objective to play for. No longer were they just going on tours or playing friendlies, they had a World Championship to win and the very first World Championship in China would be the first chance that Dorrance and his squad of players would have to show how far they'd come and how much work they'd put in to being the dominant force they and the USSF had planned them to be.

Media attention on the tournament was sparse and the only major sponsor was the food company Mars, who decided to help by officially naming the tournament the 'FIFA World Championship for Women's Football for the M&M's Cup', with FIFA reluctant to use the World Cup as the name. They had also decided that 80 minutes was suitable for the women and not the usual 90.

The tournament got under way and with two points for a victory in the group stage, the USWNT romped through the opening three games undefeated against Sweden, Brazil and Japan, scoring 11 and conceding twice, and having both Michelle Akers and Carin Jennings score three goals each. The undefeated streak carried on in the quarter-finals when they met up with the weak but spirited Chinese Taipei, who restricted the US to just the seven goals, with Akers getting five and setting a record that still stands, prior to the 2019 World Cup, of most goals in a single World Cup game. Akers was unstoppable and Dorrance had managed to form a team that gelled perfectly together and had peaked at precisely the right time, and before the semi-final against Germany most of the mainstream American media started to take notice and realised that the women were about to make history. The *New York Times* and *Sports Illustrated* sent over reporters to cover the games, but Dorrance almost preferred the anonymity because it allowed him and his team to work without the pressure of media attention, although media pressure probably wouldn't have affected this group of players because they were all so mentally strong. The squad had a 'take it one game at a time' approach set by Dorrance, and it worked brilliantly, despite the sudden attention and praise. The game against Germany didn't faze them and it showed after a superb 5-2 victory with Jennings scoring a hat-trick and cementing herself as one of the favourites for the tournament's MVP race. The USWNT were stronger, smarter, quicker and just outright better than the Germans on the day, who possessed a strong midfield and had conceded the same number of goals as the US up until this game (two), so they were no slouches. With Germany out and the US in the final, it seemed like destiny and fate were aligning for the USWNT. With their 'triple-edged sword' up front (the nickname given to Akers, Jennings and Heinrichs), the Norway side were no match for the USWNT, who took the honours home thanks to two goals from Akers in a 2-1 win, with Akers scoring the winner in the 78th minute. History had been made, and at the very first attempt the USWNT had done what they had set out to do: dominate women's soccer, and they did it with the best player of the tournament (Carin Jennings) and the top scorer (Michelle Akers with ten goals). Undoubtedly, they had been the best team in China, and it wasn't even close, yet while the USWNT had made history and some media outlets had jumped on the bandwagon of the team, the fanfare wasn't there when the team landed at JFK in New York. Swiss Air staff lined up to greet them, as did three reporters and some USSF officials. The USSF actually tried to get some local schoolgirls to cheer for the team, but they never showed up. Why? Because the USSF couldn't actually get the girls out of school, despite the fact a world championship-winning team was arriving. Friends and family were there, as was USMNT coach Bora Milutinović, who wanted to congratulate Dorrance on the success (also, he was staying in New York because the qualifying draw for USA '94 was being held at Madison Square Gardens). There wasn't a parade, there wasn't mass hysteria on the streets, there weren't any brand deals or even fame. It was just an historic victory that proved the United States had the best women's team in the world and had the best players to match. After taking this giant step forward, the big question was how would the USWNT continue to dominate, or if they would even dominate at all.

While media coverage for the USWNT was sparse, the significance of the 1991 World Championship wasn't lost on the powers that be. Because 1991 was so successful, FIFA decided to host another tournament in 1995, this time in Sweden, and this time actually naming it the FIFA Women's World Cup (no M&M's this time). There was also an extra incentive that every quarter-finalist would automatically qualify for the 1996 women's soccer tournament at the Atlanta Olympics. For the USWNT, this meant nothing because they already qualified due to being the host nation, but to the rest of the competition it meant a whole lot more. Not only did the Americans have to contend with teams trying to take their World Cup crown in a different time zone, but they also had to deal with teams gunning for a place at the next year's Olympics in their backyard! It was a different kind of pressure to 1991, and the resignation of Anson Dorrance didn't help matters as he handed his notice in in 1994 due to a lack of urgency to regularly get the USWNT together from the USSF, who believed that if there wasn't a tournament to play, there wasn't any point. Dorrance went back to being an NCAA juggernaut and was replaced by Tony DiCicco, the goalkeeping coach of the '91 side and assistant to Dorrance at the 1991 World Championship. DiCicco was experienced coaching this group of players and had no trouble taking them into the 1995 World Cup, even if the team had a target on their back. They were the champions, they were the shining example of how to dominate women's football, and each nation wanted to show that they took it just as seriously as the US did. In Group C were the US, China, Denmark and Australia, and it was somewhat of a tough group, but that didn't faze the USWNT as they finished top thanks to wins over Denmark and Australia, although they only managed a draw against China, a thrilling 3-3 in the group opener. FIFA extended the women's matches from 80 minutes to the full 90, and it didn't seem to affect the USWNT, who skipped past Japan in the quarter-final stages 4-0, thanks to goals from Tiffeny Milbrett, Tisha Venturini and a brace from Kristine Lilly, to set up a semi-final clash against Norway in a rematch of the 1991 final. Norway, who had beaten the US's group mates Denmark in the quarters, looked dominant throughout the competition. In the group stages they beat Nigeria 8-0, England 2-0 and Canada 7-0, with both Kristin Sandberg and Ann Kristin Aarones getting hat-tricks in the Nigeria and Canada wins. They were, perhaps, the only team who had the firepower to beat the US, and they had the further incentive of exacting revenge on them. And they did when Aarones rose highest to head in the only goal after just 10 minutes and infuriating the United States with their choreographed 'train' celebration. It was heartbreak for the United States, who felt like they were capable of making it back-to-back World Cup wins. The US hit the crossbar twice and played the last 20 or so minutes with an extra player after the sending off of Norway's Heidi Stoere, but it just wasn't to be their day. Sometimes in soccer, you can try your hardest and the stars won't align in your favour, and in 1995 this was that moment for the US. By no means was it an embarrassment to lose, certainly not against a good Norway side, but it could have been a big moment. Media coverage still wasn't there, but players like Hamm and Akers were becoming more popular and more well known in mainstream sports fans' consciousness (Hamm, in particular, due to her endorsement deal with Nike) and the *Tampa Tribune* said on the tournament:

'When the United States won the first Women's World Cup in 1991, it was probably one of the best kept secrets in sports. Maybe it had something to do with the fact the tournament was held in China, not exactly a media hub. Or maybe it had something to do with two things that are virtual poison to the vast majority in the American sports media – women's sports and soccer. Put those two items together and watch how fast a sports editor can roll his eyes and yawn. But things have changed a bit in the last four years. Women's sports are starting to get a little more coverage and with the help of last summer's men's World Cup, sports editors are begrudgingly beginning to realise that people do follow the sport in this country.

Soccer was the cool new thing in 1995, and even though the USWNT didn't bring home the World Cup it still inspired tons of people around the country. Those who had caught glimpses of these women had role models, mainly young girls who finally had a team that they could aspire to be like. Did the 1995 World Cup affect the reputation of the USWNT? Not particularly, if anything it made them more human, it showed that they weren't invincible and unstoppable.

The US loves a good winner, but they love a redemption story more, and the USWNT had the perfect chance to rectify their 1995 World Cup semi-final loss the following year at the 1996 Atlanta Olympics. For the first time, women's soccer was entered into the Olympic Games and it promised to be a huge event. With the eight best teams from the '95 World Cup, there wasn't much better opportunity to showcase your talent, and with crowds ranging from 17,020 to 76,489 the fans were very interested in the women's tournament, which was all the more impressive considering NBC didn't televise any of it. Drawn against Denmark, Sweden and China, the United States had expectations of glory given the talent they had and the home advantage, and they delivered in the group stage with two wins against Sweden and Denmark and ending the group with a 0-0 draw against China, finishing second due to China's superior goal difference. The second-place finish meant that a revenge match against Norway was on the cards (for the third tournament running), who were still looking like a tough team to beat, and *the* team to beat if the US wanted the gold. The Norwegian's had scored the most goals in the group stage and still had the core from '95 in their ranks, but it didn't seem to bother the USWNT, who dispatched of their new rivals 2-1 after extra time, coming from behind to win. Norway took the lead after 18 minutes and it looked like it would have all the signs of a repeat of the 1995 semi-final, but the sending off of Agnete Carlsen changed the game in the US's favour. Unlike '95 when they couldn't take advantage of the extra player, they made the most of it and Akers scored the tying penalty moments after the red card and Shannon MacMillan scored the golden goal. The US had overcome their World Cup opponents to reach the gold medal match on home soil against a China team that they couldn't get past during the group stages, but this match looked to be bigger than just a final. In front of 76,000 fans who were hooked on the tournament – despite NBC not showing the final even with a US side in contention to get a gold – this was the chance the US had been waiting for. A win here would make stars out of their players, giving them more iconic moments in front of more fans than they'd ever played in front of before. There was expectation, and with expectation comes pressure, but this tight group of women never felt pressure, and it showed during the match. MacMillan, off the back of her semi-final winner, opened the scoring just before the 20-minute mark before China pulled level before half-time. With the game going into the final 20 minutes, Milbrett scored into an empty net to deliver the gold for the US. Was it easy? No. Was it simple to win gold? No, but the team were so talented that they made anything look easy, and when they went to the Olympic podium to collect their medals, it changed the women's game in the country forever. The World Cup had taken over as the main male soccer competition, so the Olympics was the perfect opportunity for the women to shine and show what they could do. Ask any American soccer fan who won a medal in the men's soccer tournament in 1996 and chances are they won't know more than five, despite the likes of Kanu, Jay-Jay Okocha, Roberto Ayala, Hernan Crespo, Ariel Ortega, Diego Simeone, Javier Zanetti, Dida, Roberto Carlos, Juninho, Bebeto and the original Ronaldo all taking part. But ask them about the women's team that summer and chances are they'll know multiple players because that team made such an impact, not only in a mainstream way but for soccer across the country. Michael Johnson, Andre Agassi, Charles Barkley, Shaq, Carl Lewis and Mia Hamm all have the same thing in common, despite one major difference. They all picked up gold in 1996, and that wouldn't be the end of the success for Hamm and the USWNT. In fact, the success in Atlanta drove them on to be more successful, it gave them the taste for winning and every single member of that team was hungry for more medals, and they wouldn't have to wait too long for another chance to taste success.

If the 1996 Olympics were massively important to women's soccer in the US, the 1999 FIFA World Cup in the United States was set to be even bigger and more important for the legacy of the players involved, the legacy of the sport and the future of the sport at the same time. With calls for a professional league akin to the fledgling MLS in the men's game (a league came close in 1998 but, despite players committing to the league, financing fell through at the last minute and a league was halted), women's soccer was at boiling point and the promotion for 1999 meant that the USWNT had the chance to be iconic in the eyes of the fans and to be historically dominant. There was no other sporting event going on in the United States during that summer (the NBA finals coincided with the opening of the tournament, but despite the New York Knicks going up against Tim Duncan and the San Antonio Spurs, no one cared. The MLB season was in the middle of seeing the New York Yankees win yet another title, but everything important happened *after* the World Cup), so all eyes were on the USWNT. The 1999 World Cup marketing team went all in on this tournament, spreading the word of this group of young, talented, determined young women who were dominating their sport, and ultimately decided to host games in major stadiums across the country. The organisers thought that if you hosted a tournament in smaller venues, the idea of what you're trying to sell becomes second class, but if you hosted games in stadiums like the Rose Bowl or in The Meadowlands, it adds a level of interest to your product. At a time when the women's game was still trying to convince investors to start up a league, this was a genius idea and it worked wonders when coupled with rabid fans who wanted to see a squad of players who many in the crowd saw as role models and athletes they could look up to. The likes of Adidas, Budweiser, Gatorade and Nike were on board with the advertising and ran multiple ad campaigns on television and billboards in the lead up to the tournament, so there was ultimately more pressure than ever before. They'd already won a World Cup and had won the Olympics on home soil, but with the latter of those two victories prompting the upturn in support for 1999, not only was the expectation to win, but to win convincingly, with the eyes of a nation watching. In fact, the opening game between the United States and Denmark was seen in person by 78,972 fans at the old Giants Stadium, making it the most-attended female sporting event ever and, at the time, the second-largest crowd for a single event in Giants Stadium history, coming second to when the Pope came to visit in 1995 (U2 would go on to break the record in 2009), and it proved to be the start of a very straightforward and simple group stage, as the team beat the Danes 3-0 before smashing seven past Nigeria in front of 65,080 fans at Chicago's Soldier Field before finishing the opening round off with a comfortable 3-0 win against North Korea in Foxborough. The tag of favourites – or at least one of the favourites – didn't affect how the US played and they almost relished the fact that so much was expected from them. The USWNT had that edge in this World Cup, and in front of their own fans, who were breaking records to see them, no one was going to beat them. The only major trouble they had in the tournament was in the quarter-finals against Germany when a different side of the team came out to play. After going behind after just five minutes courtesy of a Brandi Chastain own goal, the Americans had to fight back and levelled things up when Milbrett equalised, but they went into the half-time break behind when Bettina Wiegmann put the Germans ahead. It was only the second time in the tournament that the US had fallen behind in a match (Nigeria took the lead after two minutes in their 7-1 loss, which only seemed to anger the USWNT) and they faced an uphill battle. Germany, perhaps not as individually gifted as the United States, had the team spirit to fend them off for a period of time, but the quality of the US shone through eventually when Chastain equalised, atoning for her own goal, and Joy Fawcett won the game just after the hour mark. It was a scare for the women to go behind twice, especially so early on, but the spirit in the team and the will to win pushed them over the edge into the semi-final against Brazil, a team that had the top scorer of the competition – Sissi – in their ranks and were coming off the back of a golden-goal victory over Nigeria. But the US didn't give them a chance. Five minutes in and they'd already taken the lead through Cindy Parlow, and 10 minutes from time Chastain sealed the win from the penalty spot. With relative ease, the USWNT had reached yet another final and had seemingly done it without breaking a sweat. The sheer talent of the players combined with the togetherness of the group (humorously shown in a Nike advert where members of the squad, one by one, state that, 'I will have two fillings' to a dentist – it's on YouTube, go watch it) got them to this position, and the number of fans who packed the stadiums to witness history spurred them on even more. But while the tournament had been easy enough for the US, the final posed a completely different kind of test. China had developed into one of the two best women's soccer teams in the world at this point and were favourites alongside the US prior to the World Cup beginning, and there wasn't too much to separate the sides. The US scored goals for fun and were defensively solid, as were China. The US had been playing together as a core for a number of years, as had China, so you understand how close this game was going to be. Not only was it going to be exciting off the field, but it made history – yet again – off it as the Rose Bowl in Pasadena (where the 1994 World Cup Final was held) broke the record set earlier in the tournament for most fans at a women's sporting event ever, and the match itself provided women's soccer with a few iconic moments that changed the course of the sport forever. Bizarre then to think that there was a strong chance this game may never have happened.

In May 1999 the Chinese embassy in Belgrade was bombed when five United States Joint Direct Attack Munition bombs hit the building, killing three Chinese journalists. The US and President Bill Clinton claimed that the attack had been an 'accident', while the Chinese government claimed that the bombing was a 'barbaric act'. The relations before the incident were tense, but the bombing intensified matters, with some feeling that the Chinese women's national team would pull out of the World Cup because of it. As we know, that didn't happen and China made the final to face the US, with both President Clinton and the President of China in attendance, and having them at the game to watch a soccer final and to try to rectify some good relations out of a bad situation, it just added more drama and history to an already (potentially) historic game. But even with 40 million fans watching at home, two juggernauts of the political world in the stands, alongside a record crowd for a women's sporting event, the game didn't really kick into gear, mainly because the two teams were so good that they cancelled each other out. They knew each other's strengths and weaknesses and it made for a tense, tetchy and very even 90 minutes. With no major chances of note, the game went into extra time. The US had pushed further up the field as the game went on, cutting off supply from the China midfield to superstar striker Sun Wen, the tournament's top scorer and goalscoring machine. Without the supply from the midfield, she had very little to work with, and the Americans, who defended deep enough to make very few chances of their own, didn't manage to make much of an impact, but with the golden goal rule in this extra time period, all it needed was a single chance to go in and you have your world champion. While China came close to taking the tournament in extra time, Kristine Lilly had other ideas. The general consensus when defending corners is to keep someone on your goalposts so they can clear off the line, and for the USWNT Lilly had been put on the front post due to her lack of height and her inability to compete in the air. After 10 minutes of extra time, Fan Yunjie connected with a strong header that looked like it was destined to go in, with goalkeeper Briana Scurry unable to clamber over to clear the header, but Lilly was on the post and cleared without moving a muscle, saving the day with the one skill she wasn't recognised for – heading. Penalties beckoned for the two sides who couldn't break one another down. Carla Overbeck and Joy Fawcett scored the opening two spot kicks for the US, with China matching them both to level the scores at 2-2. Scurry made a good save to deny Liu Yung from giving China an advantage, and the advantage swung in the US's favour when Lilly – who had already been the saviour once this game – tucked her penalty away. Zhang Ouying, Mia Hamm and Sun Wen all scored their penalties to give Brandi Chastain the chance to win the World Cup with one kick, but the road to this penalty had been a long and bumpy one for Chastain, who had been in a similar position in the Algarve Cup earlier in the year. She hit her penalty straight at Gao Hong to give China a 2-1 win in 90 minutes, and even in this shootout she wasn't due to take a penalty anyway. USWNT assistant coach Lauren Gregg had Chastain down as the sixth penalty taker, but DiCicco changed that, mainly due to the fact he'd advised Chastain to change her style. He advised her to change her preferred foot to avoid her penalty being predictable, and in the biggest situation of all it was time to see whether his advice was right. As Chastain stepped up, she looked confident. She didn't look like a player that had missed a penalty against the very same goalkeeper she was up against right now, she didn't look like a player who had put an own goal past Scurry in the quarter-final, she looked like the defender who helped lock down the World Cup's top scorer. She looked like a defender who was about to win the World Cup on home soil in the biggest piece of history that US soccer had ever seen – and that includes the men's game. A lot was riding on this spot kick, but Chastain smashed the ball past Hong into the top-right corner to send her team-mates into bedlam and to win their second World Cup, cueing up perhaps the most iconic image in US soccer history: Chastain on her knees on the penalty spot with her sports bra on show, screaming with clenched fists and pure emotion. It was made for the front cover of *Sports Illustrated* and it was a huge moment in history. As her team-mates bundled her in the penalty spot, it was important to take a step back and realise that the United States had the best women's team on planet Earth and had proven it during this tournament and this final. This team had popularised women's soccer in the US and had given millions across the country role models to look up to and a new kind of hero, becoming the *Sports Illustrated* Sportswomen of the Year. This quote from Karen Bokram says all you need to know about how popular this USWNT team had become:

> This team did a remarkable job of seeping into the culture quicker than any US sports team in memory. The Americans quickly transcended their sport, then approached the kind of mythical status reserved only for beloved Olympic teams, like the 1980s men's hockey team that upset the Soviet Union and won the gold medal.

They were being compared to the US men's hockey side that were involved in 'the miracle on ice' (the 1980s ice hockey gold medal match was a bunch of US amateurs against Soviet Union professionals in which the US won), a team and moment that was named by *Sports Illustrated* as the greatest sporting event *ever*. (Just for background, *Sports Illustrated* had the 1999 Women's World Cup Final at number 24 on the list, two spots behind Lou Gehrig's famous 'luckiest man on the face of the Earth' speech, and it was one of four soccer moments on the list which included Pelé's 1958 World Cup performances, Diego Maradona's goal against England at Mexico '86 and one other moment that you'll have to wait for further on in this chapter.) The difference between the miracle on ice and the Women's World Cup, though, was that most of those ice hockey team were amateurs who had respectable, and in some cases successful, careers, but this group of women had the chance to be *truly* special.

A new league was formed off the back of the '99 success – even if the league went bust in 2003, the fact it was created was a positive sign – and the team plus the success just seemed to strike lightning in the bottle. It was the perfect team for the perfect competition in the perfect year, but would it be the same in the 2000 Olympics? The core of the '99ers (as they were now called) was still intact, and even with coach DiCicco stepping down and being replaced by April Heinrichs, the captain of the 1991 World Championship-winning side and a member of the 'triple-edged sword', they went into the Olympics as one of the favourites. Once again, the seven best teams from the previous World Cup, along with host nation Australia, were entered into the tournament, with the US drawn in a group with Norway, China and Nigeria. With their stars still in the squad and new players brought in such as Cindy Parlow, a 22-year-old striker who had been a part of the '99 squad but began to play a more prominent part in future squads following the 2000 Olympics, the experience showed throughout the competition. Dispatching of Norway 2-0 seemed to be easy enough, with Milbrett and Hamm essentially killing the game off within a six-minute spell before the half-hour mark, and the win against Nigeria in the final group game meant that the USWNT finished top by a point, ahead of Norway, despite a 1-1 draw against China in between. The US scored six goals in the group stage and had six different scorers (Milbrett, Hamm, Foudy, Chastain, Lilly and MacMillan), and they were the only team to have that many different players hit the back of the net, pointing to the incredible depth of talent in their squad. When Hamm scored the only goal in the semi-final win over Brazil, it looked like a certainty that the US would go on to win. It may seem presumptuous to suggest it, but they had already beaten their opponents Norway in the group stage – quite comfortably too – while Norway had only managed to advance thanks to a German own goal in the 80th minute in their game. It looked for all the world that the USWNT would stroll to another title and win yet another major competition, and just five minutes in it was looking good … but Norway had other ideas. The Norwegian side weren't in the final to simply roll over as the United States announced their complete dominance over the 90s and the 00s, the Norwegians came to play, and despite falling to a 1-0 deficit thanks to an early Milbrett goal, they got themselves into a 2-1 lead which they held until the dying minutes of the game when Milbrett equalised in stoppage time. The USWNT had managed to claw a draw out of the clutches of defeat, but with extra time looming there was no time to be complacent. The US had to go ahead and kill off Norway, who were shocked to throw away their lead right before the final whistle. As fate would have it, the USWNT did not go on and push home their advantage, but instead Norway struck again through Dagny Mellgren. The score finished 3-2 in favour of Norway in a pulsating, exciting and controversial match between two superb teams. The end of an era went out with a whimper as they picked up silver, but the motivation to get back on top was immediately burning inside of them. With Michelle Akers and Carla Overbeck retiring from the national team and other veterans being weened out of the set-up, a new era was on the horizon.

The Women's United Soccer Association (WUSA) was founded in 2000 with the aim of having the league follow the same path as MLS, although the WUSA folded in 2003 with $100m in losses, despite having players like Sun Wen and most of the USWNT involved and investors such as Time Warner, Comcast and the co-founder of Discovery Corp John Hendricks. The league itself started off quite well, with TV figures and attendances meeting their expectations, but ultimately it just seemed a little bit of 'too much too soon'. A pro league was certainly seen as the next step in the progression of women's soccer in the United States but when finances hit a low point, it takes a lot to bring things back to where they once were. Nevertheless, during the preparation for the 2003 Women's World Cup in China, the WUSA gave the women a league to play in regularly, with 2003 set to be the ultimate swansong for most of the original members. However, China pulled out of hosting the tournament due to an outbreak of the SARS virus – severe acute respiratory syndrome that caused the deaths of 774 people in 37 countries from late 2002 to 2003 – which meant that FIFA had to quickly relocate the tournament to a country that could host without any major issues. Of course, the United States were more than happy to oblige and were named as the new host of the 2003 Women's World Cup, giving them the perfect stage. This was meant to be the story book ending for most of their players: a final World Cup on home soil and going out as winners. That was how it was all meant to end, but despite the feeling of 'out with the old, in with the new' things didn't go quite according to the script. Off the bat, there was concern over the viewing figures and attendances due to the new schedule that saw the World Cup being played from September to October, with an article from the *New York Times* saying:

> While the 1999 Women's World Cup, held in June and July, faced little competition from other sports, this year's scaled-down tournament will take place during the baseball play-offs, college and professional football seasons, and the youth soccer seasons of potential World Cup fans. The conflict with football will determine, in part, the television scheduling and could put the final on a Sunday in direct competition with the National Football League.

And while the initial point was true, 20,000 plus fans still poured in on average to watch the tournament, and the only major sporting event that clashed was the American League Division Series and the National League Division Series play-offs that didn't last too long with only two series going to game five. The organisers were worried about the prospect of coming up against other sports, but they needn't have, because the tournament went off without a hitch and people were excited to see the USWNT play and wanted to give some of their heroes a good send-off. The group stage went smoothly for the US, picking up three wins out of three and being one of only two teams to have a perfect record. A 3-1 win against Sweden was soon followed up by a 5-0 thrashing of Nigeria, which saw relatively new star Abby Wambach get on the scoresheet. Wambach had only made six appearances for the USWNT before 2003 and was touted as one of the stars of the future and one of the deadliest strikers in the world. A comprehensive win against North Korea saw the US go into the quarter-finals to face off against their old rivals Norway. Wambach was key in this situation again, coming up with the only goal in the first half to send the US through to face Germany in the semi-final. For some people, this was basically the final. These were the two best teams in the tournament, and while the US had been dominating across the globe, Germany were slowly putting together a great side that was ready for their own kind of domination. The semi-final (despite it perhaps having the quality of the final) started in the worst possible way for the US. After 15 minutes, Germany took the lead when Kerstin Garefrekes headed home off the crossbar after losing her marker from a corner. It was just so simple from the Germans that it looked too easy, but this German team was different to any other that the US had faced in this tournament so far. While the US were pressing on for a quick response, the Germans stood firm and restricted the team to long shots and forced them to make quick decisions. In the stereotypical German fashion, they weren't flashy, they just did what they needed to do. They stopped the US from attacking too often and, apart from a missed penalty call from referee Sonia Denoncourt (Milbrett went to take down a lofted pass over the German defence, only to be crashed down by the goalkeeper Silke Rottenberg in a very Harald Schumacher-esque fashion) they didn't really get close. As the score stayed 1-0 until injury time, the US forced players forward in search of that elusive and valuable leveller, but it never came, instead Germany scored two more deep into injury time to turn a somewhat fortunate

1-0 win into a comprehensive 3-0 victory. And just like that, the fairytale ending was over. The US were out on home soil and couldn't retain their World Cup crown, they hadn't managed to give their veterans a perfect send off, and they were now staring down the barrel of a full-blown rebuild. But ... the rebuild could wait one year. The fairytale ending that wasn't so great now had the sequel that fans had hoped to see. The 2003 World Cup wasn't the end of the line for certain veterans, instead the end of the line would be in 2004 at the Athens Olympics where they had one final chance (it's definitely the last chance now) at glory. And they were determined to make the gold medal theirs.

The 2004 Olympic tournament in Greece was the first women's soccer event to include qualification that was separate from the FIFA World Cup results. No longer was it just the teams that went far in the previous World Cup that got a place, and the qualification format opened it up to the six continental confederations that are a part of FIFA and allowed each team who had a women's side to qualify, with the group draw being split into three categories: pot one was Europe, pot two was the Americas and pot three was the rest of the world. Greece qualified automatically as hosts and it wouldn't be long until the USWNT joined them after beating Mexico in the CONCACAF final, with the Mexicans also qualifying. With six of the USWNT squad being 32 or over and only having three players under the age of 23, this was a pivotal tournament. The 2004 Games would be the gateway to a new era, whilst simultaneously ushering out the successful generation of Mia Hamm, Joy Fawcett, Brandi Chastain and Julie Foudy. There was a new generation of stars on the brink of joining the ranks, but they knew that their chance was coming and the veterans knew this was their last chance of success. Drawn into Group C alongside Brazil, Australia and hosts Greece, the United States went undefeated with two wins and a draw, beating Greece and Brazil while being held to a 1-1 tie against Australia. It perhaps wasn't the most exciting of group stages, but when you've got someone as lethal in front of goal as Abby Wambach, a win is almost certainly in the bag. And another win was the order of the day when Japan faced off against the US, with Wambach scoring the winner in a 2-1 triumph, putting her on three goals in four games. Up until this point, the 2004 Games had been straightforward for the US, with no issues or any unconquered hurdles, but when the semi-final against Germany came around the entire squad sensed that revenge was on the cards. Sweet revenge. They knew that to go out in style, they had to beat a Germany side that had looked impenetrable all tournament. They put eight past China in their opener and had come from behind in their quarter-final match against Nigeria to set up this game. This game promised to be entertaining, enthralling, passionate, hard-hitting, all the soccer clichés you can throw at a big game, and all the clichés were applicable. The US were, at times, dominant in the game, and by and large better than Germany, but in typical German fashion, they didn't bow out without a fight. Kristine Lilly opened the scoring in the 33rd minute and the US held the lead until the very last second, when it looked like the fat lady was just about ready to sing her first note. But when the first note was at the tip of her tongue, Germany equalised through Isabell Bachor. It was a somewhat fortunate goal considering the deflection the ball took off Joy Fawcett, which saw it move slightly away from Scurry's reach, but it was testament to Germany's hard work and determination. The US could have won the game about 10 minutes earlier when Steffi Jones deflected a Heather O'Reilly shot on to the crossbar, and while that name may seem unfamiliar at this point in the journey, it won't be the last time you hear about O'Reilly in this game. The youngest player on the 2004 Olympic roster, O'Reilly was a 19-year-old forward who was coming off the back of a broken fibula from a year before, and she was set to be a pivotal part of the USWNT's future going forward. She was a part of the under-19s side that won the FIFA Women's World Cup and was set to take part in the biggest game of her career (so far). With her father up in the stands, O'Reilly embraced what the entire squad was feeling. As a second-half sub, O'Reilly hit the post before the Germany equaliser, but she did not, and nor did any of her team-mates, drop her head in disappointment.

They kept attacking, and O'Reilly was the one who made the breakthrough just nine minutes into extra time. The girl who grew up idolising Mia Hamm, wore the same number as Hamm, went to the 1999 World Cup and cheered for Hamm, went to the same college as Hamm and won a NCAA title at North Carolina in her freshman year just like Hamm had now scored the goal to send herself – and her hero – to an Olympic gold medal match. It was the fairytale way to help end a fairytale career for Hamm and a fairytale way to start one for O'Reilly (don't let anyone ever tell you that soccer isn't inspirational).

Brazil was all that was standing between the US and another gold. It was a very talented Brazil side containing Marta, a future World Player of the Year winner, who had only been part of the national team set-up for around a year, top scorer Cristiane and Pretinha (Pretinha in Brazilian translates to 'little black girl' with Pretinha herself saying the reference to skin colour in Brazil isn't seen as problematic). This was not a team to take lightly because they could hurt you in many different ways, but after the buzz of the extra-time win over Germany, the US felt like they could take on anyone. And just like the game against Germany the US took the lead before half-time when Lindsay Tarpley, another young star, opened the scoring with a long-range effort. Brazil did hit back, however, and much earlier than Germany did, courtesy of Pretinha, and once again the USWNT were taken into extra time. The Americans were sapped of all energy. Two consecutive games totalling a massive 240 minutes of soccer played with very little rest took a mental and physical toll on the players, but if there is anything that we know about the USWNT it's that, when glory and success is at stake and it's right in front of them, they always find a way to muster up the energy to win the game. When Abby Wambach mustered up enough energy to leap into the air, seemingly defying gravity for a matter of seconds, to reach Lilly's cross, that was all it took to change the game. A matter of a few gravity-defying seconds was the difference between silver and gold, and thankfully the USWNT were taking home the latter, thanks to Wambach's fourth goal of the Games. The

US held out again to win yet another gold medal and finally managed to give their legends a send-off they deserved (they would actually go on a ten-game 'farewell tour' after the 2004 Games, but in terms of actual competitions this was their official send-off) and also created new legends in Wambach and O'Reilly to lead the future generation to more glory. Mia Hamm, clearly emotional, said:

> This team never gave up and every single player made a difference. These guys deserve it. They always put the game first. They always thought about leaving a legacy and leaving a better place for all the young girls that are in the stands. These girls deserve it and I am so proud to be on this team. I'm just one person. America should be proud of this team. We are going to enjoy it.

Whether Hamm meant they'll enjoy the triumph or the retirement is irrelevant, but one of the main takeaways from 2004 was that despite having a core group of legends leave the future was in good hands with ready-made replacements. In 2005 April Heinrichs resigned as manager of the USWNT and was replaced by Greg Ryan, one of the assistants from the 2004 Games. The future looked rather bright for the USWNT, even if there were expected to be a few bumps in the road ahead, but at the 2007 Women's World Cup was an opportunity to show the world that they could rebuild and still conquer at the same time.

Most of the newer members of the USWNT already had a decent number of caps under their belt and certainly weren't stepping into uncharted waters, but their importance to the team was emphasised a lot more than ever before. Take Hope Solo, for example. Solo was the third-choice goalkeeper at the 2004 Olympics, despite being eligible since 2000, but with Brianna Scurry being reliable between the sticks and Solo's injury issues, there was never any need to rush her into the team. After being advised to find game time in Europe, Solo made the most of her spells with Göteborg in Sweden and Lyon in France to establish herself as the US's number one towards the back end of 2005, with her Algarve Cup appearances all resulting in clean sheets and kick-starting a great run of performances. Solo took over in goal and Abby Wambach was still performing at a ridiculously high level and asserting herself as one of the team's main leaders alongside veteran presence Lilly, who was still captain. Heather O'Reilly was just 22 by the time the tournament rolled around, but she was also a vital cog, but the new main attraction for this rebuilt team was a talented 25-year-old midfielder who had impressed from an early age and had been expected to be one of the main talents for years to come. Making her debut in 2005, Carli Lloyd was awarded the MVP of the 2007 Algarve Cup, scoring four goals as she was also named the tournament's top scorer, with this edition of the Algarve Cup making everybody aware of what they probably knew already. The US were going to win the World Cup. It may have been in China (FIFA gave China the tournament as a way to pay them back following the SARS disease that prevented the country from hosting the previous World Cup) and there may have been many other great teams heading into this competition too, but none looked quite as dominant as the US. The USWNT had a 51-game unbeaten streak prior to the tournament, and given their performances in the build-up it certainly didn't look like they were ready to relinquish the streak any time soon. Drawn in the groups against North Korea, Sweden and Nigeria, the United States drew their opening game against North Korea 2-2 but managed to slip past both Sweden and Nigeria 2-0 and 1-0 respectively. Perhaps not the most exciting of group stages, but you don't get extra points for style and the United States certainly didn't care about it because they had managed to win their group – again – and waited to take on England in the first knock-out round. This was an England team who had beaten Argentina 6-1 and held Germany to a goalless draw, which is impressive in itself, but the reigning world champions were coming off the back of demolishing Argentina 11-0 (poor Argentina) with Birgit Prinz and Sandra Smisek both scoring hat-tricks. By no means were England an easy game, but the 3-0 scoreline in favour of the

US made it look easy enough, but when you can call upon the reliable and experienced talents of Wambach and Lilly – both of whom scored in this game – it can make any game look just that little bit more straightforward. The win against England set up a mouth-watering tie between the US and Brazil in a repeat of the 2004 Olympic gold medal match. While both teams were stacked with top-class talent, it was also clear by looking at the ages of the Brazilians that they were also setting themselves up for the future, spearheaded by the incredible Marta who had an amazing partnership up front with Cristiane, with the two combining for 70 goals in all competitions prior to the World Cup. Brazil got through the group stage with complete ease, winning all three games against New Zealand, China and Denmark and scoring ten goals in the process and conceding none. The quarter-final match against Australia proved to be a harder test, but with both Marta and Cristiane getting a goal each, the 3-2 win put them in the semis and gave them a chance at revenge against the Americans. For Brazil, this was the perfect chance to show how their rebuilding job was going, and, with the best female player on the planet, they were about to stake their claim to be a force in this generation, but for the Americans their tournament was about to drive itself straight off a cliff ...

There had been some rumours in the build-up to the semi-final that coach Greg Ryan was set to change the starting goalkeeper from Hope Solo to veteran Briana Scurry due to the veteran's performances against Brazil in the past (12 games, 12 wins, but it should be noted that it was 12 games without facing Marta and Cristiane, 12 wins). Scurry, who was 36 by 2007, hadn't played all tournament and was about to step into the fire in place of the poster-child of this team, whom she was acting as a guiding figure for, so it was never going to be an easy decision to make or to take and the only way it could be ratified was if the US beat Brazil and went on to win the World Cup. Instead, what happened next was perhaps the biggest humiliation the USWNT has ever faced. After just 20 minutes, Brazil took the lead when Leslie Osborne tried to clear from a corner kick and inadvertently scored an own goal, and the Brazilians soon doubled their advantage seven minutes later through Marta. Two goals down at half-time isn't the end of the world for a team as good as the US, but when Cristiane made it 3-0 it looked like lights out. A fourth from Marta was soon delivered and the US were sent packing courtesy of their biggest defeat ever, yet the scoreline wasn't what made the headlines. It was the outburst from Solo after the game that stole the show. Speaking to a reporter after the game, Solo said this about the decision from coach Ryan:

> [Starting Scurry] was the wrong decision. And I think anybody that knows anything about the game knows that. There's no doubt in my mind I would have made those saves. And the fact of the matter is, it's not 2004 anymore.

Whether or not she realised it at the time, Solo had just created a frenzy with her comments. The veterans of the team called her out in a private meeting after the game, the squad seemingly banished her from team activities and effectively suspended Solo for the third-placed play-off against Norway (which the USWNT won 4-1). When teams lose, they tend to go after one particular individual to blame the loss on (see Steve Bartman and the 2003 Chicago Cubs and Bill Buckner for the 1986 Boston Red Sox), but on this occasion this individual had left herself wide open by just stating her mind. She was outspoken, she was – what could be considered – very unprofessional, but she was good enough to earn her place back at some point in time. But the question wasn't about earning her place back on talent, it was about earning the trust of her team-mates again. So the controversy surrounding Hope Solo overshadowed anything that happened at the 2007 World Cup, and the first stage of the rebuild wasn't exactly going to plan. The next generation's goalkeeper had undermined her entire squad and Greg Ryan was sacked as head coach. The replacement for Ryan would be Swede Pia Sundhage, the former assistant to the

China women's team who had served as a scout for the USWNT during the 2004 Olympics. It seemed like a perfect match early on, with Sundhage winning the 2008 Algarve Cup, and it set the USWNT up well for the bounce back from a disappointing World Cup in 2007.

With the 2008 Olympics just ahead and firmly in their sights, it was perfect timing. It was perfect for Solo and her next generation of stars to stake their claim as the real deal, while it gave Sundhage the perfect opportunity to show what she could do as a head coach and how she could deal with the incredible array of talent she had at her disposal. It wasn't going to be easy, but it would go on to have an important lasting effect on the future of the team, regardless of how this tournament went. If the USWNT won, it validated the fact that this new breed were about to really kick into full flow, but if they lost, it would've set the programme back a few years unnecessarily. With the 2008 Olympics arriving, Sundhage named her squad. Veterans Christie Rampone (now Pearce) and Kate Markgraf were named as joint captains and were the two most experienced players in the squad. Hope Solo, Carli Lloyd and Aly Wagner provided the balance of experience in big games and youthful exuberance, while a few new members were added to the line-up. A 20-year-old midfielder called Tobin Heath entered the fray, as did speedy forward Amy Rodriguez, to test themselves out for the future. One notable omission from the squad was Abby Wambach, the prolific scorer, who'd suffered a mid-shaft oblique fracture of the tibia and fibula in a game against Brazil beforehand, meaning she had to sit it out. It was heart-breaking for her and for the rest of the team because they knew how much she wanted to be at the Games, but also – from a purely soccer perspective – they knew they had a much better chance to win the gold with her in the side. Nevertheless, strength comes from adversity, and without their main source of goals the US had to find a different way to win. In their group against New Zealand, Japan and Norway, the USWNT got off to the worst possible start imaginable. In the opener, Norway beat the US 2-0 with two goals in the first four minutes, which really shook the US. They were beaten and they struggled against Japan too, winning by the one goal. A 4-0 win over New Zealand made things look a little bit more rosy, but it just seemed to paper over the cracks somewhat. Up next in the quarter-finals was Canada, and it took until extra time for the United States to get over the Canadian line, thanks to Hawaiian Natasha Kai, the supersub of the team. With Lilly out pregnant and Wambach out due to her injury, the strike force of the United States was looking threadbare. Young Rodiguez was tasked with leading the line alongside veteran midfielder Angela Hucles, a midfielder who was transformed into a striker by Sundhage, and, as Heather O'Reilly explains, was nicknamed 'Butter' because 'she was always extremely poised'. The semi-finals saw the US come up against a Japan team that they struggled against in the group stage, but the team looked like a different side from the group rounds. After the late Canada win, the team looked buoyed and a lot more confident knowing that they had the tools in their arsenal to win games, and it was a much better game against Japan this time around. Ohno opened the scoring for Japan, but the US went on to score four, Hucles grabbing two before Japan got a consolation in the dying seconds. Before the tournament there was genuine concern over how the US would cope without their main source of goals and how they would cope without key veterans from past winning teams, especially after the whole episode with Solo and the appointment of Sundhage. There were a lot of questions pre-2008, but after the knockout rounds when the US made the gold medal match, a lot of the questions had been answered. Sundhage looked like the perfect appointment, Solo had regained the trust of her team-mates and was now becoming one of the more vocal leaders in the team, while the team found a way to adapt to their striker issue by getting goals from other sources.

The Gold Medal match was against 2007 World Cup opponents Brazil, and the wounds were still fresh. Brazil still had Cristiane and Marta – who was in the middle of her incredible run of five FIFA Women's World Player of the Year awards in a row (Marta would be on the podium for this award from 2004 to 2014, only finishing third twice) – and were starting to look more and more like the unstoppable force of women's soccer. They had their own brand of soccer that the direct style from the Americans hadn't been able to handle in 2007, so how would they deal with it a year on? Well, this is why Sundhage was the perfect appointment for the US because she had managed to change the way they played. This US side was able to keep the ball and take possession right out of the Brazilians' hands (or rather their feet), which was led by a pivoting midfielder duo in the form of Lloyd and Shannon Boxx. Lloyd and Boxx were the main cogs in this wheel and were instructed to feed the energetic, yet exhausted, Rodriguez, who chased every ball with the same gusto. Some vital saves from Solo kept the United States in the game and a brilliant performance from right-back Heather Mitts – a player who had to watch the 2007 World Cup Final from the ESPN studio because she tore her ACL earlier in the year, and she also missed the 2003 World Cup with a broken leg – and it frustrated Marta, and it took her off her game. As extra time rolled on, Brazil began to open up a bit more and Lloyd started to make runs to support the attack. She found a pocket of space around 20 yards away from goal and smartly back-heeled it to Rodriguez, with the striker holding the ball off three Brazilian defenders and feeding it back to Lloyd. Lloyd's first touch was absolutely perfect, taking her past any defender near her and allowing her enough time to wind back her left leg, pinpoint exactly where she wanted the ball to go and, just like that, with the wave of her magic wand of a left foot, Lloyd scored a cracker.

The ball bounced just before it got to the goalkeeper, which made it near-impossible to save, but no one from the US cared, because they were about to win yet another gold medal. A team that was essentially counted out before the Games, who were missing their star striker and who had a ton of questions hanging over their heads prior to the tournament had gone all the way and proved, once again, that the team to beat in the women's game was still the United States. If this was them in a state of transition, imagine how good they'll be when they get all the pieces together?

With the 2008 gold medal in the bag, and with players like Solo and Wambach becoming leaders on the pitch and role models off it, one could argue that the status of the USWNT had never been better. With the help of social media and wider coverage of soccer in the United States, these women were becoming stars. They weren't afraid to speak their mind, which appealed to millions, but they could also back up their words with their actions, which earned them even more admiration, and with a new generation of players due to make their mark on the 2011 World Cup in Germany, now was the most important time in the careers of the leaders in the team. Six players in the 2011 World Cup squad had over 100 caps (Hope Solo had 95 heading into the tournament so reached her ton during the competition) and 12 members of the squad were 26 or younger, with the more experienced members of the squad such as Lloyd, Solo, Wambach, Rampone, Mitts and Boxx all playing crucial roles as mentors and as key players on the pitch. Pia Sundhage knew that it would be a good chance to challenge, while bringing in fresh faces, and one fresh face in particular was making a name for herself as one of the best in the world, even if she was the youngest member of the squad. At the 2008 under-20s Women's World Cup, there were two Americans atop the best player rankings. One was Sydney LeRoux, and the other was Alex Morgan. Morgan – described by FIFA on their official website as the following: 'The American striker's good looks and eye for goal quickly marked her out as a favourite of the Chilean fans and media alike' – was clearly the prized possession in US women's soccer in that age group, and while she was only 21 when she got the call-up to the World Cup, she looked certain to be a key player at the tournament. Her four goals at the under-20 World Cup showcased her eye for goal, and while she wasn't quite a starter for the main squad just yet, she was a valuable asset to have on the bench. No other nation had the quality to bring off the bench that the US did in Morgan and 23-year-old Tobin Heath, a midfielder who made her debut at the 2008 Games and who was probably the most naturally gifted player in the squad. While the US were reigning Olympic champions, the number-one ranked nation in the world and had arguably the best goalscorer in the competition with Wambach, they weren't the only ones considered favourites. Hosts Germany had a knack of performing well at World Cups, and this one was expected to be no different, as well as Brazil who were still led by Marta and Cristiane. These three were probably the favourites to take home the trophy, and with Germany and Brazil winning their groups with maximum points, the United States were the odd ones out. Two straight-forward wins against Colombia and North Korea meant that the final-day clash against Sweden was a shootout to see who would finish top, and despite Wambach pulling a goal back in the 67th minute to cut the deficit down to 2-1, the Swedes held on and the United States were forced into second place and forced into the tougher route in the knockout rounds. If they had beaten Sweden, a game in Augsburg against Australia was waiting with a potential semi-final against Germany or Japan after that, but instead the US got Brazil in the quarter-finals, followed by either England or France.

There's never an easy way to win a World Cup, but one route looked substantially less difficult than the other, but when you're the best-ranked side on the planet you should have the talent to get through the knockout stages, regardless of what stands in front of you. For the US, Brazil was just another chance to show how good they could be and why they deserved to be the number-one nation. In fact, it only took two minutes for the United States to take the lead when Daiane scored into her own net after a devilish cross in from Boxx. The sell-out in Dresden was eagerly anticipated by fans across the globe, and the match delivered, and one of the players who had expectation heaped on to her was World Player of the Year Marta, who was Brazil's main outlet. The Brazilian controlled a long ball down inside the US box, with two defenders hassling her, and produced a magnificent piece of skill to take the ball over her markers and earn herself a penalty – sending Rachel Buehler off in the process. Daiane stepped up to take the spot kick, but Solo was equal to her effort; however, the referee ordered a retake after Rampone encroached into the penalty area, and Marta made no mistake in putting that one away. It was a tough way for the US to lose the lead, but such was the closeness of the game that it went into extra time. These were two of the best teams in the world and they were playing like it. But given the quality of the teams, the second Brazil goal wasn't particularly glorious or amazing, but it seemed to catch everyone in the United States backline out. A cross was played into the box, and while it seemed to be an easy one to deal with, Marta stole a march on her defender and looped the ball goalward, but Solo wasn't able to deal with the danger and the ball went in off the post. It was poor concentration from the USWNT and one they would've been sick to their stomach for conceding, but the end of the line wasn't the Marta goal because while Brazil's main goal threat had her say on proceedings the US's goal-getter was about to have hers.

Megan Rapinoe – a winger who missed the 2007 World Cup and 2008 Games through injury – played in a beautiful cross to the back post that was just begging to be headed home, and when Andreia failed to claim the cross all Wambach had to do was make good contact on the ball and it would be 2-2, which she did without hesitation in the 122nd minute. It was a dramatic way to clinch a draw out of the claws of defeat, but the US don't do things lying down, and a penalty shootout would, ironically, be the only way to separate these two. Unfortunately for Brazil, the only missed penalty during the shootout would fall their way as Daiane missed once again, with Solo saving again. The US advanced to the semi-finals to face France, who also went the distance and beat England on penalties, but while both teams took their games the full 120 minutes and more, the semi wouldn't be as close as the United States ran out 3-1 winners. Some big saves from Solo kept the United States ahead until just before the hour mark, but goals from Wambach and a sub goal from Morgan meant the US advanced to the final against Japan, a team who had a tough road to get to this final.

After losing to England in their final group game, Japan had to face Germany in the quarter-finals and dispatched of them 1-0 after extra time, and in the semis they faced off against Sweden in Frankfurt, with the score being a 3-1 win in favour of the Japanese. Maybe historical factors had a say in who was considered favourites for the final, but when push came to shove there wasn't much separating Japan and the US, at least based on what was seen during the tournament. It certainly seemed like destiny that the United States would win their third Women's World Cup, especially after the win against Brazil, and given the fact that this was Japan's first Women's World Cup Final. Of course, history and experience only matter if you can transfer your talents on to the pitch on the day, along with a good slice of luck, and for 90 minutes the one thing that the US lacked was luck.

If you watch any World Cup Final, you will not see a more one-sided affair than the US vs Japan from 2011. Japan sat deep, allowing the US to press on to them, and the US didn't hesitate one bit, but they just couldn't find the magic touch until the second half. Lauren Cheney saw her effort go agonisingly wide of the post, while Wambach had a rocket of a shot that deserved to be a goal but could only cannon back off the underside of the crossbar. Alex Morgan was brought on as a second-half sub to see if she could work her magic, and her first major involvement was to stab an effort onto the post, before Wambach forced a great save with a looping header. It looked like it was going to be one of those days for the US, but super-sub Morgan had other ideas when she let rip with an effort on the edge of the penalty area that beat Ayumi Kaihori all ends up. The US dominated the game for the most part and were more effective on the counter attack, but a defensive mix-up from the US backline allowed Aya Miyama to poke her effort past Solo from the edge of the six-yard box. If the woodwork didn't show that the US's luck wasn't in, this goal certainly did. Nine times out of ten the US would clear the ball, but the one occasion they didn't just happened to occur during the most important time of the tournament. Extra time loomed, and just before the extra-time interval, Wambach headed the US back in front with what looked to be the winner, deflating an already tired-looking Japan, but somehow it wasn't. Captain and talisman Homare Sawa managed to flick the ball on at the front post from a corner that beat Solo all ends up and took the game to penalties. The Japanese hadn't had a penalty shootout in this tournament, while the Americans managed to convert all five of theirs against Brazil in the quarter-finals and had the best goalkeeper at the tournament to make the important saves. Surely now, with hitting the woodwork twice, the defensive mix-up for the Japan equaliser and the fact that they'd led twice, and so late into extra time as well, this meant their luck would now be in. You'd think that by the law of averages the United States would get a break in the penalty shootout, but it wasn't to be. In fact, it probably couldn't have been much worse. Boxx, Lloyd and Tobin Heath, the late substitute, all missed, while Japan converted two of their three penalties. The ever-reliable Wambach tucked her penalty away, but with Solo needing to save Saki Kumagai's penalty, Kumagai placed her shot perfectly into the top-left corner to win the World Cup for Japan and break US hearts. It was now 12 years since the last World Cup triumph, and the squad were naturally disappointed, but there wasn't an inquest like last time. There was no controversial outburst from a player who was dropped, there was just disappointment. The support for the USWNT grew after the final loss because of how they performed during the rest of the tournament. After going a player down in the second half against Brazil, and then going a goal down in extra time before equalising with the latest-ever goal scored at a World Cup (men's or women's World Cup, beating Alessandro Del Piero's record from 2006 of 121 minutes by a solitary minute), you'd have thought that some doubt would have crept into the players' minds, but they were calm, because they were confident. The calmness and the confidence transferred into the stands. Hope Solo had been accused of being arrogant at the last World Cup, but that 'arrogance' was vital in the 2011 shootout against Brazil. But actually what Solo had wasn't arrogance, it was confidence, and everyone in the squad had it. Yes, the stars looked like they had aligned for the US, but they had aligned for Japan as well, who were playing for a much bigger cause. Four months earlier, Japan suffered in the tragic tsunami and earthquake which caused so much damage, and these women were seen as heroes. They were seen as the shining light to bring some form of hope to a country on its knees, and given the fact they had never beaten Germany before – their quarter-final opponents – given the fact they had never beaten Sweden before – their semi-final opponents – and given the fact they had failed to beat the United States in 25 attempts – their final opponents – it just seemed like their name was on the trophy. And sometimes, in soccer, you just cannot do anything about it.

Hope Solo had established herself as the best goalkeeper on the planet, while the arrival of Alex Morgan and Tobin Heath took the load off Wambach and Carli Lloyd. Players like Lauren Cheney, Megan Rapinoe, Amy Rodriguez, Rachel Buehler and Stephanie Cox were now more integral to the entire squad. Heading into the 2012 Olympics in London, the squad wasn't likely to be altered too much, with maybe one or two extra key players brought in, but there was no need to change things too much. Sundhage had built a great side, they just needed luck to be on their side, and whilst the 2011 World Cup was destined to go to Japan, the next few years were destined to belong to the new USWNT dynasty that looked certain to dominate, as they had all the tools and talent needed to do so.

While 2011 was a major disappointment, it wasn't seen as the end of the world, rather it was seen as a good building block for the future, and the 2012 London Olympics gave the USWNT a great opportunity to flex their muscles. The large majority of the 2011 squad stayed intact, and the addition of Sydney LeRoux made their attack look more formidable, with Wambach moving up to third in the all-time USWNT top scorers list just behind Mia Hamm. Alex Morgan had become a more integral part of the team, with 27 goals before the start of the tournament, and other players who had played major roles in reaching the World Cup Final were now more experienced and contributing more than before, such as Megan Rapinoe, Tobin Heath and Lauren Cheney, all of whom were 27 or younger. There was a youthful vibe to this squad and there was also an air of invincibility around this team as well. They were talented, they were confident and it was almost like they knew they were on their way to winning yet another gold medal, but that confidence didn't translate on to the pitch straight away. In the opening game against France, the US found themselves in a hole. A two-goal hole, to be precise, as the French went 2-0 up after 14 minutes, leaving the US in a sticky predicament. But as per usual, and just when they needed her the most, Wambach pulled one back 19 minutes in before Morgan levelled things up after the half-hour mark. The two France goals seemed to light a fire in the US, almost like they had woken a beast that wasn't going to thrash them, just meticulously pick them off one goal at a time. The second half was more of the same as Lloyd got in on the scoring proceedings to put the US 3-2 up, and Morgan completed the comeback with her second and the US's fourth of the game. A comfortable 3-0 win over Colombia followed, with Rapinoe, Wambach and Lloyd scoring, and the 1-0 win over North Korea (another Wambach goal) saw the US qualify as group winners and into the quarter-finals to face New Zealand. Having played at Hampden Park in Glasgow and Old Trafford in Manchester, a trip to Newcastle and St James' Park was next up as the US looked for another convincing win. Another goal from Wambach and a first Olympic one for LeRoux put the United States through in a game that they never really looked like losing and never looked challenged, and it was probably this match that convinced the world that this was their gold medal, especially after Brazil were knocked out by the hands of Japan in the quarter-finals. With New Zealand out of the way, up next for the United States were their neighbours and main rivals, Canada. The US vs Canada will always add an extra level of spice to whatever event it is, but this match in particular will live long in the memory because it is one of the most spectacular, dramatic, exciting and entertaining games you will *ever* see. At the Theatre of Dreams, it was wall-to-wall, non-stop action, with Canada taking the lead after a wonderfully taken goal from Christine Sinclair, their captain. She danced past two US defenders before slotting past Solo to give the Canadians a 1-0 half-time lead, but the second half would be where the action commenced. Just nine minutes after the restart, Megan Rapinoe scored directly from a corner as Sinclair tried to clear off the line, but the ball had fully gone over before she could get a touch to it. Then Sinclair put Canada back in the lead after 67 minutes. The second Sinclair goal was the flame that lit the match because the next six minutes were pure bedlam. Once Sinclair had scored, Rapinoe had the ball on the right flank, cut back inside and fired her shot off the left post to equalise, and then just three minutes after that – and six minutes after her initial header to kick-start this frenzy – Sinclair completed her hat-trick after her arching header went over the woman on the goal line and in for a 3-2 Canada lead. It was pandemonium and pure end-to-end stuff, but it wasn't over with the third Sinclair goal. Next in this epic encounter was a controversial penalty, but it wasn't just a regular controversial penalty, it was a penalty unlike any that most people have ever seen, including Pia Sundhage, who said after the game, 'I've never seen that before'. But rather than just explain what happened, this brief excerpt from the match report from Canadian website *The Star* tells the story perfectly (at least from a Canadian perspective):

> Around the 78th minute, the ball found its way back to Canadian goalkeeper Erin McLeod. The American forwards were pressing high up the pitch. McLeod was looking for a chance to outer the ball to a full-back, rather than to launch it up the field. Eventually, she gave in and hoofed it forward. But [referee Christina] Pedersen had blown her whistle.
>
> She called a foul on McLeod for a six-second violation – time wasting in other words, though no one was foolish enough to begin eating the clock with 20 minutes to go. No warning was given, according to McLeod. That's the form – warning first. You want another theme? This has

been the Army Olympics, the Empty Olympics, and the Angry Olympics. Now it's the Making Things Up As You Go The Hell Along Olympics.

Regardless of the warning, how often is that call made? 'I've never seen that before,' US coach Pia Sundhage said afterward. Sundhage has worked in the game since they used mammoth tusks for goalposts. She's never seen it because that call is never made. Never.

And in a one-goal game in which a gold medal hangs in the balance, it should be made near to the power of infinity. On the ensuing free kick inside the Canadian area, the ball cannoned into the protective arm of Marie-Eve Nault. That's probably a penalty. That's how Pedersen called it. The problem was that Pedersen and her crew had ignored an even more blatant handball in the area by American Megan Rapinoe 10 minutes before.

After the call, Canadian players rushed Pedersen. I said, 'I hope you can sleep tonight. Put on your American jersey. That's who you played for today,' [Melissa] Tancredi said, voice shaking. 'I was honest.'

As captain, Sinclair asked Pedersen for an explanation, 'She actually giggled and said nothing,' Sinclair said. 'Classy'.

After the controversy managed to boil itself down, Wambach tucked the penalty away to level the score, before Morgan scored a winner in the 123rd minute of the game. It was heartbreaking for Canada, but it was jubilation for America, and it was pure soccer entertainment for the neutrals. Those in attendance at Old Trafford witnessed a treat, and with the gold medal match against Japan on the horizon, the fans had witnessed a determined and rampant USWNT team. With the world-famous Wembley Arch hanging above their head, the US and Japan walked out to face one another just a year after they had done the same in the World Cup. This time, however, the stars aligned for the USWNT as a double from Carli Lloyd managed to bring home the gold. Lloyd opened the scoring after eight minutes, but the US rode their luck a bit in the first half, with Solo tipping a header on to the cross bar and the referee somehow missing a blatant handball in the box. But while Lloyd doubled the score and Yuki Ogimi pulled one back, the win was all the US deserved, and it was their second consecutive gold and second consecutive game where Lloyd proved to be the difference. She was a truly iconic player for the national team and had come in clutch on more than one occasion, but the entire tournament showed how versatile the USWNT could be. With Hope Solo in goal, it would've taken something special to beat a special goalkeeper, and with Christie Rampone and Heather Mitts at the back they had the experience, talent and brain to outclass any opposition forward. With Lloyd, Rapinoe, Tobin Heath and Heather O'Reilly deployed as midfielders/wingers, you'd be hard pressed to find a weak link at all, and with Wambach, Morgan, LeRoux and Cheney in attack, you had goals coming from everywhere. They weren't the perfect team, but they were about as perfect as you could get. Could you score against them? Yes, but could you stop them scoring? Not a chance. With Olympic glory in their back pocket, the US had another target in their sights. They wanted their World Cup back, and in 2015 they had the chance, already having a firm grip on the trophy following their impressive showing at the Olympics.

Following the Olympic triumph in London, there was an air of change about the USWNT. Pia Sundhage announced that she would depart as head coach, following the celebration tour in September 2012, to take the role as Sweden national team coach. She was replaced by Glasgow-born Tom Sermanni, who had been the head coach of the Australian Women's side from 2004 up until 2012. Sermanni had the required experience to take over the role. He finished 2013 unbeaten in his first year as coach and won the 2013 Algarve Cup, becoming just the second USWNT side to remain unbeaten for an entire year (they did it back in 2006). But 2014 wasn't as productive for Sermanni and the USWNT as they finished seventh in the Algarve Cup after failing to win a single group game, despite starting the year off with a 1-0 win over Canada and a pair of 7-0 and 8-0 drubbings against Russia. In April of 2014, Sermanni was sacked as USWNT boss and replaced with Jill Ellis, a former USWNT assistant and previous interim boss. Ellis was born in Portsmouth, England, but never had the opportunity to play women's soccer until she moved to the United States, so she had to make do with playing with the boys in her youth, saying:

> Soccer was in my blood, but there were no formal opportunities for girls. Soccer was for the boys. So, I played with the boys.

Her mother described the sport as 'unladylike', so soccer was out of the question when she was in England, but when her father John Ellis – a former Royal Marine commando who also coached soccer – took up a coaching position with the Annandale Boys Club in North Carolina in 1981, Ellis's life changed. Ellis didn't have a position when she joined her first team and was captain of her secondary school team, who won the state championship in 1984, so she had considerable talent and a considerable love for the game. When it became apparent that women's soccer in the US wasn't about to launch a fully fledged league in the 80s/90s, Ellis used her time to study for her masters and became the assistant coach of the North Carolina State women's soccer team, a move that shaped her destiny forever. She entered the USSF system in 2000 as coach of the USWNT under-21 side, before working her way up the ranks through various age groups – development director for the USSF, USWNT assistant and interim, before finally getting her crack at the full job prior to the 2015 World Cup.

It was a tough job considering that the US had never failed to reach the semi-finals of a World Cup, and without having won the competition since 1999 there was an expectation to bring home the trophy with this special set of players, aided by the incentive of it being north of the border, hosted by their good friends Canada. With the introduction of hawkeye and goal line technology, along with every game being played on artificial turf, it proved to be a World Cup that everyone would talk about for years to come. Drawn in Group D alongside Nigeria, Australia and Pia Sundhage's Sweden, the US finished top despite not exactly looking on top of their game. A 3-1 win against Australia was enough for the opening game three points, with a double from Rapinoe and one from Christen Press. A 0-0 against Sweden seemed almost fitting, while the final game against Nigeria resulted in a 1-0 win, with Wambach scoring the winner. But while the US didn't look on top of their game for the entirety of the group stage, they entered their knockout round mode and started to churn out win after win, looking formidable. Two second-half goals from Morgan and Lloyd won the game against Colombia in the next round, which saw them move on to face China in the quarter-finals. Another Lloyd goal after 51 minutes, this time a wonderful leaping header from the penalty spot, sent the US through in a game that they never, ever looked like losing. They never looked like losing mainly due to the performance of Hope Solo, a player some would argue shouldn't have even been in the squad, let alone starting a knockout game, because in June 2014 she was arrested on two counts of domestic abuse, and she was reportedly shouting insults at officers when she was being arrested. Solo defended herself on multiple platforms and even went on *Good Morning America* to tell her side of the story, but the problem was her story and the police report didn't entirely match up. Solo accused her 17-year-old nephew of abusing her, while the official report was placed by her nephew and Solo's sister-in-law.

Eight months after the incident, the case was thrown out, but that wasn't the end of Solo's off-field incidents. Not long after the domestic abuse case, Solo's husband and NFL player Jeremy Stevens was charged with a DUI whilst driving a USWNT team van ... whilst Solo was in the van with him. The USSF suspended Solo for 30 days, but the incidents didn't seem to affect anyone in the camp. Solo eventually regained her place in the starting line-up and was still as incredible between the sticks as before, keeping another clean sheet in the semi-finals against a very tough Germany side. The theme for the USWNT this tournament was slow starters that grew into the impenetrable force they had always been throughout the knockout stages, and whilst wins against Colombia and China were what was needed, the semi-final win over the top-seeded Germany was the statement that they truly needed to make to assure the neutrals that the US were coming home as world champions, regardless of what any other team had to say about it. The US should've been 2-0 up by the break, but a missed penalty from the Germans in the second half handed the US a lifeline that they didn't need to think twice about taking, because Lloyd converted her penalty – her third goal of the tournament. Kelley O'Hara sealed the game for the US with a close finish to set up yet another game against Japan in the final, a potentially historical final for both nations. For Japan, they had the chance to become the second team to win the World Cup – male or female – twice under the same manager (Italy did it in 1934 and 1938 with Vittorio Pozzo) and they could have been the first nation to retain their World Cup title since Germany retained their crown in 2007. For the US, a win would see them become the first team to win three women's World Cups, thus placing them above Germany in the all-time wins rankings. After facing each other in the 2012 Olympic gold medal match, the 2011 World Cup Final, a 1995 World Cup quarter-final and 1991 group stage match, the two were more than familiar with each other, and with the Americans taking the 2012 game and Japan taking the 2011 final, there was more at stake than just a trophy.

Whoever won would be the dominant side of the early 2000s and in historical terms would be remembered for decades to come, so it was safe to assume that a tight, cagey, feisty, dogged affair was in order. The US hadn't conceded a goal since the opening game, whereas Japan were undefeated yet scraped through against England courtesy of a late own goal. Most people had assumed that it wouldn't be full-throttle soccer from the opening whistle because of the nature of the two teams, so naturally the game started in dramatic fashion.

The USWNT had clearly been working on set pieces during training because their opening two goals came from low crosses into the box, with Lloyd scoring both. Five minutes in and the US were 2-0 up, with Japan, understandably, shell-shocked and frozen in a shared state of panic and confusion. It would take nine agonisingly long minutes for the US to add a third, when Lauren Holiday capitalised on some terrible Japan defending before the most extraordinary World Cup Final goal you will ever see. We've seen players score from the halfway line against Luton in the FA Cup, Wimbledon in a meaningless Premier League game, but never a World Cup Final. So when the United States won the ball back in their own half, hardly anyone expected Carli Lloyd to glance up, swing her right leg at the ball and watch in awe as the ball dipped in off the post. It was her hat-trick goal and it set a new record of the quickest hat-trick in World Cup history (the fastest in men's and women's World Cup history). Now, 4-0 down before the 20th minute is far from ideal, and it was pretty much the end of the game, although Japan did manage to pull it back to 4-2 in the 52nd minute, but any hopes of a comeback were dashed when Tobin Heath scored the fifth and final goal of the 2015 World Cup Final, and a pulsating one at that. In emphatic fashion, the United States had regained their World Cup crown and made history in the process. Not only that, but they had the Golden Ball winner in Carli Lloyd, the joint winner of the Golden Boot in Lloyd, the Golden Glove winner in Hope Solo and six members in the fan-voted Dream Team. It was an explosive return to the top of the world, but not an unexpected one considering what they had achieved in recent years. The growth of women's soccer had been there for everyone to see, with the success of the USWNT and the introduction of the National Women's Soccer League (NWSL) –launched in 2012 – which gave the USWNT stars a professional and stable league to ply their trade. It provided them with a place they could call home without having to go to Europe to play for the likes of Lyon, PSG and Chelsea. Players like Carli Lloyd, Alex Morgan, Marta, Christine Sinclair, Tobin Heath and Megan Rapinoe have all been able to call the NWSL their home, and they've benefitted massively from it. But the 2015 World Cup also spelled the beginning and end of different eras in the USWNT. Abby Wambach retired as a legend, being 2012 Women's World Player of the Year and all-time USWNT top scorer, with 184 goals in 256 games. Probably the deadliest striker in women's soccer history, it was only fitting that she went out with a win. Players like Hope Solo, Carli Lloyd, Ali Krieger, Becky Sauerbrunn and Megan Rapinoe were all 30 and above and approaching the end of their international careers, while the likes of Julie Johnston, Crystal Dunn, Morgan Brian, Lindsey Horan and Mallory Pugh were drafted in with eyes looking towards the future.

Rio 2016 was the first stop on the journey for the next generation. Wins against New Zealand (2-0) and France (1-0) saw the US through to the knockout rounds, despite their 2-2 draw against Colombia, where they would face Sweden. Sweden, who got out of their group as one of the best-ranked third-placed teams, did not look like a threat to the United States. The US, the reigning Olympic and world champions, should not have had an issue beating a side that couldn't even win their group, but as fate would have it the United States were given a rude awakening. For the first time in their history, they failed to make the semi-finals of a major competition, as underdogs Sweden defeated them 4-3 in a tense penalty shootout. In a bid to become the first nation to win the World Cup and Olympics in consecutive years, the Americans went a goal down when Stina Blackstenius gave Sweden the lead, before Alex Morgan equalised in the 77th minute. Morgan stepped up to take the first US penalty of the shootout and failed to convert, and their dreams of making yet more history were ended when Christen Press couldn't find the back of the net. Carli Lloyd spoke after the game with regards to the loss, saying:

> It's hard to go back to back – that's why no one has done it. It's unfortunate. We had the talent. We were playing well. That's the way soccer goes sometimes.

But while the collected thoughts of Lloyd were your standard soccer player response, Hope Solo had other ideas and decided to blast the Swedes, saying post game:

> I thought that we played a courageous game. I thought we had many opportunities on goal. I think we showed a lot of heart, but I also think we played a bunch of cowards. The best team did not win today. I strongly believe that. They didn't want to pass the ball. They didn't want to play great soccer. It was a combative game, a physical game. Exactly what they wanted and exactly what their game plan was. I don't think they're going to make it far in the tournament. I think it was very cowardly, but they won, they're moving on and we're going home.

Sweden boss Pia Sundhage simply replied to Solo's statements by saying:

> It is okay to be a coward if you win.

Sweden would go on to finish fourth in the Games, while Solo was suspended for six months and had her contract terminated. Solo believed the reason she was suspended was her vocal role in wanting equal pay for the women in comparison to the men, saying:

> Seventeen years on this team and then to be treated this way in the end is not surprising from US Soccer, to be honest. I feel like I'm being pushed out because it can't be based on performance or my health. It can't be based on anything but they don't like me, because they know I've been fighting so hard for equal pay.
>
> They're going to use my comments as an excuse to get rid of me forever so that they don't have to deal with such a strong voice and opposition to field conditions and playing conditions and pay. I think I'm just a thorn in their side and it's time for them to cut their losses.

With Solo out of the set-up and the much larger issue of equal pay in the public spotlight (more on that in the conclusion chapter), the attention of the USSF was shifting. The women in the USWNT were becoming more vocal about what they believed in and used their status in sport to spread their message, like Solo and her message about equal pay and Megan Rapinoe in 2017, who was the first white American athlete to take to her knees during the national anthem in support of NFL quarterback Colin Kaepernick.

The USWNT had the privilege of going down New York City's Canyon of Heroes following their return from the 2015 World Cup, following in the footsteps of astronauts, soldiers and royalty. These women were more than just soccer players at this point, they were role models to young girls in the same way that Derek Jeter was a role model to every shortstop in the country. They were the first women to go down the Canyon since 1984, when Mary Lou Retton and Cheryl Miller, two gold medalists who joined the US's team – men and women – on a ticker tape parade. The 2015 USWNT might possibly be one of the first-ever women-only sports team to get a parade. It was inspiring for young girls across America, and they wanted to see their heroes given the attention and adulation they deserved, and while some people may not 100 per cent agree with taking a knee during the anthem or shouting about equal pay, these women used their status to get important talking points into the mainstream consciousness, like true athletes and true role models.

After the 2015 World Cup and 2016 Olympics, the USWNT became a much bigger point of focus, more than ever before. More people were interested following these tournaments, and even though experimentation after the Olympics debacle meant that they lost three home games in a row, the US bounced back in 2018 with wins in the SheBelieves Cup and Tournament of Nations, while picking up their 500th win, against Portugal. As this chapter is being written, the United States are entering the 2019 Women's World Cup as favourites and, depending on when you read this, they may be world champions again or they may have lost what they firmly believe is their and their only. It will likely be the last tournament for Carli Lloyd – who turns 37 after the end of the World Cup – and Megan Rapinoe, who'll be 34 two days before the World Cup Final itself, and the duo are probably planning on going out on a high, just as their former team-mate Abby Wambach did.

While some look past the accomplishments of the USWNT in a general American sporting sense, it's impossible not to acknowledge how dominant they've been in soccer. Three World Cups, four Olympic gold medals, ten Algarve Cups and possessing some of the greatest female talent this game has ever seen. Don't put the USWNT down for whatever reason, acknowledge them for what they truly are – a true dominant sporting dynasty up there with the New York Yankees, the Los Angeles Lakers, the New England Patriots and the Boston Celtics. In such a short space of time they've been just as successful as these juggernauts of sports, so why aren't the USWNT recognised as a dominant force? Well, there probably is one major reason why, but there is a high possibility you already know what that reason is, and it has absolutely nothing to do with gold medals or World Cups ...

Chapter Nine

The Introduction of MLS and the 25-Year History of the League from 1996 to 2019

THE year 1988 was quite a significant year in cultural history. Rick Astley released the song 'Never Gonna Give You Up', one that gave kids in the 2000s a viral meme to send to their friends, George Michael released 'Faith', and the world was one year away from the emergence of a cartoon family called *The Simpsons,* so America had put up with wonderful shows such as *Roseanne, The Cosby Show* and *Cheers*, while *Wrestlemania IV* at Trump Plaza in Atlantic City saw Macho Man Randy Savage beat Ted DiBiase after a FOUR-HOUR tournament. In sports, Liverpool won the English First Division but shockingly lost to Wimbledon in the FA Cup, with John Aldridge becoming the first player to miss a penalty in an FA Cup Final. The Washington Redskins beat the Denver Broncos in Super Bowl XXII, the Los Angeles Lakers defeated the Detroit Pistons in game seven of the NBA finals, the Los Angeles Dodgers beat the Oakland As in the World Series – courtesy of an iconic

Kirk Gibson home run in game one – and in total it was a big year in the world of sport and culture. It was a good year for Los Angeles with two titles heading their way, but the state of California was about to receive the biggest prize in sport. The United States had a feeling that it was on top of the world with regards to sport, but for all the Magic Johnsons and Larry Birds in the country, the true global attraction was the FIFA World Cup.

The World Cup is the *be all and end all* of sporting events, bigger than anything in the world, and what better country to have the World Cup staged in than the land of Hollywood, the land where everything is bigger and better than everywhere else on the planet? The World Cup wasn't hosted in the US until 1994 (see chapter seven) but there was a lot more that had to be planned and integrated before the World Cup reached the US. The US had the funds to pay for what FIFA charged, they had the stadiums to hold the matches to perhaps the grandest scale it's ever been staged on, and it had the infrastructure to cope with masses of fans from across the globe entering their country and travelling to and from different states to watch games. From the logistical side, the US was the perfect country but for many outside of the United States who weren't familiar with the history of soccer in the country, it didn't seem like a good fit sporting wise.

Looking briefly at the previous few countries who had hosted the tournament prior to 1994 and you see Italy, Mexico (twice), Spain, Argentina, West Germany and England. All of these countries have a deep love for soccer (*Calcio, Football, Fussball, Futbol*) and, with the exception of Mexico, they had all been incredibly successful at a national and domestic level. Italy, England, Argentina and West Germany had all won the World Cup or performed well at previous tournaments as had Spain, and the leagues in these countries were some of the best in the world, housing some of the best teams and players in the world. The United States had none of that. In 1988 the United States were making it a habit to *not* qualify for the World Cup and hardly produced players who were going abroad and making successes for themselves. Sure, they had the NASL back in the day, but the NASL at its peak compared with the demise of the league in the 1980s was a stark contrast. Besides, the league went out of business in 1984, so for four years the United States didn't have a first division. Once the NASL ceased to exist, indoor soccer started to experience a slight surge in popularity, but you can't have an entire soccer culture based around indoor soccer, it's bush league stuff.

While a professional league was a few years off actually happening, baby steps needed to be made in the formation of a full league in order to secure the rights for the 1994 World Cup. It was the only condition that FIFA imposed on the US bid, so it was something they had to get right, and while 1988 was quite a dull year for US soccer on the surface, it proved to be potentially the most important day in their modern history.

The US won the bid, of course, due to their commitment to creating a professional first division. In the civil action papers for the Fraser vs MLS court case – an anti-trust file made by eight MLS players in 2000 against the league, the investors and the USSF claiming that the single entity nature of the league devalued players – it stated that:

> In the early 1990s, Alan Rothenberg, the President of USSF and of World Cup USA 1994, with assistance from others began developing plans for a division one professional outdoor soccer league in the United States. Rothenberg and others at the USSF consulted extensively with potential investors in an effort to understand what type of league structure and business plan they might find attractive.
>
> He also consulted anti-trust counsel in the hope of avoiding the anti-trust problems which other sports leagues such as the National Football League ('NFL') had encountered. Eventually the planners settled on the concept of organizing a limited liability company to run the league, and in 1995 MLS was formed.

And as the file says, the formation of Major League Soccer began. The league itself wouldn't begin for a few more years, but the starting blocks were in place from 1988 to 1993, the proposed start date for the new league. Although the building blocks for MLS were set up in 1988, soccer in the United States at the time wasn't in a healthy position. Former NASL honcho Clive Toye had reintroduced the American Soccer League in 1988 (the third incarnation of the ASL name since the early 1920s – yes, there was a second incarnation ... no, there is nothing significant about that one either – focusing solely on clubs on the east coast, using former NASL names in the league to bring attention to the new ASL. The Washington Diplomats, Tampa Bay Rowdies and Fort Lauderdale Strikers joined the ASL, but it missed the point of what made the NASL so popular. It wasn't the clubs, it was the players, and while the ASL brought in USMNT players in Peter Vermes, Tab Ramos and Bruce Murray and a few NASL vets like Ray Hudson, Steve Wergerle (the older brother of Roy Wegerle, one of two men to play in both the NASL and MLS – the other was Hugo Sánchez. Roy missed the new ASL due to Rodney Marsh sending him to have a trial with Queens Park Rangers and Chelsea in the mid-80s, signing for Chelsea before eventually joining QPR in 1990) and Teofilo Cubillas (fun fact, Teofilo is one of three players to score five or more goals at two World Cups alongside Miroslav Klose and Thomas Müller), true star power, like there had been in the NASL days, just wasn't quite there. The ASL was actually considered a success in 1989 in terms of attendances, carrying on into 1989 with the hopes of being turned into the division one pro league. Remember, the building blocks for MLS were set in place around this time, which is why the ASL is significant in this story.

We know what happens, but to understand the journey is just as important. With the success of the ASL in 1988 and then in 1989, along with the upturn in fortunes for the Western Soccer League (WSL) – where the Portland Timbers were playing at the time – merger talks were started with the hope of forming the unified league to become *the* top league in US soccer. The

WSL, at one point the only outdoor soccer league in America after the closures of the NASL and USL, joined up with the ASL to create the American Professional Soccer League (APSL) in 1990 and at that point in time stood a very good chance of being the division one soccer league. The ASL had a bulk of USMNT players who were already in their league with clubs who had experience in amateur soccer and a sort of history, but the reality of a nationwide league soon hit home the following year, proving to be the biggest dent that the APSL had seen at this particular moment. Having teams in the north-eastern region worked, having teams in the Florida region worked, as did having Californian teams mixed up with teams from Washington and Oregon, but when those teams were merged together it proved costly. Sure, Boston to Washington DC isn't that bad a flight, but Boston to San Francisco? Absolutely not and certainly not in soccer in 1991. With games coming thick and fast, with wages of star players increasing steadily over time and with the amount of money being wasted on travel, teams were struggling already.

Attendances were modest – averaging around 5,000 fans per game – but the income wasn't even coming close to the expenditure, which was a lesson for the future – if you want to run a soccer league in the US, you have to be prepared to spend a fair amount of money. Teams in the APSL *wanted* to spend the money, but because of the low income they *couldn't* spend the money. Multiple teams folded at the end of the 1991 season due to financial problems, meaning that in 1992 the APSL had just five teams playing. Obviously a league can't run with just five teams, so when Miami and San Francisco dropped out after 1992, the league was in a dangerous place. They couldn't afford to keep going, yet they were so close to being the division one soccer league they had hoped to be, but, whether it was naivety on the financial side of things or just boredom from the backers at clubs, it looked like the APSL was going to go out of business. At least that's what it looked like until the introduction of Canadian teams – thanks to the demise of the Canadian Soccer League not long before.

Officially, the APSL became the top soccer division in the United States and Canada, gaining USSF division two standing, and it gave them a massive boost in their quest to become division one before the 1994 World Cup. In 1993 the APSL was essentially running unopposed and thanks to the introduction of the Canadian teams, they looked to be in a strong position to win the bid. But while the APSL thought they were running alone in this race, behind the scenes it was looking like a second competitor was on the gallop, chasing down the APSL with all of its might and setting its gaze on the same target.

Alan Rothenberg had been the commissioner of soccer at the 1984 Los Angeles Summer Olympics, a part of the Games that had been widely successful, to the surprise of pretty much everyone. With the NASL on its dying legs in and around this period, it came as a shock that the Rose Bowl sold out multiple times for soccer games and Rothenberg was credited with a lot of the success, with soccer at that Games being a massive factor into why the US won the 1994 World Cup staging in the first place. It was clear there was a demand for the sport, plus the infrastructure was in place too. Due to this, Rothenberg was elected president of the USSF and then became the chairman of the 1994 World Cup committee. Of course, one of his roles as president of the USSF was to help in the organisation of the division one league that was so badly needed, but rather than simply vote in the only league at his disposal (the APSL), Rothenberg decided to do almost the complete opposite. He decided to help create a new league from the ground up. After the division two sanctioning by the USSF, the APSL initially thought that it would help them in their bid to be division one, but FIFA put a stop to that almost immediately. They ruled that leagues that crossed border boundaries could not become division one, and seeing as the APSL had the Montreal Impact and Vancouver 86ers from Canada, that ruled them out of the race, but it did leave them as division two, which made them an impressive league despite the costs of travel and expenses.

While the APSL continued in 1994, the World Cup in America only increased the eagerness amongst fans for a top-flight league, one that would be like what they had witnessed in the summer and one that would help grow a new soccer culture in the US. The NASL had been the glitz and glamour, whereas the ASL/APSL had been the fundamentals of soccer, and MLS had to try to bring both of those together. But MLS had different ideas on how to run their league, and it was almost in direct contrast to how APSL wanted to run theirs. For starters, there was no promotion or relegation, so MLS franchises weren't going to be relegated into the APSL and APSL teams weren't going to be promoted into MLS, which made the incentive for APSL teams almost non-existent. MLS was a single-entity league, meaning it was its own product and not part of any other league, the opposite of what, for example, the Premier League and Football League are in England. Rothenberg spoke about how the single-entity idea was the right way to convince owners and investors to jump into the league, saying:

> That [single-entity idea] dates back for years and years, when I was involved with the NBA and the players were suing the league. It was clear that the structure of all the major league sports at the time was such that they had a lot of legal vulnerabilities and difficulties from a business standpoint because they were basically an association of the teams. From both a legal and business standpoint, if you had just one entity you could better control them. For example, in sponsorships, the IOC [International Olympic Committee] and FIFA own their property, and they buy the rights to give to their local organisers of the competition to prevent the markets from being cannibalised. Also of interest to MLS was somehow trying to control team salary expenditures. We'd seen in all the other sports, and also with the NASL, that you can kill yourself off, particularly in the early years, if you have [teams] that are profligate spenders and others can't keep up, and they fail financially or competitively. It just doesn't work.

The name may be different but it's all connected and all linked in the same soccer pyramid. MLS and the APSL weren't linked, at all. USA '94 had made the public and the fans hungry for more soccer, and the immediate aftermath of the tournament wasn't a great look considering MLS pushed their start date back from 1995 to 1996, there was a big disconnect between the USSF and APSL on how to develop the USMNT talent (the USSF wanted them in their own development team, while the APSL wanted to keep them in their league to build a profile and give them competitive games to play) and outdoor soccer and indoor soccer were still stuck in a rivalry with one another. The discussion of how to recruit young talent came to the forefront, with many suggesting an NCAA system like you see in other American sports – where the young player goes to college, gets an education and then joins a team – whereas others called for what was essentially an open system in which anyone from anywhere could get scouted, like everywhere else in the world. The US had been given the gift of soccer and looked unable to decide how they wanted to play with it. Do you take the traditional American sport route of no promotion/relegation and NCAA youth, or do you follow what the rest of the world does and have promotion/relegation and give opportunities to everyone instead of a select few? These were questions that were still being asked when the 1994 World Cup was over, and the introduction of MLS didn't help matters.

Rothenberg had the task of starting MLS from the ground up and immediately set about trying to find investors who would be willing to learn from the mistakes of the old NASL of not spending all your money too soon, and considering how flawed the sport of soccer is throughout its history in the United States you can forgive Rothenberg for feeling like it was a daunting task. First on the agenda was convincing investors to come into the league and, aided by the security blanket provided by the single-entity method, they were more than willing to try out this new-fangled sport called soccer. Rothenberg acknowledged that, 'if we did not have single-entity, we wouldn't have a league today,' while Todd Durbin, MLS executive vice president, said,

'The single-entity is one of our core long-term equities. It's an incredible point of differentiation between us and the other soccer leagues around the world. Our system and our structure ensures and allows that at the beginning of the season, every team has the opportunity to win an MLS Cup, and every fan knows that.' Single-entity helped attract some big names into the league, such as Lemar Hunt, a big hitter from the NASL days who had always been involved in soccer, AEG chairman Phil Anschutz, and New England Patriots owner Robert Kraft, who was said to be willing to play 'the long game' with regards to his ownership.

Once the owners were on board – all of whom were understanding of the fact that the league would not be an overnight success – a commissioner was needed, with that role going to Doug Logan, a soccer fan and owner of the San Diego Wildcards basketball team. Logan's objective was to try to entice non-soccer fans in America to MLS the same way that Robert Kraft was enticed during the 1994 World Cup. To put it simply, Logan's job was to Americanise soccer. The Americanisation of soccer helped bring more investors in, but in hindsight it probably wasn't the smartest of moves; nevertheless, the founders had to think of any way possible to drum up interest. They thought about bringing in timeouts, kick-ins instead of throw-ins, making the goals bigger to increase the chances of more goals, just in order to create interest (which, when you think about it, was all they could actually do without a game being played). So, with their investors in place, their commissioner at the helm, teams ready to play, players ready to play, television deals with ESPN and ABC in place (MLS actually had TV deals ready before teams or players were announced, getting the TV deals done in 1994), the league was ready to kick off. The ten teams in 1996 were a downgrade from the originally proposed 12 teams in 1995, but they were:

Columbus Crew
D.C. United
New England Revolution

New York Metrostars (nearly called the New York Cosmos, but the owners refused to pay for the name)

Tampa Bay Mutiny

Colorado Rapids

Dallas Burn

Kansas City Wiz

Los Angeles Galaxy

San Jose Clash

And with new teams came big-name signings to increase popularity and get the fans in the seats early on. The key allocations were a range of foreign stars and USMNT players who were designed to help grow the name of the league. Players like Carlos Valderrama, Roberto Donadoni, Hugo Sánchez, Jorge Campos and Shaun Bartlett were brought in (conveniently placed in areas where their popularity would be maximised i.e. Italian Donadoni going to New York, Hugo Sánchez to Dallas, Valderrama to Tampa Bay and Jorge Campos going to Los Angeles) and alongside USMNT players like Tony Meola, Alexi Lalas, Tab Ramos, Roy Wegerle, John Harkes, Preki, Marcelo Balboa and Eric Wynalda the league felt that they had the perfect mix to entice fans.

A lot of football stadiums were used for MLS, with the Metrostars using Giants Stadium, New England using Foxboro, RFK Stadium for D.C., Mile High Stadium for Dallas, Arrowhead for Kansas City and the Coliseum for Los Angeles. There was a foreign player limit of five players per team in order to boost the number of home-grown players getting minutes in the league, and in a bid to stand out and to look cool in the mid-1990s the kits were perhaps some of the most outrageous ones you will ever see.

On 6 April 1996 (Celine Dion was top of Billboard 100 with 'Because You Loved Me', 'Firestarter' by The Prodigy was top of the UK 100 and OJ Simpson was just a few weeks away from going on *Richard and Judy* in the UK for a fee of £1), MLS officially kicked off. The San Jose Clash defeated D.C. United, managed by Bruce Arena, 1-0 courtesy of an Eric Wynalda winner in the 88th minute in a game that was broadcast live on ESPN, with 31,000 fans in attendance in San Jose. The league was in full flow in 1996, but there were some early growing pains that wouldn't go away. Despite losing the first game, it would be Arena's D.C. United that took home the very first MLS Cup, beating the LA Galaxy 3-2 after extra time thanks to a golden goal by Eddie Pope (most fans didn't see the goal because they had left to return to their cars to warm up from the cold weather and only heard of the winner when they switched on their car radios). By and large the 1996 MLS season wasn't that inspiring. The standard of play was probably comparable to the Championship in England or any other major second division, while the attendance figures were comparable to Ligue 1 in France and behind only the Premier League, La Liga, Serie A and the Bundesliga. Fans were clearly interested in what MLS had to offer, even if the play left a lot to be desired. The fans enjoyed themselves by forming supporters' groups and tailgating before games like the old NASL fans did, and MLS had largely exceeded everyone's expectations, and had looked to consolidate their growth the following season. Kansas City changed their name from the horrible Wiz to the Wizards, the outlandish kits were redesigned, the salary cap was increased from $1.19 million to $1.3 million, games were scheduled on weekends instead of midweek and another overseas player spot was opened up. The now infamous variation of a penalty shootout where a player is one-on-one with the goalkeeper and has to score five seconds after their first touch was introduced in the inaugural season to replace draws, but it was ultimately scrapped in 1999; however, MLS was growing – slowly, but it was growing. Growing pains came along with it, but fans were ready to stick by their teams. The start to the season seemed to be a one from reigning champions D.C. United – who went unbeaten until the start of June when the Wizards beat them 6-1, ending a 22-game unbeaten run – then the Wizards themselves dominated the west, aided by the incredible form of MLS MVP and top scorer Preki, and a total of 2,399,019 fans saw an MLS game in 1997, even though the league actually suffered a drop in attendances. The league lost $40 million over the first two seasons, but they had planned on the substantial loss so it wasn't as big a deal as some had expected it to be. The sophomore season was over, and with 1998 around the corner MLS, and soccer in general, was in for some big changes.

Sepp Blatter was voted in as FIFA president, while the USSF elected Robert Contigugla as new president – Rothenberg couldn't run for a third term – and change was in the air. Bruce Arena was named as USMNT manager, the Chicago Fire and Miami Fusion were introduced into the league with Arena's old assistant at United, Bob Bradley, taking over the Fire for their inaugural campaign. MLS and the USSF introduced 'Project 40', a programme that was designed to find the best young players across the US with the purpose of developing 18–22-year-olds for MLS and then eventually the USMNT.

Bradley's Fire finished second in the west, while D.C. still romped to the Eastern Conference title, although it would be the LA Galaxy who took home the Supporters Shield (the award given to the team who accumulated the most points across the regular season) after picking up 68 points, a record that would stand until 2017. Future journeyman of the English game Stern John won the scoring title, while Marco Etcheverry won the MVP award, but the season was largely interrupted by the 1998 World Cup in France, with the majority of teams' star USMNT talent heading overseas for the tournament. In the play-offs, a surprising victor took home the MLS Cup thanks to a strong defence, and a shock in the semi-finals would tee the winners up for it. The two favourites for the trophy were the Galaxy and D.C., who were looking to continue their own early MLS dynasty that didn't rely on a certain manager to deliver success, and both made it through to their conference semi-finals, with United beating Miami and the Galaxy beating Dallas. The Columbus Crew went on to face United in the next round but fell to them after a game-three decider in Washington. The Galaxy met up with the defensively rigid Chicago Fire, and after a 1-0 first leg win from the Fire in LA, the Galaxy were eliminated via shoot-out in the second leg, setting up D.C. United vs Chicago Fire in the MLS Cup Final. In front of 51,350 fans at the Pasadena Rose Bowl, the Fire won the MLS Cup in a tight 2-0 win, where Peter Nowak's brace was enough for the triumph, and a heroic performance from the Fire's defence and midfield shut down D.C. from the off. The Fire then made even more history by being the first expansion team to win the double (MLS Cup and US Open Cup), but despite this moment of history attendances were down across the league, and when the 1999 season rolled around, it didn't look like a solution was in place to solve the issue. Commissioner Logan resigned and was replaced by Don Garber, the former head of NFL Europe, with Alan Rothenberg saying that he was, 'hopeful that he can become the second coming of Pete Rozelle'. No pressure then. With D.C. up for sale and the league losing money, Garber seemed like the perfect fit. He had increased NFL International's revenue by 250 per cent, and while he wasn't a 'proper soccer man' he knew what it took to grow a business and make it successful. In 1998 and into 1999, MLS was still a small fish in the ocean that was American sport, and the league had high and low points throughout the next few years.

Garber oversaw the very first soccer-specific stadium in the league when the Columbus Crew opened their ground, which is now named the MAPFRE Stadium (fun fact: the Crew stadium was the second-ever soccer-specific stadium built in the US, with the first belonging to the Bethlehem Steel back in 1913), while the league suffered financial losses of $250 million in their first five seasons, and more than $350 million from the foundation of MLS to 2004. However, the overall quality of play was slowly improving, and while attendance figures didn't fall off a cliff, they didn't exactly climb either. Overseas imports were more successful both on and off the pitch, bringing a different level of attention to MLS. Former Everton striker Paul Rideout joined the Wizards in 1999 before heading back to England to play for Tranmere Rovers, Walter Zenga was still in action in goal for the Revolution, Mo Johnston ended his famous career by playing for the Wizards too, along with Richard Gough, before he returned to play for the San

Jose Clash. While these names may not immediately jump out of the page like some who passed before them in the NASL days, they still added a different level of class to the league and still had enough talent to increase the competitive nature of MLS. D.C. United returned to the top of the tree in 1999 with an MLS Cup win over the Galaxy, also taking home their second Supporters Shield. That year also saw the end of the unconventional shootout format, and MLS teams were upset a few times in the US Open Cup, prompting the discussion of whether or not the teams actually cared for the competition. But while this was happening and Don Garber was trying to make the league a bigger fish in the American sports ocean, MLS lived in relative anonymity. It was a dot on the map, but some of the bigger-name players from overseas loved it, because they had been so accustomed to being stars in Europe and South America that they were just happy to be able to live their own lives. In 2000, when the New York Metrostars brought in World Cup winner and soccer legend Lothar Matthäus, the German spoke about how he found life in the US and in MLS when writing his column for *FourFourTwo:*

> New York is one of the most interesting cities in the world. I lived in a beautiful apartment in Trump International Tower by Central Park, and I met Donald Trump once when he was sat near me in an Italian restaurant. I was recognised less in New York than in Germany, but many people – often South Americans and Europeans – would still ask for a picture or an autograph. I didn't feel alone in New York City!

The players were relative unknowns at the time, unless they were superstars or in huge metropolitan areas, but the majority of the time they were left to their own devices. With the arrival of players like Matthäus and Bulgarian legend Hristo Stoichkov, who went to the Chicago Fire, MLS experienced some change. As well as dropping the shootouts, for the first time since 1974 ties/draws were introduced. A five-minute 'golden goal' period was introduced and if the scores were level at the end of the five minutes, then the game was a tie. The teams were split into three divisions – East, West and Central – to promote regional rivalries, and the draft class was changed into the 'Superdraft', which brought through players like DeMarcus Beasley and Carlos Bocanegra, combining the college soccer system and any youth player from across the country.

The Wizards would be the shock story of the 2000 season as they won both the MLS Cup and the Supporters Shield, mainly down to the defensive work of goalkeeper and MVP Tony Meola and Defender of the Year Peter Vermes. They went on to capture their first glory in the MLS era, while D.C. United floundered at the bottom of the East, finishing second from bottom of the entire league. The Wizards defeated the Fire 1-0, thanks, in large part, to their defensive solidity that had served them well throughout the season, keeping a clean sheet against a Fire side that had scored 14 goals against the Metrostars and the Dallas Burn combined in the previous two rounds, which emphasised just how good the Wizards were at the back. But while attracting players like Stoichkov and Matthaus did reasonably well to raise the profile of the league, season-ticket sales were down to 4,000, well below the 10,000 that the league had planned for. Single-game tickets were up by 18 per cent so it wasn't all negative for MLS, but attendances were down by nearly 100,000 from 1999 and the league made marketing the main focus for the next few years. They had to target the next generation of potential soccer fans, and the first step was to build soccer-specific stadiums for the Galaxy and the Metrostars and then expand the league. Soccer hotbeds such as Seattle, Atlanta and the historical area of Philadelphia were considered for expansion, but the introduction of new teams wouldn't be a reality for another few years. The league knew that they had to play the waiting game to see whether it would be a success overall, building the structure of the league around young, home-grown talent and big-name stars who would bring casual fans into the stadiums ('come for the stars, stay for the young Americans' was essentially what MLS planned to do). The San

Jose Earthquakes (who had officially changed their name from the Clash to the Quakes in '99) brought in young American star Landon Donovan on loan from Bayer Leverkusen to add to the American side of the league, but the overseas stars didn't arrive on mass for another few years. The overseas player limit was brought down from four to three, and with MLS losing millions upon millions each season, some owners were ready to back out, but Lemar Hunt – owner of the Wizards and Columbus Crew – convinced the investors to stay and fight it out, just like he had done with the old AFL before the AFL merged with the NFL in the 1960s. MLS was like the boxer that kept getting punched but always found a way to get saved by the bell, they always looked like they were one blow away from keeling over but somehow they mustered up enough energy to keep plugging away and felt that eventually they would get what they deserved.

In 2001 the season – and the world – was marred by the terrible attacks on 11 September. The MLS regular season was extended by three days in order for the final round of regular fixtures to be played, giving the league enough time to reconfigure their play-offs (MLS actually considered moving straight on to the play-offs without the final round of games being played, but due to the fact that seedings weren't finalised, they decided to delay instead of cancel). The Columbus Crew were the only team whose flights had been affected, being diverted to Birmingham, Alabama, before having to take a ten-hour bus journey back to Columbus, with their luggage still being checked over at the airport. On the pitch, the Crew were knocked out of the play-offs in the first round by the Earthquakes, who finished the season on 45 points, finishing behind the LA Galaxy. The two favourites coming out of the regular season were the Fire and Miami Fusion, who both finished on 53 points, but neither side would make it to the MLS Cup Final despite early predictions, with the Fire getting past Dallas in the first round before being bounced by a seemingly inspired Galaxy side, while Miami got past the Wizards in round one before being knocked out quite convincingly by the Quakes, who won in a 4-0 romp with four different scorers, which set up a Californian cup final between San Jose and Los Angeles. Led by Sigi Schmid, the Galaxy were favourites but had dropped their two games against San Jose in the regular season, meaning that while the Galaxy were favourites heading into this final, they just happened to come up against their bogey team. The Galaxy took the lead through veteran Mexican striker Luis Hernández before young Donovan pulled the Quakes level before the break. The second half ended 1-1, then Dwayne De Rosario scored the golden-goal winner in extra time to give the Quakes their first MLS Cup triumph, somewhat of an upset in their biggest game of the season at Columbus Crew Stadium. The league handled itself with dignity in this final, bringing in NYPD and FDNY members for the coin toss at the beginning of the game, with Don Garber saying:

> We all knew what we needed to do, to bring this league back to properly honour and show our gratitude to those people who were heroes and those who lost their lives.

It proved that with players like Donovan on show and more than 20,000 in the stands, MLS was growing. The attendance figures showed a good upward curve after 2001 and the upturn in season ticket sales was another huge positive. Financial struggles were another cause for concern, but when compared to the apparent $500 million losses that MLB had on their hands, MLS wasn't doing too badly. Two teams were set to be cut from the league in order to cut costs, meaning that the Central Division was cut from the league as well. Unfortunately for Miami Fusion and Tampa Bay Mutiny fans, their teams were the ones chosen – mainly due to low attendance figures and absent owners. Owner commitment was extended for another five years, a new television deal was agreed with ABC and ESPN2, and the Galaxy moved into their new Home Depot Centre. There was also a huge development behind the scenes that largely went unnoticed: a company was formed for the sole purpose of managing, marketing and acquiring soccer properties by the name of Worldwide Momentum, which helped AEG run D.C. United and Lemar Hunt's Sports Group run the Dallas Burn. This may seem insignificant, but it meant that for the first time in league history no team was owned or operated by MLS themselves.

On to 2002, which would be a huge year for US soccer because the World Cup would give them a great platform to show how far their talent had come in recent years, while in MLS the new wave of American soccer talent was emerging. Landon Donovan was obviously the golden boy of the generation, but Tim Howard won Goalkeeper of the Year in 2001, Taylor Twellman finished as league top scorer in 2002, DeMarcus Beasley kept on showing his talent growth, Kyle Martino won Rookie of the Year, Carlos Bocanegra won Defender of the Year, and it all made for exciting viewing both in the summer and during the MLS season itself. Once again the Galaxy kept performing at the highest level by winning the West, but the Twellman-led New England Revolution shocked many by winning an insanely tight Eastern Conference, although they probably should have won by a bigger margin than 'goal difference' because they had some extremely frustrating losses during the season, mainly due to the fact that they simply didn't gel until the final stretch of the regular season, when the team really came to life. And just as it should be, the two best teams from both conferences faced off in the MLS Cup that season in front of 60,000 fans at the brand-new Gillette Stadium in Foxboro, the home of the New England Patriots (oh, and the home of the New England Revolution). The final wasn't the most exciting, and it was decided on a golden goal for the second consecutive year as Carlos Ruiz popped up with the all-important winner. The Galaxy, after multiple attempts at trying to take home the MLS Cup, finally did it in 2002 in what also looked like a turning-point season in MLS, but in some ways the change didn't really have anything to do with the Galaxy or MLS for that matter. The USMNT's performances at the World Cup sparked an interest in the league, attendances went up post-World Cup, and so did revenue streams, and more fans became attached to the teams they saw. Also, as a knock-on effect of the 2002 World Cup, a few of the US players were taken by European clubs. Brian McBride, who had been a great striker in the early MLS days with the Crew, spent time on loan at Preston North End and Everton before joining Fulham, Kasey Keller and Brad Friedel were two of the more reliable goalkeepers in the Premier League, while Tim Howard joined Manchester United in 2003 from the Metrostars to replace Fabien Barthez midway through the MLS season, eventually becoming only the second American to win an FA Cup-winner's medal in 2004.

Being a 'selling league' was a pivotal part of MLS's strategy to grow. Unlike the NBA, NFL and MLB, it wasn't the pinnacle, but if the league could help produce players that would go on to reach the pinnacle, it would have a positive effect on the league. So, while losing talent like Howard and McBride wasn't a good thing initially, moves to bigger European clubs helped grow the league's name and image if they were successful. And it wasn't just the player transfers that helped the league's image, the opening of soccer-specific stadiums also helped, and in 2003 the LA Galaxy opened their Home Depot Centre in Carson, California.

A lot of the older USMNT players like Alexi Lalas, Peter Vermes, John Harkes and Marcelo Balboa, either retired or were let go by their respective teams, with some younger stars from 2002 – like Frankie Hedjuk and Joe-Max Moore – arriving to add some fresh blood. The 2003 season was perhaps the closest season to date, with only two clear favourites predicted from the outset (the Crew and Galaxy), but a lot of teams – more or less everyone – went against expectation (not always in a positive way). The Crew finished bottom of the East, while the Galaxy took the last play-off spot in the West, and Colorado and San Jose, two teams who were written off at the beginning of the season, managed to finish first and third in the West. In the Eastern play-offs, Chicago reached the cup final without conceding a goal and with relative ease, but all the drama was in the West, particular in the semi-final between San Jose and the Galaxy. Landon Donovan called it 'the single-greatest soccer game I've ever played in', and with most of the 2001 MLS cup-winning side still intact, the Quakes felt confident after winning the West. But this was the Galaxy. This was the big one. The first leg at the Home Depot Centre didn't go to plan for the Quakes, but for LA it was perfect. Sasha Victorine and Carlos Ruiz gave the Galaxy a two-goal lead heading into the second leg, and when the Galaxy took a 2-0 lead after just 13 minutes in San Jose it looked like it was game over and tie over. But the Quakes had other ideas, they had belief and confidence in their ability, but surely no one could have expected that they would pull off what they did next? With the Galaxy 2-0 up before a quarter of the first half was played, the Quakes needed to respond quickly. The Galaxy fans and players were acting like, at 4-0 up on aggregate, the tie was over, but San Jose weren't about to go down without a fight. Jeff Agoos fired in a free kick from the edge of the box and it gave everyone in the stadium a lift, almost like 'it's on, we can do this' was the general feeling amongst fans and players. Donovan equalised on the night from a tight angle before half-time, and at this point the general consensus was that San Jose were going to somehow take this to the wire. Five minutes after the interval and Jamil Walker, a fourth-round pick in the MLS Draft, headed in the third and the momentum had completely changed. Quakes defender Troy Dayak said, 'I think the whole stadium knew at that point, including the LA Galaxy, that we were going to win that match.' Inevitably, with the Galaxy shaken, San Jose levelled things up in the final minute. Chris Roner, who goes by his middle name Thor and was out of MLS by 2004, rose highest in the Galaxy box to level the scores on aggregate, before bit-part player Rodrigo Faria, someone who hadn't managed to score a single regular-season goal for San Jose, slotted home the golden goal. It was quite simply the most incredible play-off match in MLS history. The fans were electric, the players couldn't have played any better and the stars aligned for San Jose to win, but they still had the Conference Finals to play, where they would match up against Kansas City. Once again, however, San Jose showed their durability against the Wizards by winning 3-2, coming from behind twice and winning through another golden goal, this time from Donovan. For the Quakes, this MLS Cup was a sweet one. Not only had they performed the impossible comeback over their rivals the Galaxy, but they were one game away from winning their second MLS Cup at the home of the Galaxy, with 27,000 in attendance to witness it. It couldn't have been much sweeter, and in an exciting game the Earthquakes claimed their second title in three years when Donovan scored a double, winning the game 4-2 against the Chicago Fire. They won it in their rivals' backyard, they won it despite looking dead and buried both in the play-offs and in the regular season, and it was the perfect story that the league wanted. The underdogs, led by the American golden boy Landon Donovan, were champions and things were only going to keep getting better for MLS in the next year, with attendances rising 14 per cent from 2003 to 2004, and with the signings of two young Americans they had more stars to market the league around. Clint Dempsey was named as Rookie of the Year in 2004 after being selected eighth overall in the MLS Draft, scoring seven goals in his rookie season as he helped the Revolution reach the Eastern Conference Finals. Texas native Dempsey studied the game of Diego Maradona in his youth, and he was the standout player in his youth soccer team but had to pull out for financial reasons (he was later brought back into the team after parents of other kids raised enough funds), but his main motivation for pursuing a career in soccer was the tragic passing of his sister Jennifer, a talented young tennis player, who died of a brain aneurysm. The tragic event pushed Dempsey on and it would prove to be an amazing career, but as touching a story as Dempsey's is, he wasn't the biggest name to be signed in MLS in 2004. No, the biggest player signed in the league was a 14-year-old who had the weight of expectation placed firmly on his shoulders. To say he was American soccer's LeBron James was an understatement, because LeBron James was only expected to conquer the NBA. Freddy Adu was expected to conquer the world.

Born in Ghana, Adu came to the US when he was just a child when his mother won the 'Green Card lottery', moving to

Rockville, Maryland. From a young age, Adu was playing soccer and always stood out from the rest of the crowd, attracting offers from clubs like Lazio, Juventus and Inter Milan following impressive tournaments in Italy. Inter's youth general secretary Piero Ausillo said of Adu, 'We have never done this before – Freddy is the first American soccer player that we have ever seen with potential as a pro in European soccer. Simply, he's a great, talented player with great physical tools and wonderful technical attitude.' Perhaps the biggest moment of his life was when, at the age of just 14, he signed his first professional contract with D.C. United, becoming the youngest-ever American to sign a professional sporting contract when he was selected first in the 2004 MLS Draft. This was unprecedented in any form of soccer. To have a player this young in the senior squad either meant you were expecting him to become the next Pelé (Adu was once dubbed 'the next Pelé' by many, but it was a completely unfair comparison for someone so young) or you were setting him up for a long, hard fall. But in his first year, it wasn't like anyone was aware that he could possibly fail because he actually had an impressive year. Making his debut against reigning champions San Jose and scoring in a defeat against the Metrostars to become the youngest-ever MLS goalscorer, Adu was already a star in the league. Making 30 appearances, scoring five goals with three assists in your first season is no mean feat, let alone for someone his age. He helped D.C. United in a pretty successful season (no spoilers on how it ends just yet), and the year before he had been making waves on the international youth scene, scoring four goals in the FIFA under-17 World Cup. Adu missed out on the 2006 World Cup, citing his public frustration at his lack of game time, and he eventually went on a trial at Manchester United, but due to work permit issues a deal couldn't be done, even if Sir Alex Ferguson said, 'Freddy has done all right'. Unfortunately for Freddy, this proved to be the peak of his career. In 2007 he moved from D.C. to Real Salt Lake following a falling out with manager Peter Nowak, before moving to Benfica after an impressive under-20 World Cup. Between 2007 and 2009,

Freddy played for five clubs, four of which were loan deals, before heading back to the US with the Philadelphia Union. As of 2018, Adu has played for 14 different teams, never scoring more than 11 league goals in a single season in his career, and for a career that promised so much from such a young age, it really is a shame that it's gone the way it has. He could have been the first world star from MLS, unlike Dempsey or Donovan, but he just didn't deliver. Was it simply a case of too much too soon? Did he make the wrong move by turning down Serie A clubs? Was he just not able to perform against grown men at an age when most people haven't even left school? Or was it a mental block that stopped him? Only Freddy will know and it's one of the biggest 'what ifs' in US soccer. But in the 2004 season, the hype around Freddy Adu was warranted because he was living up to expectations. With his help, United finished second in the East behind the Columbus Crew, while over in the West it was Kansas City and LA who led the way. Top-seeded Columbus went out in the first play-off round to New England, while United, the Wizards and the Galaxy all managed to get through their respective games, with the Wizards taking down the Galaxy in the Western Conference Finals. Back out East, a thriller was played out at RFK Stadium, with New England and D.C. drawing 3-3 in normal time and D.C. advancing on penalties (Adu scored his penalty, but Dempsey missed the vital one for the Revs. Funny how things work out). United went on to win yet another great game against the Wizards 3-2, with the Wizards taking home the US Open Cup. Overall 2004 was a great year for MLS, with the influx of young American talent shining through mixed with another upturn in attendance figures, plus the confirmation of two new expansion franchises in Chivas USA and Real Salt Lake (RSL), and the addition of Adidas as the sole kit provider for the league.

The following season, in 2005 the two new expansion franchises arrived, but the years following that completely changed MLS. The first move in this huge domino effect was created by Landon Donovan, who returned to MLS, joining LA Galaxy following a disappointing spell back in Germany, while

Alexi Lalas finished his moves in San Jose as club president, moving on to the Metrostars in a bid to boost the flailing franchise in America's toughest media market – a move that started with Lalas taking over the Metrostars but by the time he left in 2006 they were renamed New York Red Bulls. Both RSL and Chivas finished in the bottom two places in the West, while the Western Conference play-offs saw the LA Galaxy reach the MLS Cup Final, only conceding two goals. The Revs took over in the East despite losing their first game 1-0 to a Youri Djorkaeff-inspired Metrostars.

At the newly built Pizza Hut Park in Texas, the Galaxy won the 2005 edition of the MLS Cup; however, in 2006 they didn't even make the play-offs as the Houston Dynamo, a team that wasn't an expansion side, but were actually the San Jose Earthquakes who had moved to Texas because of stadium issues, won the 2006 MLS Cup. But while these games were a huge part of the league's success – attendances grew over the 2005/06 period – the biggest thing to ever happen to American soccer was on the verge of completion. Bigger than Pelé, probably bigger than the World Cup in 1994, just no one around the world knew what was going to happen. No one knew how to react because it was so outrageous to contemplate, but it was a transfer that completely changed the face of soccer in North America.

> Author's note: It may seem that this section of the MLS chapter wasn't as detailed as other chapters, but the truth is not an awful lot happened. Every major event that happened in the first half of MLS was mentioned, and it wasn't a lot. Freddy Adu? Checked him off. Every winner of the MLS Cup and yearly attendance updates? Check. Key transfers, key draft signings and key players mentioned? Also check. But we had to save room for the second half of the MLS era, because it was simply more important and bigger to the wider story of MLS. The second half of the MLS era was much more interesting too, so let's not waste any more time ...

When Pelé arrived at the New York Cosmos, the soccer world was taken aback. A veteran of the game yet one of the greats was going to America instead of going to Juventus or Real Madrid, but Pelé was at the end of his career when he joined the NASL. And in January 2007 one of the most recognisable sportsmen in the world joined MLS to try to do what Pelé couldn't. He tried to put American soccer on the map in perhaps the biggest risk of his sporting career. David Beckham announced, on 10 January, that he would resign from his contract with Real Madrid, prompting speculation of where his next move would be. The whole world of soccer was thrown into a frenzy when, on 11 January, Beckham announced he would be joining LA Galaxy. Fabio Capello said that Beckham would never play for the club again (they were in the midst of a La Liga title run, which would be their first in three years), while club president Ramon Calderon said, 'He's going to Hollywood to be half a film star. Our technical staff were right not to extend his contract, and that has been proved by the fact that no other technical staff in the world wanted him other than Los Angeles.' No fury quite like the fury of a club president who just lost one of his best players! Beckham eventually found his way back into the Madrid starting line-up and proved to be pivotal in their La Liga triumph, leaving Spain as a hero to the Madristas. So good were Beckham's performances that Madrid actually tried to withdraw the transfer to the Galaxy, although they made it impossible, with general manager Alexi Lalas claiming that there wasn't a withdrawal clause in the transfer. With La Liga in the bag, it was off to Los Angeles for the most famous soccer player on the planet to try to change the face of American soccer. That's not hyperbole, that is legitimately what Beckham intended to do, saying in his press conference:

> With me, it's about football. I'm coming there to make a difference. I'm coming there to play football. I'm not saying me coming over to the States is going to make soccer the biggest sport in America. That would be difficult to achieve. Baseball, basketball, American

football, they've been around. But I wouldn't be doing this if I didn't think I could make a difference.

For Beckham the move to MLS was about soccer, or at least that's what he said in public, but the transfer was always going to be more than just soccer. He was a global icon that transcended his sport. He wasn't the best player in the world, but he was certainly the most recognisable and that fame is part of the reason the Galaxy brought him in. Brand Beckham came with the package and it was a perfect marketing plan because he brought attention to the league, and MLS needed attention to survive. According to Grant Wahl's book *The Beckham Experiment,* there were 5,000 fans, over 700 media members, a news chopper overhead and cannons ready to spurt out yellow and blue confetti and all this for ... a soccer player? Ironically enough, the only person who wasn't treating David Beckham like the saviour of sports or the second coming of Jesus Christ was Beckham himself, but he was his usual, calm self and was prepared to say what needed to be said in order to drum up interest in the 2007 MLS season – not that it needed drumming up any further, but when David Beckham says something those who fawn over him listen intently. The next piece of news to come out of the signing was Beckham's contract, which was all over the news networks even if it wasn't entirely true. Beckham's salary was listed by the Galaxy as $250 million ($2 million less than Alex Rodriguez received from the Texas Rangers in 2000), and while that was an astronomical fee and technically it wasn't a lie, it wasn't the entire truth either.

The actual salary over the course of his contract was $32 million, with AEG paying $30 million of the contract and MLS owners paying the rest – due to the new designated player rule that allowed Beckham to join the league, owners had to contribute to his salary to keep the league fair and stop teams from going bust. Beckham also received cuts of the Galaxy's ticket revenue and shirt sales, which was potentially worth more than his regular salary, with more money to be made in endorsements now that he'd swapped Madrid for Los Angeles.

For AEG, it wasn't a risk and for MLS it wasn't a risk either. For Beckham, however, it was a massive risk. If he succeeded in making MLS a bigger league he would completely justify his salary and the changes made in the league. If he failed and focussed more on growing his image in the US, the league potentially might never recover from the move and the strategy would have to be completely changed. The David Beckham era began in 2007 and it shaped the league from the very start of his journey in America. One example of how Beckham changed MLS was a time when Galaxy midfielder and 23-time USMNT international Chris Klein found a red envelope on his locker; he was used to getting mail from time to time, but mostly messages from around the Galaxy, but this was a different kind of message. Not many messages came in a red envelope with gold writing on and read, 'Tom Cruise and Katie Holmes and Will Smith and Jada Pinket Smith request your presence ...' Klein didn't realise it was a formal invitation to a party hosted by four of the biggest names in Hollywood at first, but when he did realise he knew he got the invitation because he was part of David Beckham's LA Galaxy, not because of his reliability in midfield.

The England captain's first game in a Galaxy shirt was in a friendly against Chelsea when he came on as a 78th-minute substitute, but in reality Beckham should never have been on the pitch. He wasn't fully fit following the transfer and he had an ankle injury that was nearly aggravated by Chelsea's Steve Sidwell, who left one in on his compatriot. 'Becks', as he was nicknamed, was to miss the next four MLS matches, including a trip to Toronto. Due to his presence, the Galaxy now had no choice but to fly charter instead of commercial (MLS usually forbids the use of charter flights because it might provide an advantage) because of the security surrounding Beckham. His proper debut eventually came against D.C. United two weeks after the Chelsea game. The Galaxy lost that one 1-0 and eventually failed to make the play-offs once Beckham suffered an MCL injury in his right knee. Beckham ended his debut season without an MLS goal, while the MLS Cup was won by the Houston Dynamo again, who defeated the Revolution in a 2006 rematch.

The next season, attention was still on David Beckham and how the Galaxy would perform with 'Golden Balls' (another strange nickname Beckham had) alongside the golden boy of American soccer Landon Donovan, whom Beckham had taken the Galaxy captaincy off. There was perceived tension between the two, which wasn't helped by president Alexi Lalas trying to give the Englishman everything and the incompetence of manager Ruud Gullit, an icon of the game who couldn't quite get to grips with every rule in MLS (don't worry, Ruud, not everyone did). Bruce Arena was brought in to replace Gullit at the start of the 2008 season, and a new San Jose side was set to be in town, run by Oakland As owners John Fisher and Lewis Wolff. Boxer Oscar De La Hoya purchased a 50 per cent stake in the Dynamo, meaning only AEG and Hunt Sports Group controlled more than one team. Once again the Galaxy were expected to be one of the favourites for the MLS Cup, but even with top scorer Landon Donovan firing goals left, right and centre, the team finished joint-bottom of the entire MLS with just 33 points. Columbus Crew won their first MLS Cup and Supporters Shield by beating the newly named New York Red Bulls at the Home Depot Centre, but the story of the season stayed in California with the Beckham saga. Two seasons, no trophies and nothing to show for the amount of hype and cash thrown around. Beckham controversially went on loan to AC Milan in Serie A in order to keep his fitness and maintain a push for a place in the 2010 England World Cup squad. The loan deal was originally set to expire in March before the start of the MLS season, but it was reported that Beckham wouldn't return until July, prompting Galaxy fans to greet Beckham with signs that called him a 'part-time player' and a 'fraud'. Even though the Galaxy, who had reinstated Landon Donovan as captain during Beckham's Milan adventure, were flying in the Western Conference and had beaten the Red Bulls on Beckham's return, the negative press surrounded Beckham, and fellow team-mate Landon Donovan made the following comments in the press:

When David first came I believed he was committed
to what he was doing. He cared. He wanted to do well.
He wanted the team and the league to do well. But
something changed. He flipped a switch and said uh-
huh, I'm not doing this anymore. I can't think of another
guy where I'd say he wasn't a good team-mate, he didn't
give everything through all this, he didn't still care. But
with Beckham, I'd say no, he wasn't committed.

Scathing, but it was a thought that Donovan wasn't thinking
alone. Beckham was brought in to make MLS a bigger league
and bring success to the Galaxy, and while MLS had become
a bigger name and while the Galaxy were having a successful
season – albeit without Beckham – many didn't view him as
the main reason for either of these things.

The 2009 season was another big one for MLS as the Seattle
Sounders, the former NASL team, were brought back into
Division One soccer at Qwest Field (now CenturyLink Field)
under the guidance of Sigi Schmid, former LA Galaxy and
Crew head coach. The Sounders, helped by the considerable
talents of Kasey Keller, Freddie Ljungberg, Ossie Alonso, Steve
Zakuani, Roger Levesque and Fredy Montero, finished third
in the West behind the Dynamo and the Galaxy, while in the
East the Crew (who won another Supporters Shield) finished
first, the Fire were in second and the Revolution were third.
On paper, it looked like the Galaxy's year. The Crew were
knocked out in the Conference semi-finals by RSL, while the
Galaxy reached the final thanks to wins over Chivas USA and
the Dynamo, where they'd play the conquerors of the Crew,
RSL. The unfancied RSL, who snuck into the post-season on
goal difference, weren't expected to put up much of a fight
against Beckham and MLS MVP Donovan, but they took the
game to penalties when it looked like they shouldn't have, and
with the help of MLS Cup MVP Nick Rimando, who made
heroic saves in the shootout, RSL went off-script in what was
meant to be the Hollywood moment for Los Angeles. Their
first MLS Cup with Beckham in the side and they couldn't

get the job done, bringing up more questions about his commitment, and the matter wasn't helped when Beckham went back to Milan on loan, ultimately tearing his Achilles tendon against Chievo. Beckham missed the 2010 World Cup and most of the 2010 MLS season, but did return later that season to help the Galaxy collect their first Supporters Shield title since 2002 and reach the Western Conference Finals, albeit losing to FC Dallas, who would then go on to lose in the final to Colorado Rapids.

So, 2011 was perhaps the year that MLS started to change around, thanks to an improvement in Beckham's all-round performance and the introduction of another huge European name in Thierry Henry, who joined the New York Red Bulls in 2010. In 2011 Henry finished second in the Golden Boot race with 14 goals and took the Red Bulls to the Conference semis against Beckham's Galaxy – who had won another Supporters Shield this season – only to lose 3-1 on aggregate. Beckham, who finished with 15 MLS assists, was a changed man. His performances improved, his attitude was completely different and he looked committed to winning the MLS Cup with the Galaxy. His time going out on loan was effectively ended when the Galaxy refused his move to Tottenham Hotspur, so he had to buckle down, and he did, with an incredible amount of effort and hard work.

The Galaxy won every post-season game of the 2011 play-offs as they beat the Red Bulls, RSL and then the Dynamo in the final 1-0, with a goal forged by the big three of the team. Scored by Landon Donovan, it was great teamwork from Beckham and Irishman Robbie Keane, who had signed from Tottenham Hotspur, with Beckham nodding the ball onwards to Keane, who then played a through ball into the path of Donovan, who dinked the ball over the onrushing Tally Hall. It was the moment that Galaxy fans and MLS had waited for, and seeing Donovan jump into Beckham's arms was the perfect way of showing that not only had the Galaxy done what they had intended to do, but that Donovan and Beckham had put their tensions behind them and were ready to win as team-mates. With Beckham finally giving the Galaxy 100 per cent alongside Donovan and Keane, who still had a lot to offer from a goalscoring point of view, and with players like Thierry Henry at the Red Bulls, Federico Higuaín at the Columbus Crew – who joined the Crew as a designated player in 2012 – former Dynamo Dwayne De Rosario, who was now at D.C. United following a spell at the Red Bulls, Rafael Márquez and Tim Cahill, who also made appearances with the Red Bulls, and with the reappearance of Freddy Adu at the new Philadelphia Union – who joined MLS as the expansion club in 2010 – coupled with the all-round general improvement of the league, MLS was making waves. There was still a long way to go because perception in soccer is dangerously more valuable to some than facts, and attendances dipped from the previous few seasons (although the stock market crash was a big factor in this, for obvious reasons), but in a general sense MLS was improving. The Seattle Sounders were showing the league how to act as an expansion team, with their rabid fanbase adding a different kind of atmosphere that the league had hardly seen before, and they wore memorable lime green kits with 'XBOX' written across the middle that was instantly recognisable (perhaps it was recognisable thanks to the influence of new media and the *FIFA Football* video games).

In 2011 the Sounders were named as Professional Sports Team of the Year by *Sports Business Journal* after a superb debut season that saw them make the play-offs and led MLS in attendance, beating the Cleveland Cavaliers to the award as well as the New Orleans Pelicans for having the highest average attendance. The Sounders fans would march through the streets to the game in one group, singing and chanting as they made their way, but given their history in the old NASL the Sounders were somewhat of a modern throwback. They had the modern sponsor, the modern look and modern stadium but had a throwback name and throwback history, and that history was a big part of why the Sounders were such a success. They had been in Division Two for quite some time before they entered MLS, but in order for Seattle to become a huge, huge soccer team in America it needed one other ingredient, an ingredient that didn't actually involve them directly, but it was needed to push Seattle into a more advanced position.

Merritt Paulson had bought the Portland Timbers in 2007, along with baseball side the Portland Beavers, but while the Beavers proved to be a venture that wouldn't last long (he sold the team in 2010), Paulson was fully committed to soccer. To put it simply, he was fully committed to making the Portland Timbers an MLS team. In 2009, after lengthy plans to renovate PGE Park (now Providence Park), MLS officially announced that the Timbers would be in the league and Paulson, understandably, was ecstatic, saying:

> Today is an historic day for Soccer City, USA, and it is a big win for our economy, our community, and soccer fans everywhere. Not only does it bring MLS to Portland, but it creates hundreds of jobs, protects taxpayers from risk and shines a positive national and international spotlight on Portland and the state of Oregon.

It reads more like a political rally speech than an owner who's just had his team expanded into MLS, but you get his point. The Timbers kept their name from the Division Two and NASL days and embarked on matching what their great rivals, the Sounders, had done down south. The Vancouver Whitecaps were also entered into MLS to complete the Cascadia Trio of Portland, Seattle and Vancouver, giving MLS a taste of the Cascadia Cup, a competition played between the three clubs to see who the dominant club in the area was. Portland won the Cascadia Cup in 2011, but finished 12th overall, while Seattle finished second in the West and the Vancouver Whitecaps finishing rock bottom of the entire league. But 2012 promised to be a huge year for MLS with the Galaxy looking to retain their crown, the Montreal Impact – who also joined the league in 2010 – brought in veteran Italian talent in Marco Di Vaio and Alessandro Nesta, while it was considered that the Red Bulls, despite Henry up front who came back fresh after his winter loan spell at Arsenal, would never taste MLS success with him in the line-up. The Galaxy were favourites for the title again but not by much, because there were a lot of good sides who could trip them up along the way, and given the fact the Galaxy finished eighth overall, that proved the point. The Earthquakes won the Supporters Shield while Sporting Kansas City – the new name for the Wizards – finished second, five points ahead of D.C. United. The reigning champions had to go through a wildcard game against the Whitecaps, winning 2-1, with Donovan scoring the winner from the penalty spot, while in the opposing wildcard game the Houston Dynamo, 2011 runners-up, beat the Chicago Fire on the Fire's home turf. The Dynamo once again made it to the final, while the Galaxy had to beat the Quakes in dramatic fashion thanks to a 3-1 second-leg win following a last-minute goal scored by the Earthquakes in the first leg to lose 1-0. The Sounders were up next for the Galaxy, but Robbie Keane was in inspired form to fire two goals past the Emerald City team in the first leg and one in the second leg to make it 4-2 on aggregate. So once again the Galaxy met the Dynamo, with the danger man in the game not being David Beckham, who had announced that the MLS Cup Final would be his last match for the Galaxy despite signing a two-year deal at the end of 2011, nor was it Landon Donovan, but it was Robbie Keane. The former Tottenham striker led the play-offs in scoring and looked in incredible form when the pressure was on, grabbing six goals across the play-offs, including one in the final, but the Galaxy's performance that day was the perfect way to end the David Beckham era. The score read 3-1 in favour of Los Angeles, with Omar Gonzales, Donovan and Keane overturning a 1-0 half-time deficit to take home the second MLS Cup since Beckham's arrival and the Galaxy's fourth overall. It looked like it was going to be the Galaxy's day, and it was, with the comprehensive win putting the finishing touches on what had been an incredible time in MLS for Beckham.

Two MLS Cups is no mean feat, but questions were asked early on about Beckham and his commitment. Sure, in his early days he wasn't completely focussed, or at least it looked that way from the outside, but after the tension was cleared between himself and Donovan, once Bruce Arena took charge and once Robbie Keane made the Galaxy an MLS superteam, Beckham changed. He was fully committed to the Galaxy and changed his tune, becoming a leader in the squad and proving himself as the winner that he is. He changed MLS, he changed American soccer and he changed the LA Galaxy, all for the better, but while the Beckham era was over in 2012, MLS still had to carry on. The league was entering a new era, a Beckham-less era, and one that would prove just how well run the league was. Without the major star to hang their hat on, they had to find other ways to promote and other ways to bring fans in, but that, surely, wouldn't be a problem?

By 2013 MLS had grown to 19 teams (ten in the East, nine in the West) ranging from almost every major market in America – with the exception of a handful of areas – so appeal was there, especially when you judge it by attendance figures. Thierry Henry was coming towards the end of his career, so the Red Bulls needed someone to take the goalscoring load off the Frenchman, and in the summer of 2013 the Red Bulls managed to find the perfect replacement in the English Championship. For years, Bradley Wright-Phillips had to deal with a lot. Firstly, he had to deal with the pressure of following in his dad's footsteps, being the son of Ian Wright, the great Arsenal striker. His older brother, Shawn Wright-Phillips, had been a youth product at Manchester City before earning a big-money move to Chelsea in the mid-2000s, which left Bradley as the odd one out. His father was renowned as one of the best strikers in England, while his older brother was considered one of the top talents for the future at one point in time, while Bradley had largely spent his career outside England's Premier League with Southampton, Plymouth Argyle, Charlton Athletic and Brentford. Up until 2013 Bradley's two highest-scoring seasons were 13 goals in 2010/11 and 22 goals in 2011/12, but those were the only two seasons when he scored eight or more goals. Bradley was considered a very good lower league striker, not like his father and not like his brother, but he was what would be called a player who can 'do a job'. It wasn't until Bradley went across the Atlantic that he discovered quite how good he could be, and even though he joined halfway through the 2013 season, 2014 would be his breakthrough year in MLS. Henry had gone, but Wright-Phillips stepped into his boots perfectly. Diego Valeri, an Argentinian attacking midfielder, joined Portland from Lanus, and there was an influx of English players such as John Bostock, who was tipped to become a superstar when he joined Tottenham Hotspur from Crystal Palace, and Hogan Ephraim, the two of whom joined Toronto FC, the first Canadian franchise in MLS, in 2007. With no Beckham or Henry, MLS was about to be 'starless' for the first time since 2007. Landon Donovan was a star, Robbie Keane was a star, Tim Cahill was a star, Chris Wondolowski was a star, but they weren't superstars. Donovan was an American star, Keane was a British and Irish star, Cahill was a star in Australia and was well known in England for his time with Millwall and Everton and Wondolowski was a star that MLS fans could attach themselves to. None were going to be on *SportsCentre* (other than Donovan in his role in the USMNT), none were going to be invited to a party held by Tom Cruise, so it was almost a new experience for MLS and American soccer. But the new challenge wasn't finding a Beckham-level superstar to hold the brand aloft, it was to maintain the fanbase that Beckham brought to the league. Beckham was the bait on the end of the fishing rod, dangled out to the fish in the lake to entice them and Don Garber and MLS was the rod and the fisherman trying to reel them in for the catch. The fish had bitten on the bait, it was up to the fisherman to keep them on the shore.

When 2013 arrived, change was expected in the standings. The Galaxy were expected to remain competitive, but no one was sure how the post-Beckham Galaxy would play, while out East Thierry Henry and Tim Cahill were the leaders of the Red Bulls, who would eventually go on to win the Supporters Shield and finish top of the East with the addition of Wright-Phillips. Portland won the West with Sporting Kansas City having by far the best defence in the league, managed by former USMNT man Peter Vermes. Captain Jimmy Neilsen was in goal, Ike Opara and Matt Besler were centre-backs, Graham Zusi and Benny Feilhaber were in the midfield; now *that* is a spine of a team! When you look at Sporting Kansas City in 2013, it is no wonder they did so well in the regular season and were set up the best out of all MLS clubs to go deep in the post-season. They had the experience of winning trophies with the 2012 US Open Cup and as back-to-back Eastern Conference regular season champions, but they were built on defensive solidity. Neilsen was statistically the best goalkeeper in MLS that season (although the stats are helped by his strong defence, it only furthers the point on how strong the backline was) while their top scorer, Claudio Bieler, only managed ten MLS goals, finishing outside the top ten scorers. Sporting Kansas City were the best *team* in MLS, and while their players were never recognised with individual awards (none were awarded Player of the Month during the season and Graham Zusi was the only player to win Player of the Week – just once), they didn't care. They weren't going to let awards dictate their season, only they were going to dictate their season. The Galaxy and Red Bulls had recognisable names, and while both teams did well, they were both knocked out in the first round of the play-offs. RSL beat the Galaxy after extra time and the Houston Dynamo beat the Red Bulls after extra time as well, with Houston facing Kansas and RSL facing the Timbers in the next round. In the Dynamo vs Kansas game it was predictably tight, with Kansas advancing thanks to a 2-1 second-leg win, while RSL and the Timbers played out a classy 5-2 series to make it a Kansas vs RSL final. Again, it was a predictably tight game, and it was also MLS's first-ever 'small-market media' game (Kansas were ranked number 31 and Salt Lake number 33), yet it still had over 20,000 fans there. The coldest game in MLS Cup history? And still there were 20,000 there. It was Kansas City's first chance of a trophy in any sport, since the last time they had won the MLS Cup when they were still the Wizards, and even though the game ended 1-1 and had the longest penalty shootout in MLS Cup history, Kansas City had their winners. It was 1-1 in regular time, 8-7 on penalties, and Sporting Kansas City were deserved champions, especially after the season they had put together.

While the 'small-markets' won in the 2014 season of MLS, big changes were on the horizon, with new teams and new stars joining the league. Firstly, Toronto FC made some moves to strengthen their squad under Greg Vanney in order to push for a serious MLS Cup bid. After Ryan Nelsen brought in Jermain Defoe in 2014 for a fee of around $10 million (with weekly wages believed to be around $150,000), the Englishman played just under a year in MLS before hightailing it back to England to play for Sunderland, which saw the Canadians get USMNT striker Jozy Altidore in return. Altidore, who hadn't exactly been a hit in the Premier League, was to team up with Sebastian Giovinco, a talented but inconsistent striker who had played the majority of his career in Serie A with Juventus and Parma but took the step to join MLS and was the league's highest-paid player due to the fact he was signed on a free transfer. Toronto had two top-drawer strikers in their team, as well as team captain Michael Bradley, who joined the club in 2014 from AS Roma. Two new teams were added into MLS in 2015, which added a new dimension on and off the pitch and in turn meant that Chivas USA closed down. Orlando City, armed with their star signing Brazilian legend Kaka, and New York City Football Club (NYCFC) boasting the likes of Frank Lampard, David Villa and Kaka's former Milan team-mate Andrea Pirlo, were ready to be part of MLS, although the story of NYCFC is slightly different to what people may have wanted from a New York franchise, and it's quite a complicated story. MLS had been looking for a second New York franchise since 2006, and in particular were looking for one based in the Five Boroughs of Manhattan, Brooklyn, Queens, the Bronx and Staten Island. Manhattan was almost immediately off the table seeing as it's hard enough to house citizens, let alone a soccer team. Brooklyn, Queens and the Bronx were seen as prime locations, and the New York Mets owner Jeff Wilpon was approached about the possibility of owning a soccer franchise, which he ultimately declined, thus taking CitiField off the table temporarily. With Brooklyn busy with the Nets NBA team, that left Staten Island and the Bronx. Staten Island would be a good location for a stadium, especially on the waterfront, but with the famous Staten Island ferry only travelling every 30 minutes, it would be hell on earth for fans who rely on public transport, which meant the Bronx was the only borough that could house the club. Between 2006 and 2013 MLS had been desperately trying to get investors involved to create a New York club that was actually in the state (unlike the Metrostars/Red Bulls, who were in New Jersey yet went under the New York name for marketing reasons), and in 2013 they finally found an investor who was also looking to expand their own brand in America and wanted to create a club in the biggest market in the world – Manchester City. To add context, in the years since Manchester City had been bought out by Sheik Mansour, they wanted to dominate world soccer and felt like an MLS franchise would be a big step forward, and when the owners of the New York Cosmos refused to pay the MLS franchise expansion fee, City Football Group – the group that is the official owner of clubs such as Girona in Spain and Melbourne City in Australia – were unopposed bidders for this new team. In 2010 Don Garber was also looking at a Miami franchise and spoke with FC Barcelona about the prospect of a Barcelona-style group in MLS, but the deal fell through. In 2012 the vice president of the Miami bid Ferran Soriano was appointed Manchester City CEO and he started discussions with Garber over a New York franchise led by his new club. In 2013, at a price of $100 million – $60 million more than the Montreal Impact had paid three seasons before – NYCFC was born. Or, if we are being blunt about it, NYCFC was genetically modified to act, look and sound like Manchester City lite. But City Football Group weren't the only owners of the team, with the New York Yankees and Steinbrenner family on board at a reported 20 per cent ownership stake, which solved the stadium issue. Instead of building their own stadium immediately, NYCFC would just adopt Yankee Stadium as their home in the Bronx, and just like that NYCFC were in MLS. The league had got their New York team, Manchester City had another feather in their cap of world soccer domination and the Yankees had more revenue coming into their stadium that they could keep because soccer has absolutely nothing to do with MLB. The first three major signings were World Cup and Champions League winners David Villa and Andrea Pirlo and Chelsea's Frank Lampard, who initially delayed his move to NYCFC to play on in the Premier League with Manchester City, which no doubt broke some rules, although no one is quite sure what rules were broken. But, nevertheless, some truly world-class names were entering MLS, and it wasn't just at NYCFC; other expansion side Orlando brought in Kaka and Steven Gerrard left Liverpool to join the LA Galaxy in the 'Michael Jordan playing at the Washington Wizards' part of his career. In 2014 the Galaxy had won yet another MLS Cup after beating the New England Revolution 2-1 after extra time in what was Landon Donovan's final game before his retirement (his first of three retirements). The winning goal was scored by captain Robbie Keane, who was also named MLS Cup MVP, and the Galaxy had gotten their fifth MLS crown, Donovan's sixth and Bruce Arena's fifth title. For the Galaxy, 2015 was set to be somewhat of a transition year. Donovan was gone and two designated player spots had opened up and were quickly snapped up by the arrival of Gerrard and Giovani dos Santos, the former Barcelona and Tottenham starlet who was tipped for great things at the start of his career, but for commitment reasons he never really lived up to his potential. The Galaxy offered him a new route to success, but it just wasn't destined to work out, and while the Galaxy was the only show in Los Angeles following the shutting down of Chivas USA, the more general state of MLS was wide open. Diego Valeri was putting in superstar performances with the Timbers, while Bradley Wright-Phillips was a complete goal machine for the Red Bulls, winning the Golden Boot in 2014 with 27 goals, a joint record held with Chris Wondolowski and Roy Lassiter. Toronto's big three were set to be a threat as Sebastian Giovinco had a point to prove to what seemed like the whole of Italy, as did Jozy

Altidore, to those who said he was bust because of his Premier League failure. Sporting Kansas City wanted their title back, Didier Drogba arrived at Montreal Impact to see what he could do and the Columbus Crew side were led by Gregg Berhalter and had some interesting players such as Federico Higuain, Kei Kamara, Justin Meram, Ethan Finlay and Michael Parkhurst. It was set to be a tight season, and an exciting one at that, as MLS propelled itself into a new age of marketing and promotion based around exciting, young teams with vibrant crowds, beautiful stadiums and a few stars dropped in for good measure. The Red Bulls finished top of the East, while FC Dallas finished top of the West, and the two new expansion sides finished mid-table in the East, Orlando missing out on the play-offs by four points. The play-offs saw Drogba's Montreal beat Toronto, who couldn't rely on joint-top scorer Giovinco on this occasion as they were shut out, Sporting Kansas City lost on penalties to the Timbers in an exciting shoot-out (7-6 to the Timbers, despite Valeri missing the opener) and the reigning champions losing to Seattle in an incredible 3-2 game with the Galaxy somehow reaching the play-offs despite being held back by the ageing, out-of-place Steven Gerrard, who abruptly left at the end of the 2016 season. With Portland beating Sporting Kansas City and Seattle beating the Galaxy, it looked like there was a Cascadia Cup match being set up for the Western Conference finals, but, alas, fate didn't allow it to happen. The Timbers defeated the Whitecaps, while FC Dallas dispatched of the Sounders on penalties, and over in the East the Crew beat the Impact and the Red Bulls beat D.C. United. Portland, the only third seed in the finals, beat Dallas 5-3 on aggregate, while the Crew beat first seed Red Bulls 2-1 on aggregate, giving them home advantage in the MLS Cup match. A cagey start was expected at the MAPFRE Stadium, but after just 27 seconds the Timbers took the lead through Diego Valeri in rather fortunate circumstances. Crew goalkeeper Steve Clark miscontrolled a simple back-pass, which allowed Valeri to literally slide-tackle the ball in for the quickest MLS Cup goal ever. Rodney Wallace added a second in the seventh minute to leave the entire stadium shell-shocked. Portland's high-pressing game worked to perfection, and even though the Crew got a goal back through Kamara, the Timbers were MLS Champions for the first time and delivered the first piece of silverware to the city of Portland since the 1977 NBA Championship (so long ago that it was Bill Walton's Trail Blazers beating Julius 'Dr. J' Erving's 76ers). Portland's win proved to be a pivotal moment in MLS's recent history, even if no one at the time realised it. There was no global megastar on the team, just very good and functioning players who worked amazingly well in Caleb Porter's system (looking at you Darlington Nagbe, Diego Chara and Diego Valeri). More teams looked at different markets to build their teams, mainly South America. Federico Higuain and Valeri weren't hidden away on some outer-reach planet, they just needed to be scouted, which is what it looked like teams had started doing more of, or at least they were in the process of doing.

The year 2016 was the year of the Big Apple in the regular season as they ignored the Portland way of thinking and decided to let their strikers do the talking. Wright-Phillips and David Villa were the top two scorers in all of MLS, scoring 24 and 23 goals respectively, a good way ahead of Sebastian Giovinco in third, who had 17 goals. Luis Robles of the Red Bulls had the most clean sheets (11), while Sacha Kljestan had the most assists (20, the second-highest in MLS history), so all signs finally pointed towards a successful Red Bulls play-off run, right? Well, as luck would have it, both New York sides were dumped out in the first round of the East. The Red Bulls lost to the Impact (who then lost to Toronto) and NYCFC lost to Toronto 7-0 on aggregate. Seattle, led by their stars Nicolás Lodeiro, Nelson Valdez and Ossie Alonso, had made it all the way through from the wildcard game past Sporting Kansas City, FC Dallas and the Colorado Rapids to make it to the final against Toronto, who were being led magnificently by their big three of Altidore, Bradley and Giovinco, and while Toronto held the advantage in terms of venue, the actual MLS Cup match itself was perhaps the tightest it's ever been. Toronto 0-0 Seattle was the score at the end of 120 minutes, mainly thanks to the outrageous goalkeeping from Stefan Frei to keep out shot after shot with simply astounding saves. He was like a brick wall that night, and the Swiss goalkeeper was on the winning side as the Sounders won their very first MLS Cup. The 3-5-2 from Toronto made them the more dangerous side going forward, but the two holding midfielders that Seattle implemented in their 4-2-3-1 offered them more protection at the back, which proved key through the entire 120 minutes. But the signs were looking good for Toronto to make another run at the title in the next season, with Altidore and Giovinco looking very potent in attack. Patrick Vieira – who had become NYCFC manager in 2016 – was getting a great tune out of his team, and the East was looking like it was the place to be. And when two more expansion teams were introduced, MLS got just a little bit more exciting ...

In 2014 it was announced that MLS had a new team: Atlanta United. Atlanta was generally seen as a 'non-soccer' city, being so far away from either the west or east coast. It was also thought that Atlanta wasn't much of a sporting city as the Atlanta Falcons have never won the Super Bowl and the Atlanta Braves have won just three World Series titles, with only one coming after 1957. If anything, Atlanta was more associated with Ted Turner and his exploits in World Championship Wrestling than anything else, and when soccer was around the corner, most expected it to go the same way the NHL team did – straight out the door. MLS and Don Garber made it clear that if the Falcons could clear the way to build a new stadium in Atlanta, the league would try to fit an MLS franchise into the plan, and with Garber and MLS desperate to spread to the south-east (remember, Orlando City were just a few seasons away and it didn't look like any other cities or states were getting a team any time soon), Atlanta United was just a pipe dream, unless the Falcons could seal the deal for their stadium. Thankfully for MLS, the Falcons were approved by the Atlanta state board to build a new stadium that would open in 2017. To continue the theme of the Atlanta Falcons, their owner Arthur Blank – who pitched the idea of having an MLS franchise when persuading Falcons board members to endorse a stadium move – was given the franchise mainly down to his Falcons connections, but also for his enthusiasm for soccer. It became clear that Blank wasn't joining MLS solely for the money – although it was a bonus – rather he was doing it to give Atlanta something to cheer for and something to love. Blank had tried to bid for an MLS franchise back in 2008, with a spokesman for Blank's group AMB saying:

> Filing this application represents an important next step as we continue to explore the possibility of bringing Major League Soccer to fans throughout metro Atlanta. We're also looking at how best to create a sports-and-entertainment centre that can not only serve as a premier soccer destination, but also a community resource for soccer enthusiasts at various levels of play throughout the region.

In what was quite a simple and straightforward process, helped along by MLS's desire to bring soccer to the south of the US, Atlanta United was born and thus began planning for the inaugural season in 2017. Their first season would be played at Bobby Dodd Stadium – home of the Georgia Tech College football team – until September of that year, before they moved into the incredible Mercedes-Benz Stadium (the stadium that sealed the entire franchise's existence). But to start their debut year well, Atlanta had to stand out from the rest of the league both on and off the pitch, especially entering it the same year as Minnesota United, another team who was owned by a sports group, who also owed the Minnesota Twins MLB team and the NBA's Timberwolves. Atlanta and Blank wanted the fans to help create the colour scheme, which ended up being black and red, starting the five stripes tradition. A lot of other traditions such as huge *tifo* displays, tailgating before games, supporter groups and the golden spike (which was just a spike that celebrities or sports stars could come and hit pre-game) were created, and just like that Atlanta had a team worth cheering for. The appointment of former Barcelona manager Tata Martino was a huge indicator of how the team was going to play, as were the signings of Josef Martínez, Héctor Villalba and Miguel Almirón, all for quite hefty fees. Picking up talent like Julian Gressel in the Draft, Leandro González Pirez from Argentina, Jeff Larentowicz, Michael Parkhurst and Brad Guzan meant that Atlanta came into the 2017 season ready to compete in an Eastern Conference that was absolutely stacked with great talent. Toronto and NYCFC were favourites for the Eastern title, which showed during the season when Toronto broke the single-season record for most points as they romped to the Supporters Shield, beating the record set by the 1998 LA Galaxy by one point. NYCFC finished second, while the Fire, Atlanta United, the Crew and the Red Bulls all made up the rest of the East. In the West, Portland and Seattle had a bye into the semis, while Vancouver, Houston, Sporting Kansas City and the Earthquakes made it into the post-season as the LA Galaxy finished joint bottom of the entire league with just eight wins. After their impressive debut season, which saw them play in two separate stadiums and leading the league in highest attendance figures (on average 48,000 showed up), Atlanta United went out of the play-offs in the first round against the Columbus Crew on penalties after a 0-0 draw at the Mercedes-Benz Stadium (attendance that day was 67,221, a record for a post-season MLS game at the time). Almirón, Greg Garza and Michael Parkhurst were named in the MLS All Star team of 2017, while Almiron and Martínez were in the MLS Best XI, Julian Gressel won MLS Rookie of the Year, Héctor Villalba won MLS Goal of the Year, Almirón won MLS Newcomer of the Year, Guzan won MLS Save of the Year, and Martínez had most MLS Player of the Week awards – he scored the first hat-trick of the season, the most hat-tricks of anyone that season and finished fourth in the Golden Boot standings. Quite an impressive year for Atlanta, but while they couldn't quite get over the finishing line this time around, the signs were there that the future was bright. The Crew would go on to beat NYCFC and lose to Toronto 1-0 on aggregate in a period when turmoil was brewing around the franchise, which was a great achievement, even if they went home without silverware. Seattle romped through the West again as Portland were dumped out by Houston, with the Sounders beating the Dynamo 5-0 on aggregate to set up a rematch of the 2016 MLS Cup Final between Toronto and Seattle, but this time it was expected that Toronto, a team dubbed by many as 'the best MLS team ever', were going to take their revenge on the Sounders for 2016.

On a chilly night in Toronto, the Canadians won what they felt was truly theirs, thanks to goals from Jozy Altidore and Victor Vázquez, although the breakthrough came a lot later than they had hoped. Toronto were on the front foot for the majority of the game, with Stefan Frei making a bevy of saves to keep his side in it, just like in 2016. It felt like it was going to be the previous final all over again, until after the hour mark when Altidore lofted his left-footed shot over Frei to set Toronto on their way. The goal took any steam out of Seattle and effectively won the home side the game thanks to their possession-based style that squeezed the life out of Seattle, before Vázquez popped up late on to put the cherry on top of the cake. Toronto were rightly MLS champions and became the first MLS side to win their 'domestic treble' – MLS Cup, Canadian Championship and the MLS Supporters Shield – to really cement their place in MLS history (it also helped that the *Seattle Times* ran an advertisement for a victory parade for the Sounders, essentially giving Toronto all the motivation they needed), but while history was being made on the field in MLS, history was taking place off it in Columbus, Ohio. Up until this point MLS had never had any major scandals or controversies other than player bargaining agreements. There were no drug scandals, no match fixing, nothing like that, but in an effort to create a new franchise in Austin, Texas, it was on the verge of having negative press all over it. It wasn't an overnight controversy, rather this had been brewing for several years, and it all started with a man named Anthony Precourt.

Jay Anthony Precourt, the CEO of Precourt Sports Ventures (PSV), had been a businessman his whole adult life. He has a masters in business administration and has had stints in many banking and business firms, the most notable being Merrill Lynch. It's clear that Precourt is not a dumb man; in fact, he is quite the opposite, but he made a decision in 2012 when he decided to invest in MLS and buy a team. A smart decision, but the motives, actions and decisions weren't smart – at all. Precourt purchased the Columbus Crew for $68 million from the Hunt Sports Group (unfortunately, the original owner Lamar Hunt had passed away six years before and his group/family took over operations of the Crew), which at the time was an MLS franchise sale record. If you believe in metaphors being true, then an incident at the first Crew game that Precourt attended summed up what was going to happen. As Precourt took his seat at the MAPFRE Stadium, kick-off was delayed by a few hours. Why? Because the scoreboard set on fire. To this day no one was sure how it set alight, but it prompted Precourt to spend a lot of money on 'rebranding' the Crew. New stadium facilities, new food at the stadium, new naming rights for the stadium and training complex, a change of club badge, new players and new staff. Gregg Berhalter was brought in as the new manager, and Precourt wanted to be competitive and he wanted to change the Crew's look – to an extent. He said in an interview on Fox Sports:

> We're looking at ways we can evolve and change our logo. We want it to represent the Columbus we've come to know. I don't think a construction crew is really representative. [Columbus is] not a blue-collar, manufacturing, industrial town. It's a smart, young, progressive university town with world-class businesses. It's a white-collar town. We want to be representative. We don't see Columbus in the crest. There are things we can do to represent the capital city better.

And thus the change began. At first it was a new badge, which wasn't a major concern. Lots of teams have changed badges in a bid to 'modernise' their clubs. Manchester United, Tottenham

Hotspur, Chelsea, Arsenal, Liverpool, Manchester City, they've all changed badges and no one complains, so no one thought it was out of the ordinary when the Crew did it. Another change came in the form of a slight name change, from 'Columbus Crew' to 'Columbus Crew SC' (with SC standing for Soccer Club). Again, it didn't seem too out of the ordinary because it wasn't a huge change, just two letters added on to the original name. On the pitch, the Crew were flying. Berhalter was working his magic, and with star players performing at their best the Crew reached the 2014 MLS Cup, so it looked like they would be healthy for a few more years. On the face of it the franchise had been modernised, the stadium had been improved, the team had a great manager and some really good players and they were knocking on the door of silverware. That's what it looked like on the face of things. But behind the scenes, there was a lot of plotting and scheming going on that was going to change MLS forever if it happened.

On 16 October 2017, Grant Wahl broke a story in *Sports Illustrated* about how Anthony Precourt and PSV were contemplating a move to Austin, Texas, if they were not granted permission by Columbus City Council for a new stadium in Downtown. It seemed unreal, almost like a fantasy. For someone who supposedly 'loved' Columbus, how could they just up the team and leave because they didn't get what they wanted? Teams have folded in the past like Chivas USA, but the Crew weren't folding or going out of business, they were just being moved. It was something that drew comparisons to Wimbledon's move to Milton Keynes, although this was slightly different. London-based club Wimbledon had been threatened with bankruptcy for years and the only way they could survive was if they were bought out by Pete Winkleman, a record producer based in Milton Keynes, a town 70 miles north of Wimbledon. The original Wimbledon moved to Milton Keynes before Winkleman could purchase the club, and when he did, saving them from administration, he 'rebranded' them. Wimbledon were now the Milton Keynes Dons, and instead of playing in London they played outside of it. The Crew weren't faced with financial difficulty, they just had an owner who was desperate to set up a team in Austin. The news hit the fans hard, and while some were depressed and extremely upset over what had come out, a select few decided that until the Crew were gone, they were still *their* Columbus Crew. Less than a day after Precourt announced his intentions to move the team to Austin, fans set up a movement that was unlike anything seen in America at the time, and it all started in Hendock's Pub by one fan who was simply fed up with seeing his friends and fellow Crew fans down over the news. Morgan Hughes, one of the founders of the 'Save The Crew' movement spared time to talk to me about when the news broke in February 2018, saying:

> The story kinda broke at night, Grant Wahl tweeted out that it was happening so I found out about 45 minutes before that. I got a text message from one of my buddies and he said, 'Dude, I'm hearing a lot from good sources that the Crew are moving,' and I'm like, 'Dude, get fucked! I'm not in the mood for one of these message board jokes from 2003.' So I started texting local journalists and contacts and it seemed like it was real and when I saw the tweet it felt like this can't be real. There's no fucking way. The first 18 hours felt like that for me, it was unimaginable. It means too much, you can't be taking this thing from us, it's like stealing someone's identity. It was very surreal and that is what the first 18 hours was like. We went through all the stages of grief as a community and I was just fucking done with it, it wasn't going to happen.
>
> The hardest part of this has been not knowing what the right move is. I knew immediately that I was gonna have to reach out to everyone I could to try and find at least one angel who knew more than I knew. And I needed to align myself with them from an information standpoint. I emailed hundreds of humans I knew, I emailed hundreds of humans that I've never met and I said, 'My name is Morgan and we're not gonna take

this. What do you have for me? No information is bad information, I just need some help,' and it took off from there.

And in an organic fashion, the campaign to save the Columbus Crew was underway, with fans of various MLS teams holding up banners pledging support for the cause. PSV didn't expect the movement to spring up, and MLS certainly didn't see it coming because Don Garber was so used to fans in the NFL just accepting relocations. Fans like Morgan were so passionate about keeping the Crew in Columbus that they started to spread the message immediately, creating one of the tag lines 'Tell Everyone You Know, This Isn't Over'. Precourt stayed away from the MAPFRE Stadium once the news of his intentions was announced, and the movement kept on gaining momentum. Despite people telling them that they were set to lose their team (it's just how things go in sports in the US – to quote Childish Gambino, 'This Is America') soccer wasn't a sport that bowed to conventional US sport tropes. With the Save The Crew incident, MLS had the chance to separate itself from any other league in America. Relocations happen in American sports all the time (49 times across the NBA, MLB and NFL, excluding the Raiders's move to Las Vegas). The New York Yankees haven't always been the New York Yankees (moved from Baltimore in 1903 under the Orioles guise) and the Los Angeles Lakers were once the less fashionable Minneapolis Lakers, but soccer was different, and the Crew were about to buck the wrong kind of trend. They were *the* original MLS team, they had *the* first soccer-specific stadium in all of the US, and it was all about to be taken away from them in one instant. It wasn't right and everyone knew it, and while some people shrugged their shoulders and looked the other way, people were fighting for the Crew. Off the pitch, the Save The Crew were spreading the word and creating plans on what they'd do if the Crew were saved, and on the pitch Gregg Berhalter and his squad were performing minor miracles to fend off the off-field issues. A lot of people at the club, playing staff and front office combined, weren't sure what their futures were and the 2018 season was proving to be perhaps the biggest in MLS history. Aside from the Crew, Los Angeles had a new team led by a superconsortium that contained Lakers legend Magic Johnson, comedian Will Ferrell, Mia Hamm, Vincent Tan and 27 other people, who bought the rights for the new franchise named Los Angeles Football Club, or LAFC for short. In their wonderful Banc of California stadium – a stone's throw from the LA Coliseum and an hour and a half drive from Hollywood – LAFC recruited Bob Bradley as their head coach and Mexican star Carlos Vela as their first Designated Player, setting up a great rivalry in LA with the Galaxy, who weren't staying quiet at all. In the midst of their poor period following the end of the Arena/Beckham/Donovan/Keane era, the Galaxy had problems. Defensively, they were terrible. Romain Alessandrini, Giovani dos Santos and Jonathan dos Santos weren't quite cutting it as Designated Players in attack, so they had to find a different star to not only ignite their season but to keep them relevant in their own city. LAFC were on fire at the start of the season and posed a threat to the Galaxy, but the Galaxy hit back with a huge signing, one that blew LAFC and MLS out of the water.

Zlatan Ibrahimović, released by Manchester United following a near career-ending injury, joined the Galaxy and made the best debut possible against, of all teams, LAFC. His incredible hat-trick completed an amazing comeback (it doesn't need tons of detail, you know which hat-trick this is), and while LAFC made the play-offs – only to be bounced in the first round by RSL – the Galaxy missed out on the final day in heart-breaking fashion. Over in the East, the Red Bulls broke the record for most points in a season (71), while Atlanta looked set to win the whole thing with Josef Martínez scoring 31 goals, breaking the record for most goals in a single MLS season. The Crew made the play-offs, as did a D.C. United side led by a reinvigorated Wayne Rooney who joined from Everton, but the spoils of the season, despite a ton of memorable moments, went to the record-breaking Atlanta United side. Atlanta had made the world take notice of MLS, and in their 2-0 win against the Timbers they also broke the record for highest attendance in any MLS game, with 73,019 showing up. So 2018 was a huge year for MLS, with new star players arriving and some leaving (Miguel Almirón to Newcastle, David Villa to Vissel Kobe) and records being broken seemingly every week; the league had never been hotter. However, there was still one thing looming over them that could undo any good work in the snap of a finger – the Columbus Crew. Nashville, FC Cincinnati and David Beckham's Inter Miami had all be granted access to MLS in the coming years, while there was seemingly room for one more. Room for one more in Austin, Texas. There were rumours that a new Austin franchise was going to be announced in early 2019, but questions remained about whether it would the Crew moving to Austin or a new franchise led by PSV. On 28 December 2018 all the questions would be answered, as Jimmy and Dee Haslam, the owners of NFL's Cleveland Browns, bought the Columbus Crew. Saying in an official statement:

> Throughout our conversations, it's been overwhelmingly clear that Crew SC belongs in Columbus, and we are thrilled to have reached an agreement in principle to assume an ownership position in Major League Soccer and to operate Columbus Crew SC. As the stewards of Crew SC, we will always be focused on building a championship-calibre team that makes the city proud, creating dynamic and memorable fan experiences and deeply engaging the community to make a positive impact.

The Crew were saved. The Columbus Crew would remain in Columbus, Precourt got his Austin franchise and MLS kept one of its original members. History was preserved and created on the same day in Columbus, and, much to the delight of those around the country, and the world, who were hoping that the organic, grassroots Save The Crew movement would come through, it was a joy to see that they'd saved their team. The Save The Crew movement was perhaps equally as important as David Beckham moving to MLS, but for different reasons. It showed that soccer fans in America cared deeply about their teams, enough to prevent the norm from occurring. Something like this had never happened before in American sports and it saved MLS a lot of face. Rather than dealing with a summer based around a departing Columbus Crew, they dealt with more important things instead, like the stars they had on offer and ensuring a healthy future for their league. The idea of MLS has been around since the late 1980s, and after going through every major event that has occurred during those years, here's hoping that MLS becomes a force. The feel-good story of the Crew being saved should be the start of a new era in MLS. This era won't have a title, nor will it have a poster boy like David Beckham. It'll just be the era when soccer becomes a major sport in the United States and while, obviously, things need to change, MLS is at the forefront of US soccer. The USMNT, the USWNT, MLS and the history of the game may all be different entities, but they're all under the same umbrella. They all contribute towards soccer in the United States and hopefully they can continue to create history and moments that fans will never, ever forget.

Chapter Ten

Conclusion

A conclusion at the end of books is usually answering questions about what the reader has just read, going through what has been on the page, but no questions have been asked in this book, and while questions may need answering about the future of MLS or the USMNT/USWNT, in some cases there are no correct or accurate answers. In some instances, there are only opinions, which is what this section will be: my opinions on certain topics, but in the simplest terms in a bid to not waste anyone's time further. This is probably more of a rant/getting thoughts out in the open as opposed to a clever and witty conclusion, so just play along with me here ...

As I said in the MLS chapter, the future has perhaps never been brighter for the league. There are teams that are fashionable to like, they have star players that people enjoy watching and they have players, like Miguel Almirón, who are being watched and bought by major European clubs. There is absolutely nothing wrong with MLS becoming a selling league because if you sell five players to – for example – Tottenham, Chelsea, Bayern Munich, Juventus and Paris Saint-Germain, then the whole league benefits. Miguel Almirón just joined Newcastle, and while people won't just look at him and assume that MLS is a great place to buy talent, if it happens on a regular basis opinions will probably change. Of course, you need to have a steady supply of capable talent ready to replace the outgoing players, but good scouting can do that. But the elephant in the room with regards to MLS and US soccer is promotion and relegation. There is no doubt that promotion and relegation is needed in the United States, but at the same time it can't happen just yet. Why? Because of financial and cultural differences. To start with, owners would not be interested in having a team that leaves MLS, and sports fans in general (excluding soccer fans because you guys are here for the long haul – I hope) wouldn't be able to understand why it is in place. It isn't in the NFL, isn't in the NBA or MLB or NHL, so why MLS? Because soccer/ football culture is different, and that's why it'll take time. It would do wonders for the league, but only when everyone is ready, because if they introduced it now or let's say in 2020 MLS would fall off a cliff. Owners would panic about not having an MLS franchise and would back out immediately, because they're not used to it in US sport. Teams would get relegated and struggle to find a way back in to MLS, and likewise some teams would get promoted and struggle to find a way to stay up. Once American culture changes and accepts that MLS is different to every other league in the country (MLS needs to realise this as well and stop pretending to be the NFL or NBA), then things can change. It would add a different level of excitement and intrigue not just to MLS, but to every other league in America. You wouldn't have to spend millions on an expansion fee, instead you can just play good soccer and earn your way to MLS. It would create history for every team in America and it would be amazing to see, but not just yet. Let this era of MLS simmer for a bit, let owners and fans get emotionally invested into soccer and let teams in the USL stabilise themselves and support themselves financially before making such a big jump. Imagine the New York Cosmos in MLS, with their derby against NYCFC and the Red Bulls? It would be an amazing sight! But while the timing may not be right in 2019, it has to happen in the future.

Youth soccer is a huge talking point at the moment, and so it should be because the way it works is an absolute joke.

The college system does not work in soccer and it's plain to see why. Did Lionel Messi and Cristiano Ronaldo get picked up out of college in a draft? No, they worked hard to overcome adversities and earned their spot at the top of the mountain from the youth academies of clubs to where they are now. They weren't shunned because they couldn't afford to play for their local team or because they weren't in the right college. Lionel Messi wouldn't be picked up by an MLS youth academy because he's not Russell Westbrook. He isn't the prototypical athlete that is on Nike commercials, he may not be able to do the NFL Combine, but he's a better athlete than anyone else in any other sport (except maybe LeBron). He's got a god-given talent but because he doesn't look the part, or he couldn't play for a soccer team when he was a kid because the fee was too much, he wouldn't be picked. Again, it goes back to culture. Not every soccer player can be Russell Westbrook, and if they were built like him they probably wouldn't be any good. Pay-to-play is a terrible idea because of how much the costs are: $3,000 for a season? Make that $80 a season and I bet that millions of boys and girls grow up to be soccer players (provided they're any good).

Split youth academies into sections so you have a north-west section made up of players from Washington, Oregon and close states, a west-coast one for California, a south-east one for Carolina, Georgia, Tennessee and Florida and so on and so on. Imagine being the best region in the state and having scouts watching you play against literally every other region. The USSF needs to do a lot more to encourage soccer in youth communities because it is losing a lot of potential young players to sports like basketball as those sport are more accessible, which shouldn't be the case. Soccer is the world's game and it needs to be treated as such in the United States, not treated as the cooky, quirky foreign sport.

The change in culture would benefit the USMNT massively, too (I'm not including the USWNT in this because they're the best anyway). Scout the nation, find players who are technically amazing and bring them in to the USMNT set-up. Nationalise them, if you must, but take the best talent you can find and give them a clear structure and idea on how their career path in the national team should be. Give them minutes in the youth team and if they perform at youth level and at their clubs, give them caps at the USMNT level. It isn't hard, it really isn't, but neglecting it is just plain lazy. The US is lucky to have so many different nationalities in their country that they have so many different cultures to choose from, and the majority of those cultures will have an affection for soccer. Nurture those kids, make them feel wanted and special and embrace the variety of cultures you have in your country. Efrain Alvarez of the LA Galaxy, get him signed up as quickly as possible because he's going to be a star. Scour the southern regions and west coast because there may be a lot more Efrain Alvarez's kicking around than you expect, playing with a battered ball in a cage or against a graffitied wall. But it's okay, he can't be picked by the US system because he didn't pay $3,000 a season to play for his team. Forget that he's incredibly talented, he didn't pay so he can't play. Sounds ridiculous, doesn't it?

The USWNT? They're the best, so pay them like they're the best. American sports is quick to give bang-average Bryce Harper $330 million over 13 years, but they'll baulk at giving any World Cup-winning, Olympic gold medal-winning USWNT star a decent contract because ... well I don't really know why. 'But Bryce Harper plays in a bigger sport?' Yes he does and he brings in a heck of a lot of cash for MLB, but would Alex Morgan not be as valuable if she and her sport were promoted properly and treated like it wasn't a side show in a circus? Probably. I'll tell you who she would be more valuable than, and that's every single player on the USMNT roster, because not only is she, and her team-mates, better than them, they're winners. You should have your own opinions on equal pay in US soccer, I'm not going to try to persuade you otherwise, but understand that the USSF needs to do more to bridge the pay gap, especially at a time when the talent level and success level of the USMNT and the USWNT has never been further apart – in favour of the women.

History is an amazing thing. You can learn everything and nothing from history, and hopefully you've learnt everything and a bit more reading this book. If you learnt about the origins of American soccer, or the American Soccer League or anything that followed, thank you. It's been a thrill learning about the early origins of soccer in the United States, and while I wished there was more information on the early days that I could use without copying other writers' work, I hope you enjoyed reading about it as much as I enjoyed research and writing about it. I didn't use my opinions in this book, I left that to the introduction and conclusion sections because I didn't want to influence how someone saw an incident. My goal was to inform, to tell a story and hopefully I did both. I hope that this book gets used in the future the same way that I fawned over Colin Jose's work or Ian Plenderleith's *Rock and Roll Soccer*. I want this book to be a reference point for those who are interested in soccer in the United States, and I just hope that if you've gotten this far, you either enjoyed the book, thought, 'I've gone this far, I may as well just bloody finish it', or you've used it as a coaster for your drinks, for which I hope the circular stain around the front cover is vivid because at least then you didn't swap it for another book!

Bibliography

Allaway, R. (2015). *What was the Soccer War?* [online] Society for American Soccer History.

Allaway, R. (2001). *West Hudson: A Cradle of American Soccer.* [online] Homepages.sover.net.

Almond, E. (2014). *World Cup: United States' Chris Wondolowski just misses dramatic goal against Belgium.* [online] The Mercury News.

Baxter, K. (2014). *What's behind Landon Donovan being left off U.S. World Cup roster.* [online] latimes.com.

Bagli, C. (2018). *Hunt for New York City F.C.'s Stadium Site Is Back Where It Began: the Bronx.* [online] Nytimes.com.

BBC Sport. (2017). *Trump NFL row: Megan Rapinoe on why she backed Colin Kaepernick.* [online] BBC.com.

Benjamin, B. (2014). *The story of the 1930 World Cup.* [online] These Football Times.

Bell, J. (2007). *Real Madrid Club President Says a Mouthful.* New York Times.

Bell, J. (2013). *Columbus Crew sold to Precourt Sports Ventures, which pledges to keep team in Columbus.* [online] Bizjournals. com.

Billingham, N. (2014). *USA vs Iran at France '98: the most politically charged game in World Cup history.* [online] FourFourTwo.

Blanchflower, D. (1968). *Just One Truth For Me.* Sports Illustrated (23).

Blau, M. (2014). *Atlanta likely selected to get new MLS expansion team | Atlanta Creative Loafing.* [online] Atlanta Creative Loafing.

Bolster, J. (2014). *The unheralded heroes of American soccer at the 1990 World Cup | THE WORD.* [online] MLSsoccer.com.

Borg, S. (2014). *USA Greatest World Cup Moments, No. 5: Torsten Frings handball that may have cost a semifinal.* [online] MLSsoccer.com.

Bird, H. (2018). *American Menace: When Fall River ruled U.S. soccer | Boston.com.* [online] Boston.com.

Brancati, F. (2015). *2007 Women's World Cup in China.* [online] Soccer Politics / The Politics of Football.

Brennan, T. (2017). *How MLS's single entity status works and its relationship with antitrust law.* [online] LawInSport.

Briggs, S. (2010). *England v USA: Fabio Capello's men need to fear lesson of Belo Horizonte.* [online] Telegraph.co.uk.

Davis, N. (2013). *Everybody loves Shep Messing.* [online] SBNation.com.

Davis, N. (2013). *Why Pelé's Cosmos Were the Best and Worst Thing to Happen to American Soccer.* [online] The New Republic.

Dure, B. (2016). *Messi, Lahm and ... Sidwell? How much would Pelé's New York Cosmos cost today?* [online] The Guardian.

Dure, B. (2018). *Carli Lloyd at the death: Ten years on from the USWNT's most improbable win.* [online] The Guardian.

Editors, H. (2009). *Great Depression History.* [online] History.com.

Eligon, J. (2005). For MLS, The Future Is In The Eye Of The Beholder. *New York Times.*

ESPN.com. (n.d.). *Toronto FC sign Italy's Giovinco.* [online]

ESPN.co.uk. (2010). *The Miracle on Grass.* [online]

ESPN (2012). *David Beckham's LA Story.* [video]

Farnsworth, E. (2014). *Looking back at the U.S. soccer team's historic 2002 World Cup.* [online] https://www.philly.com.

FIFA.com. (1996). *Phillip Sloane – The Lone Survivor.* [online]

FIFA.com. (2008). *Morgan and Leroux, blazing a trail.* [online]

FIFA.com. (2019). *History of Football – The Origins.* [online] FIFA.com.

Foltman, B. (1999). MLS Boots Commissioner, Turns To NFL For Successor. *Chicago Tribune.*

Football, P. (2018). *The nine stages of Freddy Adu's career: From wonderkid to wanderer Football.* [online] Planet Football.

Foudy, J. (2015). *Ending the drought – What the USWNT learned from 2011 World Cup loss.* [online] espnW.

Foulds, A. (2005). *Boston's Ballparks & Arenas.* Hanover: University Press of New England, p.23.

Foxsports.com. (2014). *Atlanta lands Major League Soccer expansion team for 2017.* [online]

Fraser v. Major League Soccer [2000]97 F.Supp.2d 130 (United States District Court, D. Massachusetts).

Gee, A. (2014). *The bra that shocked the world: Why Women's World Cup champion Brandi Chastain bared her bra.* [online] BBC News.

Glendenning, B. (2013). *World Cup stunning moments: Andrés Escobar's deadly own goal | Barry Glendenning.* [online] The Guardian.

Goff, S. (1995). All Grown Up, Hamm Comes on Strong. *Washington Post.* Glanville, B. (2010). *The Story of the World Cup.* London, England: Faber and Faber.

Gonzalez, R. (2018). *Geoff Cameron says USMNT would have reached World Cup with Jurgen Klinsmann.* [online] CBSSports.com.

Graham, B. (2018). *USA 94: the World Cup that distracted Americans from Oprah and OJ.* [online] The Guardian.

Helms, A. (2014). *The U.S. Beat Belgium in The Very First World Cup.* [online] The New Republic.

Heneage, K. (2016). *The day USA beat Argentina in Copa América: 'Simeone threatened to kill us'.* [online] The Guardian.

Hirshey, D. (2019). *ESPN.com – E-Ticket: When Soccer Ruled The USA.* [online] Espn.com.

Holmes, B. (2012). *Oneida Football Club, the first team to play high school football.* [online] BostonGlobe.com.

Holyrod, S. (n.d.). *The Year in American Soccer – 1969.* [online] Homepages.sover.net.

Hunter, A. (2010). *Landon Donovan – I was wrong to criticise David Beckham at LA Galaxy.* [online] The Guardian.

Jackson, M. (2015). *Four years later: Abby Wambach's 2011 header heard round the world.* [online] espnW.

Jose, C. (1998). *American Soccer League, 1921–1931.* Lanham, Md: Scarecrow Press.

Jones, G. (2001). *MLS Season, Playoffs to Be Adjusted.* Los Angeles Times.

Jones, G. (2009). *Beckham agrees to return to Galaxy in mid-July.* Los Angeles Times.

Kelly, C. (2012). *London 2012: Canadian women robbed in soccer semi: Kelly | The Star.* [online] thestar.com.

Kenn.com. (2019). *Attendance Project: NASL.* [online] kenn.com blog.

Kenn.com. (n.d.). *NASL TV: A Short History.* [online] kenn.com blog.

Klein, C. (n.d.). *The Forgotten Golden Age of American Soccer.* [online] HISTORY.

Kunti, S. (2018). *40 Years Ago, Pelé and the New York Cosmos Helped Shape US Soccer as We Know It.* [online] Remezcla.

Lalas, G. (2012). *For USMNT, 9/11 proves special day to 'get right result'.* [online] MLSsoccer.com.

Lamb, B. (2017). *Charles A. Stoneham | Society for American Baseball Research.* [online] Sabr.org.

Lamle, K. (2017). *46,000 fans a game: Atlanta United's strange success far from soccer's heartland.* [online] The Guardian.

Larson, K. (2017). *'BEST. TEAM. EVER.': Toronto FC wins MLS Cup, completing record-breaking season.* [online] Toronto Sun.

Lea, G. (2015). *The relationship between Mussolini and calcio.* [online] These Football Times.

Lewis, M. (2015). *How USA was chosen to host World Cup 94: the inside story of a historic day.* [online] The Guardian.

Lewis, M. (2016). *Henry Farrell, the man who helped the US soccer team make Olympic history.* [online] the Guardian. Available at: https://www.theguardian.com/football/2016/aug/18/henry-farrell-us-olympic-socc

Lewis, M. (2018). *How the birth and death of the NASL changed soccer in America forever.* [online] The Guardian.

Lisi, C. (2010). *The U.S. Women's Soccer Team.* Lanham, Md: Scarecrow Press.

Lisi, C. (2015). *A History of the World Cup.* London: Rowman & Littlefield.

Litterer, D. (2011). *Women's Soccer History in the USA: An Overview.* [online] Homepages.sover.net.

Longman, J. (2003). US Replaces China As Host Of Soccer's Women's World Cup. *New York Times.*

Longman, J. (2006). *American Attack Falls Flat.* [online] Nytimes.com.

Longman, J. (2006). *Only a Few Surprises as the U.S. Picks Its World Cup Roster.* [online] Nytimes.com.

Longman, J. (2009). How A 'Band of No-Hopers' Forged US Soccer's Finest Day. *New York Times.*

Longman, J. (2011). *Bob Bradley Fired as Coach of U.S. Soccer Team.* [online] Nytimes.com.

MacAskill, E. (2010). *World Cup 2010: How the USA's 1950 amateurs upset England and the odds.* [online] The Guardian.

Major League Soccer (2018). *The Greatest Playoff Game Ever.* [video]

Marthaler, J. (2018). *Remembering 1994 World Cup and Eric Wynalda's brilliant free kick that stood as biggest shot in USA soccer history.* [online] Star Tribune.

Martin, D. (2012). *Giorgio Chinaglia, Italian Star and the Cosmos' Leader, Dies at 65.* [online] New York Times.

Matthaus, L. (2018). *Der Kolumnist.* FourFourTwo (294), p.30.

Megdal, H. (2013). *How the Wilpons repelled Major League Soccer, and why they may regret it.* [online] Politico PRO.

Memmott, J. (2012). *Pia Sundhage Steps Down as Coach of USWNT.* New York Times.

Mifflin, L. (1982). *NASL Likely To Oust Woosnam.* [online] New York Times.

Millward, R. (2007). *Agent: Beckham Sticking to Galaxy Deal.* Washington Post.

New York Times (1914). *SCHWAB CORNERS FOOTBALL STARS.* [online]

New York Times (1982). *Colombia Won't Be Cup Hosts.*

New York Times (1983). *Mexico Chosen As World Cup Hosts.*

Nytimes.com. (2014). *The World's Ball.* [online]

News.bbc.co.uk. (2002). *BBC SPORT | WORLD CUP | Mexico v USA | USA see off sorry Mexico.* [online]

Oliver, L. (1996). *The Ethnic Legacy in American Soccer.* [online] Homepages.sover.net.

Ozanian, M. (2013). *The Economics Behind New York's $100 Million MLS Team.* [online] Forbes.com.

Ozanian, M. (2013). *Columbus Crew Sold By Hunt Sports Group For Record $68 Million.* [online] Forbes.com.

Parker, G. (n.d.). *Commissioner Don Garber on the Young Guns of MLS Ownership.* [online] Grantland.

Pendleton, K. (2007). *A Worthy Experiment: The NASL and the 35-yard offside line.* [online] US Soccer Players.

Phillips, B. (2010). *The Secret History of American Soccer.* [online] Slate Magazine.

Plenderleith, I. (2014). *Rock 'n' Roll Soccer.* 1st ed. London: Icon Books.

Politi, S. (2008). *Ledger Archives: Heather O'Reilly lifts team into the finals.* [online] nj.com.

PortlandTimbers.com. (2009). *MLS awards team to Portland for 2011.* [online]

Rivera, A. (2014). *MLS 3.0 Series: A History of MLS 1.0 – Last Word on Sports.* [online] Last Word on Sports.

Ruthven, G. (2016). *Steven Gerrard was a much better tourist than a player in LA.* [online] The Guardian.

Sanchez, R. (2015). *U.S. Women's World Cup champs get ticker tape parade.* [online] CNN.

Searcey, I. (2019). *Soccer, the game? I've never heard of that (1994).* [online] Channel 4 News.

Seattle Sounders FC. (2010). *Seattle Sounders FC recognized as the 2010 professional sports team of the year.* [online]

Shaw, P. (2015). *Dettmar Cramer obituary: Coach who took Germany to World Cup glory.* [online] The Independent.

Sibor, D. (2015). *An Oral History of Major League Soccer's Frenzied First Season.* [online] Complex.

Soccer Politics / The Politics of Football. (2015). *2003 Women's World Cup.* [online]

Soccer Politics / The Politics of Football. (2015). *2011 Women's World Cup in Germany.* [online]

Solo, H. (2012). *U.S. goalkeeper Hope Solo details benching in 2007 World Cup.* [online] espnW.

Sports Illustrated's 100 Greatest Moments. (n.d.). *The 100 Greatest Moments in Sports History | Golden Girls.* [online]

Tassell, N. (2016). *When the NASL rocked America: Elton John, Jagger and the age of excitement.* [online] FourFourTwo.

Telegraph. (2003). *Wimbledon go into administration.* [online]

Telegraph. (2009). *David Beckham booed on LA Galaxy return.* [online]

The Bethlehem Globe (1925). EXPECT A HOT SOCCER MEETING U. S. F. A. Will Hold Annual Conference in New York Next Week AMERICAN LEAGUE IN JUNE.

The Bethlehem Globe (1928). REGRET LEAGUE ACTION AGAINST THREE CLUBS Local Management Amazed at Drastic Punishment of League President NEW LEAGUE IS NEAR.

The Evening News (1980). *Cosmos Triumph Over Strikers In NASL Soccer Bowl.*

The Guardian. (2010). *World Cup 2010: Bill Clinton praises USA team's persistence.* [online]

The Guardian. (2016). *USA's Hope Solo given six-month ban for calling Sweden 'a bunch of cowards'.* [online]

The Milwaukee Journal (1983). *NASL Results: 1 Team Lost, 1 Saved.*

Trecker, J. (2014). *Alexi Lalas: 'Before USA '94 I was a punk who never thought about my place'.* [online] FourFourTwo.

Trubey, J. (2013). *Bonds approved for Falcons stadium land purchase.* [online] ajc.

Ussoccer.com. (2002). *Where It All Began: The Story of the 1930 U.S. World Cup Squad, 'The Shot-Putters'.*

Ussoccer.com. (2004). *U.S. Wins Gold Medal on Wambach Overtime Strike.* [online]

Ussoccer.com. (2005). *U.S. WNT Flashback – 20th Anniversary of First-Ever Match: Who Scored First?* [online]

Ussoccer.com. (2005). *U.S. WNT Flashback – 20th Anniversary of First-Ever Match: OOOSA!* [online]

Ussoccer.com. (2011). *Klinsmann Named Head Coach of USMNT.* [online]

Ussoccer.com. (2013). *U.S. WNT Defeats Brazil 4-1 in Orlando to Complete Undefeated 2013 Campaign*

Usatoday30.usatoday.com. (2011). *Falcons owner Blank puts in bid for MLS franchise –* [online] *USATODAY.com.*

Wagman, R. (2001). *MLS fans in several cities wait nervously for contraction decision.* [online] Soccer Times.

Wahl, G. (2010). *The Beckham experiment*. New York: Crown.

Wahl, G. (2017). *Columbus Crew Angling Toward Relocation to Austin in 2019*. [online] SI.com.

Ward, B. (1995). Women's World Cup gains U.S. exposure as 1995 World Cup kicks off in Sweden. *Tampa Tribune*.

Washington Evening Star (1928). US Team Eliminated From Olympic Soccer.

Withers, T. (2018). *Browns owners agree to buy Columbus Crew, keep team in Ohio*. [online] AP NEWS.

Yannis, A. (1973). *Cosmos Atoms In H Deadlock*. [online] New York Times.